Human
Value
Management

Jac Fitz-enz

Human Value Management

*The Value-Adding
Human Resource Management Strategy
for the 1990s*

Jossey-Bass Publishers · San Francisco

HUMAN VALUE MANAGEMENT
The Value-Adding Human Resource Management Strategy for the 1990s
by Jac Fitz-enz

Copyright © 1990 by: Jossey-Bass Inc., Publishers
350 Sansome Street
San Francisco, California 94104

For sales outside the United States, please contact your local Simon & Schuster
International Office.

Library of Congress Cataloging-in-Publication Data

Fitz-enz, Jac.
  Human value management : the value-adding human resource
management strategy for the 1990s / Jac Fitz-enz.
    p.   cm. — (The Jossey-Bass management series)
    ISBN 1-55542-228-4
    1. Personnel management.   I. Title.   II. Series.
HF5549.F557   1990
658.3 — dc20   89-43457
                                                              CIP

Jossey-Bass Web address: http://www.josseybass.com

Manufactured in the United States of America on Lyons Falls
Turin Book. This paper is acid-free and 100 percent totally
chlorine-free.

JACKET DESIGN BY WILLI BAUM

FIRST EDITION
HB Printing   10 9 8 7

Code 9022

*The Jossey-Bass
Management Series*

Contents

Preface

GREAT SPIRITS HAVE always encountered violent opposition from mediocre minds.

Albert Einstein

I have been talking and writing about the subject of human resources measurement and value-adding practices since the late 1970s. At times, I have despaired of the human resources field because I encountered so many of Einstein's mediocre minds. Yet, writing this book has been a cleansing and refreshing exercise for me. I have had the opportunity over the past two to three years to work with, interview, or simply revisit a number of brilliant and creative human resources practitioners. These are the great spirits of our profession.

They are the women and men who have the courage to try, the patience to persevere, the determination to succeed. I have worked with some and observed others who have made magnificent contributions to their organizations and to the thousands of human beings who toil therein. I can only try my best to communicate a small portion of the value they are creating for their organizations.

The most encouraging aspect of my investigation is that I found these great spirits every place I visited, and their numbers are growing. Ten years ago they were very difficult to locate. But today, they inhabit organizations of all sizes, from megacorporations to small businesses. They are in every industry within which I have worked. I have found them on every continent that I have traversed. This book tells their story. You will see their work displayed throughout the chapters that follow.

Basic Approach

I could have gone into much more detail as to what these marvelous people are doing. But it was not my objective to write another handbook of methodology. My first book, *How to Measure Human Resources Management*, used a detailed, descriptive format because the subject required that kind of approach. The present book is a call to arms. It is meant to shake up some people and provide encouragement to others. My goal is to provide a stimulant, along with a general model, for those, like you, who would like to do more but who don't know quite where or how to start. I can tell you how to calculate any measure of human resources value. But only you can determine the measures to use, because only you know your purposes and objectives.

The tactics of measurement can be described in logical, linear methodology. But the strategy of value management is best drawn broadly and sprinkled with examples of what others are doing. The examples must remain sketchy or the reader's focus will be drawn to method rather than to concept. Imagination is the key to value management. It is the one trait that is common to every value manager I know. Those spirits are the type of people who can visualize a house in an acorn. Anyone can see wood if I point out a tree. The trick is to see a cabinet or a chair within a seed. If I go into too much detail, I will draw the picture for the readers, and they will never learn to build their own models. My job is to point out the acorn and show what some people have been able to make from it. Ultimately, however, each person must learn lumbering and carpentry for themselves. And, I believe, the more space I give them, the more practical and beautiful will be the results.

There are many books and seminars on the art and science of management. I am trying to provide the vision of what could be, to point readers in the right direction, and to toss in a few examples to stimulate them to decide for themselves the type of plan that will work in their own situation. My approach versus the how-to approach might be likened to the difference between radio and television. Radio provides clues and then requires you to fill in the details from your experience, intuition, and imagination. Television gives you the whole experience—sound and pictures—and allows you to become a potato.

Human Value Management

As I watched and worked with the leading spirits of the human resources profession, I gradually became aware of the model that they all followed, and I felt I could articulate it. The model is called human value management. It is the most concise description that I could put together of what I have seen.

Human value management looks upon people as constituting one of the most important assets of an organization. The action word is *management*. The modifier is *value*. What I see happening is that human resources professionals are starting to manage the "people" side of their organizations in such a way as to create value for the organization as well as for the employee. Ultimately, of course, this will also create value for society as a whole.

My protagonists are professionals and managers who go beyond their daily administrative duties to look for ways to make the world a better place in which to live, work, and enjoy and fulfill oneself. To me, they are a source of constant inspiration. There is so much talent and energy in our field that it makes me proud to be associated with it. I want to thank these professionals and managers for continually picking up my spirits after I had encountered still another mediocre mind.

Organization of the Book

At the outset, Chapter One comments on material that I gathered while consulting and lecturing from 1986 through early 1989. It points out a basic problem that human resources must deal with; that is, a lingering perception on the part of managers that human resources does not add value to the organization. To me, the critical issue is to change that negative perception — a perception held not only by some of our customers but by some of our colleagues as well.

Chapter Two then comments on the rapidly changing marketplace and the implications that this has for human resources management. Chapters Three through Ten cover the human value management model. They deal with the model as a whole, strategic management, a new vision for human resources, how to reposition human resources, market and customer analysis, assessing the capacity of the human resources department to serve the market, identification of key success points, and how to do value measurement. Each of the nine chapters is a mix of general principles, illustrations of these principles, and, in cases where it is important, forms that can be used to gather the data needed to turn the acorn into building materials. Following each chapter are two short cases that provide somewhat more detailed examples of the central principle of that chapter. Throughout each chapter there are also many shorter examples of how the brighter, more insightful among us are solving problems in the value management way. Chapter Eleven describes a few state-of-the-art projects that I believe are pushing the frontier of knowledge forward. Again, my intent is simply to outline the main thrust of these projects. The purpose of this book is not to tell you how to do something, but to stimulate your imagination and to move you to use your talents to add value.

Acknowledgments

Many people helped me write this book. Their contributions are described through their comments and work examples in the book itself. Beyond that, I have talked informally for hours with many of these colleagues, and their insights have been invaluable. You will see their names throughout the book so I will not try to list all of them here. My only regret is that I could include only a few examples of what they are achieving.

I appreciated the help of Bill Hicks, my editor at Jossey-Bass. It was Bill who encouraged me two years ago to write this book. The staff at the Saratoga Institute has been supportive all along. Carol Walton offered ideas when I was stuck. Mike Smith and Nikhil Mirchandani printed draft after draft of my manuscript late at night while I was trying to finish it between consulting trips to far-off places. Finally, Genny Hall helped by taking some of my work at Saratoga Institute so that I could finish this work. My memory at times like this is faulty so I apologize to anyone I may have missed. But one person I could never miss is my partner in life, my wonderful wife, Ellen Kieffer. Between building our company and my writing this book we have not had much social life lately. Perhaps now I can make it up to her.

In selecting the people and cases for this book, I no doubt left out thousands more who are doing similar work and achieving similar results. I wish I could have met them. If you are doing something that is adding value to your organization, I invite you to call or write me. I want to know you and your work. You can reach me at Saratoga Institute, P.O. Box 412, Saratoga, California 95071. Telephone: (408) 446-4788; FAX (408) 446-4874.

Saratoga, California   Jac Fitz-enz
February 1990

*To Ellen, a great spirit
who inspires me.*

The Author

Jac Fitz-enz is the founder and president of Saratoga Institute, a consulting, research, and software firm that specializes in quantitative and qualitative measurement of staff functions.

In the mid 1970s, Fitz-enz pioneered the total system approach to measuring professional and administrative performance. His 1984 book, *How to Measure Human Resources Management*, is the standard text on quantitative evaluation of human resources. He is the leading consultant on the design and implementation of human resources strategic management and measurement systems, with clients in over twenty countries. Saratoga Institute maintains a data bank going back to 1985 on eighty human resources process and output measures. Annual surveys and reports are published on these measures in the United States. Work on the first international survey began in 1990.

Prior to founding Saratoga Institute, Fitz-enz held vice-presidential positions in human resources at Imperial Bank, Wells Fargo Bank, and Motorola Computer Systems. He has published over fifty articles and edits Saratoga Institute's many regional and national surveys. He holds a B.A. degree (1955) from the University of Notre Dame in political science, an M.A. degree (1969) from San Francisco State University in communications/industrial psychology, and a Ph.D. degree (1974) from the University of Southern California in communications/industrial relations.

Human
Value
Management

1

Changing Perceptions About Human Resource Management

IN MY FIRST book I said get rid of the personnel department. Then, you changed the name to human resources. In my next book I am going to say, get rid of human resources.

Robert Townsend

If I asked you, Why does the human resources function exist? what would you answer?

For the past several years I have been preoccupied with investigating the purpose and value of the human resources function. Although there are a few common perceptions about human resources, I can assure you that there is no consensus. When I ask human resource professionals why their organizations support the function, I get a very wide range of answers. They run from "We are a necessary evil" to "We improve the bottom line."

Every time that I have spoken to a human resources group in the past few years I have asked them to give me three arguments for supporting a fully functioning human resources department. In fact, I have posed this question to over 1,500 human resources practitioners in North America, Australia, Brazil, South Africa, and several European countries. Following are the top seven responses, in order of frequency of mention:

1. Keep the company out of court.   209
2. Provide standards, consistency, and equity.   171
3. Improve productivity and profits.   162
4. Develop people.   153
5. Provide recruiting services.   139
6. Improve employee relations and communications.   128
7. Support line managers.   117

1

What most fascinates me about the statements above are the underlying visions that prompted them. Nothing is more fundamental than one's raison d'etre, and nothing is more central to an individual than his or her value system. Let's use the extremes that I mentioned before as an illustration. Individuals who believe that their career field is a necessary evil for an organization obviously have a totally different vision of themselves and their profession than do individuals who tell you that their efforts improve the bottom line. Therein lies the basic problem that the human resources function has always faced. Many people both within and outside the field see only vague, limited benefits emanating from human resource activities.

A Case in Point

Some time ago I asked a favor from several human resources managers. I had hired Mike, a recent college graduate, to work on our company's software and survey systems. Since he lacked hands-on experience in human resources, I asked those friends to let Mike spend a couple of hours observing their various functions—for example, staffing, compensation and benefits, employee relations—so that he could see how things are done. Well, young Mike is a very insightful fellow. In the course of looking at operations, he asked everyone two questions.

Mike's first question was, How did you get into human resources? The answers to this question ranged from "a fluke" to "by bad luck." Further explanations revealed that most people came into the field by default. Women reentering the work force without current professional skills and experience found that the human resources department was one of the few units that would hire them. Humanities majors were shunted into human resources jobs rather than into marketing or production. No one had come in through a formal degree program. No one had grown up wanting to become a human resources professional.

The second question was, How do you see the fit between human resources and the organization? Is human resources part of the organization or outside of it? The answers here fell into two distinct categories. While the chief human resources officer often saw the function as an integral part of the organization, almost every other respondent saw human resources as sitting on the outside looking in. They said that they did not feel as though they were part of the organization and they did not think that line people saw HR as part of the organization either. Although they saw some movement toward integration, they thought it was very slow in coming and that it would be years before it actually occurred. As a result, they reinforced the separation by sticking together. They seldom had lunch or socialized with people from outside their department. They chose not to be a part of the company.

Changing HR's Self-Perception

A positive vision of the human resources function is foreign to many practitioners as well as to many of their customers. If the human resources department is to survive into the twenty-first century, however, it will need to adopt a new self-perception. The image must be one of human resources as a value-adding function. There simply isn't room for any other view.

The place to start changing a vision is within the value system of the person himself. When Mike asked what the culture and atmosphere were like in the human resources departments he was visiting, the typical reply was "We work a lot of long hours"—a reply that was almost always followed by an audible sigh of resignation. There was a fatalistic acceptance that said "We work hard and don't get much appreciation." If they are to turn self-deprecating perceptions into something more positive, people must first want to change. They must be willing to accept the anxiety of change over the comfort of the status quo. Most importantly, they must believe that a better approach is possible.

Once the desire is there, people need a path to follow. That is, they need a vision of what could be and a method that will take them step-by-step from the known of today to the unknown of tomorrow. Therein lies the purpose of the book.

Changing the Customer's Perception

The second perceptual field that has to be altered is the view that our customer has of human resources. What do most managers think of our field? In my travels I have asked some 1,200 managers to give me the three strongest images that they carry of the human resources function in their company. I have asked this not only in the United States but also in Australia, Brazil, Canada, Denmark, France, Great Britain, and South Africa. The responses of these managers were remarkably similar. Human resources seems to have a very consistent global image, and it isn't a good one. The following list gives the images of human resources most commonly held by line managers. The order in which they are listed is based on frequency of mention:

1. Human resources is too costly.   401
2. It doesn't add value.   287
3. It's bureaucratic and unresponsive.   184
4. We can do it ourselves.   163
5. Human resources people are time wasters.   159
6. They interfere with operations.   155
7. They don't know the business.   118

How is it that a group of supposedly professional practitioners on five continents have created such a consistently negative impression on their marketplace?

I was given an insight into the development of this global image by the director of personnel for a major investment banking firm. He noted that through the 1950s the human resources department was often a dumping ground for ineffective employees. Paper processing, a little hiring, and party planning were the chief duties of the personnel administrator. There was no profession as such. Only a very few colleges offered a personnel administration program. Most people came to personnel by default rather than by plan.

In the 1960s, the era of Woodstock and the Great Society, the personnel function swung heavily to the side of the individual. Well-meaning personnel people, who were naturally sympathetic to social injustices, often became self-appointed corporate consciences. It doesn't matter what your or my opinion is about this position: the fact is that sometimes human resources practitioners shifted so much in favor of the employee that they became adversaries of the organization that employed them. As a result, they came to be seen as do-gooders who only got in the way of management.

During the 1970s the federal government, along with state and local governments, became even more deeply involved in the business world through the creation and empowerment of regulatory agencies and the enforcement of social legislation. The personnel department, which was just beginning to look for a new identity, now took on the role of compliance officer. In many cases, instead of helping their organizations find paths through the legislative mine field, individuals in personnel and human resources departments used the laws as a source of personal power. But in doing so, they further alienated themselves from line managers, who were trying to cope with business problems that had been exacerbated by the new restrictions.

It was only in the 1980s that some human resources professionals began to find effective methods for playing the dual role of guardian of the employee and champion of the organization. By that time, however, the animosity that had developed over several decades had coalesced into a generally negative image of the value of the human resources function.

If reality matched the image, there would be no question but that top management should abolish the human resources function. It would be unconscionable to continue to fund such a function if it actually had a totally negative impact on the organization. Logic tells us that the truth and the image must not match. By that I mean, the human resources department must be doing something valuable or it would no longer exist. This leads me to believe that our problem is not one of survival but rather one of quality. No one is going to eliminate human resources. The critical question is, How do we improve our position?

Solving the Vision Problem

Every problem contains within itself the seeds of its own solution. Truly understanding a problem is the first step to solving it.

The way to change the vision of human resources is to change our self-concept first and then change our image in the minds of our customers. Although I am continually confronted with evidence and testimony to the contrary, I don't want to believe that anyone joined the human resources field solely because he or she finds a great thrill in administering plans or running programs. I hope and believe that you and I, and most other people who find themselves in human resources work, have higher ideals. Deep inside we know that we can help make organizations better places for the people who work in them. However, somewhere along the line that vision may become blurred. Maybe we get so mired down in our daily activities that we lose sight of why we entered the human resources profession. Sometime back, perhaps in the middle of long hours, negative feedback, and limited resources, some of us may have misplaced our original notion about the value of human resources work. We forgot why organizations need a human resources function.

Your employer doesn't need you to administer specific programs or plans. Some companies have moved many personnel administration duties back to the line where they used to be. Your organization doesn't need you to train or recruit employees. The market is loaded with consultants and headhunters who can be hired for a specific job and dismissed as soon as they complete it. No, your organization needs you for a much more important task: to make it a place where people can achieve their personal goals while at the same time helping the institution accomplish its mission.

The path to recapturing the vision lies before you. There is only one barrier to following that route to a better future. It is human resource practitioners themselves. As that great philosopher Pogo once said, "We has met the enemy, and it is us."

When I talk with people about recapturing their vision, they tell me that they can't do it. They say they don't have the time, the budget, the staff, or the authority to do so. These are simply excuses. These are reasons born out of fear and frustration. Lack of resources is not the problem. Lack of faith is.

Several years ago I met a woman who had worked with me in a personnel function in the past. I asked her how she liked her new job and her new boss. She said that he was a really nice person to work for. Then I asked her if he was getting anything done. She replied with a line that I shall never forget. She said, "He really wants to be proactive, but he doesn't have time."

No one who habitually acts in a reactive mode really wants to be proactive. You don't wait to be proactive until you have time. You don't seek permission to behave proactively. You don't ask someone if you can make positive changes. Proactive people simply make the changes and apologize later for not getting permission. Once they point out the improvement that they have made, objections usually disappear.

If you have faith in yourself, you can replace lack of money with creativity. You can replace lack of staff with commitment. You can replace lack of time with focused energy. You can replace lack of authority with action. There is nothing standing between you and your career goals in human resources except yourself. Faith in yourself will allow you to recapture the vision of human resources that once inspired you.

Human Value Management

I'm not asking you to perform managerial acrobatics without a safety net. There are already a number of organizations that are reshaping human resources from the inside out. A relatively small but fast-growing and dedicated group of your professional colleagues believes that human resources is a business function. In their view it is as integral to the operation of a business as are sales, production, research and development, accounting, and information processing. Furthermore, they have followed up their vision with a new, more pragmatic, and more opportunistic style of human resources management.

There is an international wave in motion. I've seen it happening in São Paulo, Seattle, and Sydney. Human value management (HVM) is alive and growing in Capetown, Caracas, and Copenhagen. It's operating in London, Leavenworth, and Los Angeles — Tampa, Tokyo, and Toronto — Madison, Melbourne, and Montreal. Human resource professionals in Abu Dhabi, Birmingham, Chicago, Dallas, Duisburg, Durban, Haifa, Johannesburg, New York, Paris, Perth, Portland, San Francisco, Stockholm, and hundreds of other cities worldwide are adopting the principles of human value management. HVM is now functioning in at least a dozen countries on six continents, and the number of its practitioners is growing daily.

Human value management is an operating philosophy to some, a strategy and a set of tactics for others. It is a belief system that has VALUE as its foundation. People talk about it in many ways, but its underlying idea can be expressed as follows:

> Creating value is a matter of eliminating waste. Anything
> that does not add value is waste.

Operationally, HVM assumes that the purpose of the human resources function is to add value to employees and the organization through the application of technical, interpersonal, professional, and managerial skills at the human and organizational interface. HVM presumes that its practitioners will examine their programs, products, services, and operations for examples of value-adding processes, outputs, and impacts. Those behaviors that do not add human, financial, or production value will be reduced or eliminated, and resources will be reassigned to other, value-producing activities.

There are many examples of this new vision. They exist in service, manufacturing, and natural resource businesses. I've seen evidence of them in food-processing in Australia, investment banking on Wall Street, information services in England, utilities in San Francisco, insurance in Canada, electronics in Japan, telecommunications in Sweden, construction materials in Alabama, chemicals in Brazil, and other cases too numerous to list. During the course of the book I will describe the vision and processes that HVM professionals and managers are developing and how they are repositioning their human resources departments within their organizations. I will highlight cases and practices from around the world to show you how to change your organization, your career, and your life by means of this new, positive, and practical approach called human value management.

Conclusion

It takes courage, energy, creativity, and, most of all, perseverance to change a human resources department. Although it will be a frustrating experience at times, change is possible, and the rewards outweigh the effort a hundredfold. The following are only a few of the benefits that you and your staff will obtain from this new, more positive image:

- Human resources is repositioned within the organization.
- Management begins to view the function more positively.
- The department becomes a party to strategic decision making.
- The staff gains respect as a critical player in the management game.

But you are the key to making all this happen. My ancestors come from northern Luxembourg near the Belgian border. There is a proverb from that region that seems to fit the situation in which so many human resources people find themselves today:

> It is a waste of time to wait for your ship to come in if you haven't sent one out.

But some practitioners are not waiting vainly any more. They are changing the modus operandi of personnel administration. They are truly human asset investment advisers for their companies, and their departments have become as valuable a part of their organization as are any of its other functions.

> Nothing in this world is so powerful as an idea whose time has come.
>
> Victor Hugo

2

The New Laws
of the Marketplace:
Evolutionary Change
at Revolutionary Speed

AMERICAN BUSINESS, IN fact the whole economy, is facing
its biggest change and challenges since the industrial
revolution two hundred years ago.
Malcolm Forbes

As broad as this claim is, it is an understatement. Mr.
Forbes could have included businesses worldwide and the
global economy. Quite simply, the answer to the question What's
happening to the world economy today? is Everything!

Evolutionary Change at Revolutionary Speed

The changes that have taken place over the past several
decades and the predictions of the changes coming in the next
ten years are so well known that it would be redundant for me to
repeat them. I just want to make sure that one basic point has not
been missed. It is that we are at the meeting point of two massive
forces: complex change and an accelerating rate of change. Ever
since the mid 1970s there has been a convergence of political,
economic, social, and technological forces on the global economy. Our world continues to struggle with the most profound
changes imaginable. We find ourselves living in an era shaken by
transformations as broad and deep as those brought on by the
industrial revolution in the first years of the nineteenth century.
The event that decisively initiated this massive transformation was the sharp increase in oil prices engineered by the

Organization of Petroleum Exporting Countries (OPEC) in the early 1970s. Whether justified or not, this sudden rise in cost of that most basic commodity, energy, hit the world market with a shock that is still reverberating. It devastated the fundamentals of many national economies. No one was untouched when the price of oil went to $30 per barrel. All nations, both developed and underdeveloped, floundered in their attempts to recover from this awesome economic blow. Politically, governments first regulated and nationalized major industries. In time, however, they learned a basic economic lesson: Government bureaucracies do not create wealth, they absorb it. Within less than a decade, many of these same governments reversed course and began to deregulate and privatize industries. Essentially, they kept changing the rules of the game of business without any clear recovery plan. Industries that had long enjoyed government protection and subsidies were suddenly cut loose and forced into the free market. Transportation, banking, utilities, and telecommunications—in other words, the most fundamental economic and social industries—are still struggling to learn the new rules of the marketplace.

The picture becomes even bleaker when we note the effects of knee-jerk tariff and trade programs, the heavy debt load of developing countries, and the huge federal deficit in the United States. Sudden shifts in the balance of trade bring floods of imports into previously stable markets. Margins erode and international courts are filled with litigation over dumping charges. Discontinuity clearly has been the signature of the 1980s.

Technological innovations are allowing and—in some cases—forcing organizations to restructure their operations and cultures. The ubiquitous electronic workstation and the increasing development of networks are doing more than improving employee productivity and communications. Once employees grasp the capabilities that electronics brings to communications and data manipulation, they find themselves empowered as never before. By communicating directly with each other rather than through a structured chain of command, they are able to redesign their jobs. Work flows are being restructured. New relationships, alliances, and values — the corner-stones of organizational cultures — are emerging because of the introduction of electronic technology. Make no mistake, organizational culture is changing profoundly.

It has been projected that, by 1993, three hundred and seventy million computers will be in use in business around the world (Strassman, 1985). Access to a keyboard and a transmission system frees workers from the control of their supervisors. These developments pose basic questions. What will be the new role of supervisors? Will we even need middle management by the year 2000?

Socially, there are major events occurring not only in the work force but also in society as a whole. Equal rights movements are a global phenomenon. Demographics are changing. Waves of baby booms and busts are passing through all nations. For example, the population in Third World countries is substantially younger than the population in northern European countries. This is generating labor shortages in some economies and massive unemployment and underemployment in others.

Education, or lack of it, is also impacting the employability of large segments of many societies. In the United States, of every 100 children entering high school at least 55 will not be available for employment by businesses. Correlation of various industry and government reports yields this picture: Federal and local governments and the armed forces will take at least 20 graduates from the value-adding work force. An additional 20 students will never graduate from high school and will therefore be relegated to the lowest levels of jobs and the ranks of the chronically unemployed. Some young women will choose to become full-time mothers and homemakers. A small percentage of the graduates will be chronically ill and disabled, and another 2 or 3 percent will self-limit their career opportunities through lack of ambition and education. In total, it seems that no more than 45 out of 100 high school graduates will ever reach the labor market. Of those, perhaps half will pursue advanced degrees and prepare themselves for technical, professional, and managerial positions. It does not seem likely that America can sustain a position of leadership with this level of available talent.

Table 1. Worker Happiness Factor.

	Mean Score		
	Japan	U.K.	U.S.
How important is work?	2	4	8
Where does work rank in terms of satisfaction?	4	6	7

Note: 1 = high, 10 = low.
Source: "The Happiness Barometer," 1988.

In the developed nations, where both parents usually work outside the home, there is a growing demand for child care and other social betterment subsidies. Changing personal values also represent a strong and growing reality. For example, work is no longer the top priority in many people's lives. A small study of 1,000 workers each in Japan, England, and the United States may be indicative of where work fits into people's lives today. The subjects were asked to comment on how work ranked against nine other factors in terms of life satisfaction. The results are shown in Table 1.

Finally, concern for the environment is growing. Such environmental issues as pollution, drought, and deforestation are on everyone's mind today. These issues will affect the way in which organizations deal with their employees and their communities.

Globalization

Dealing with these massive evolutionary forces provides a challenge of the greatest difficulty to both line and staff managers. But even these forces are not the whole story. There is still another development that is fast overtaking many organizations, namely, globalization.

The world has become one marketplace and any company can invade practically any market. The issue of globalization adds particularly to the challenge of organizational management. The '88 Tokyo Forum brought together representatives from five of the world's leading economic think tanks. Futurists from the Brookings Institution, IFO, Royal Institute of International Affairs, L'Institut Français des Relations Internationales, and the Nomura Research Institute concluded that there are a number of global economic problems and opportunities that will reshape world markets. Thus, as more companies move aggressively beyond their borders into world markets, they will be faced with the need to develop world-class products and services at the lowest possible cost. This will mean changes in the design, production, and distribution of goods and services.

The conclusions of the Tokyo Forum led to a Global Human Resource Management Symposium, held in the spring of 1987. Participants came from Europe, the United States, Australia, and the Asia-Pacific region. They developed an agenda for the 1990s based on four challenges that had been identified at the Tokyo Forum:

1. Global product and service market strategies
2. Global coordination and integration
3. Strategic alliances
4. Global staffing and development

The symposium participants proposed that each of these challenges had implications for human resource management. They outlined these implications and developed an agenda for human resource management executives, as follows:

1. Global Product and Service Market Strategies

Issues: Develop new kinds of design teams, better able to use strategic sourcing, and establish world-class standards for design, service, and performance.

Agenda

- Ensure human resource involvement in formulating global strategy.

- Develop competencies in human resources to contribute to globalization.
- Take the lead in developing processes for top management as it develops global strategy, including information processing, decision making, and learning processes.
- Facilitate the implementation phase by identifying skills, assessing competencies, and developing sourcing strategies.

2. Global Coordination and Integration

Issues: Improve communication and cultural integration processes and alter human resources systems.

Agenda

- Provide new concepts and paradigms for global organization design.
- Develop a blend of hard and soft (direct and indirect, quantitative and qualitative) mechanisms; be process experts.
- Provide action research learning feedback loops for global integration experimentation.

3. Strategic Alliances

Issues: Establish partnerships to gain market entry, to achieve price competitiveness, to develop technology, and to arrive at new insights about management techniques.

Agenda

- Develop models of types of alliances and rationales for their use.
- Come to an understanding of the joint-venture process.
- Design strategic alliance management processes for handling joint strategy formulation, developing structural linkages, providing daily coordination and communication, establishing a positive climate, and protecting the bargaining power of each party.

4.   Global Staffing and Development

Issue: Develop leaders with global vision.

Agenda

- Globalize the human resources staff.
- Link human resources plans to global business plans.
- Conduct analyses of which key functions, jobs, and skills are needed to operate globally.
- Develop programs that "internationalize" people, not just operations.
- Develop information systems to support global human resources management.
- Develop a plan for attracting the most capable management and professional people in the world market (Tichy, 1988).

What does all that mean to the average human resources manager slugging it out in the swamp every day? To me, it says that while he is wrestling with the alligators, he shouldn't forget to spend some time on land reclamation. In dealing with today's problems, a human resources manager has to help position his organization to deal with tomorrow's opportunities and challenges.

Clearly, a bureaucratic mentality and a tactical methodology will contribute nothing to the solution of the types of problems or the exploitation of the kinds of opportunities that were highlighted at the '88 Tokyo Forum. The 1990s and beyond will belong to those who can recognize and deal with the key forces shaping the new world marketplace. It was Charles Gow who noted that seeing is different from understanding: "Observation is more than seeing: it is knowing what you see and comprehending its significance."

Organizations are beginning to take note of the need for change. In October of 1988 Merck held a week-long meeting of its human resources managers in Montreal. Over 100 men and women came to Montreal from the company's facilities worldwide to talk about how the pharmaceutical giant was responding to the need to improve productivity and quality in the emerging global market. Chief executive officer Roy Vagelos and his team discussed "Key Strategic Issues and Challenges Facing Merck and the Impact of Globalization." Speakers were brought in from Fiat, Mobil, the London School of Business, Harvard University, and Saratoga Institute. They described in detail some of the issues that Merck would need to address to become more competitive in the global market. The very fact that Merck called this conference made the point that its management was not only committed to human value management but that it was aware that the price of leadership in today's market is constant effort and innovation. The structure of the conference agenda provided an example of how organizations are taking to heart the notion that effectiveness must be defined in new ways.

New Rules of Organizational Effectiveness

What does all this strategic, global turmoil mean for the management of organizations? I believe it adds some new dimensions to the concept of organizational effectiveness. The rules of business have clearly changed. We must now deal simultaneously with numerous changes that are evolutionary in scope. The exacerbating problem is that all these changes are coming at revolutionary speed. It is no wonder that we are stunned and confused. When you stop to think about the depth and breadth of these changes, you begin to realize that we are undergoing an organizational metamorphosis. The industrial model is being replaced by the informational model.

Moreover, just as we were getting comfortable with the concept of automation, along came Shoshana Zuboff, author of *In the Age of the Smart Machine*, with the notion of "informating" (Zuboff, 1988). She argues that information technology can empower ordinary working people with overall knowledge of a given process, thereby making them capable of executing critical judgments and taking responsible actions to solve production and distribution problems. Zuboff's position is that we don't yet know how to configure organizations that can successfully exploit the opportunities that "informating" offers. It is not just a matter of moving more data more quickly. The key is to use data in different ways to create value. Clearly, the organizational policies and practices that worked so well in the predictable, relatively low-tech world economy of the 1950s to the 1980s have little utility in "informating" organizations. The magnitude of these types of changes makes it clear that many organizations will be forced to transform their cultures in order to cope with the new market challenges. As we look forward through the 1990s to the possibilities of the twenty-first century, it becomes obvious that many organizations aren't ready for the changes that lie ahead.

The rules of the business game continue to change daily. Management's problem is that no one has published the new rules. Herein lies the human resources department's opportunity. Any time that massive change strikes an organization it begins to stretch and strain as it tries to adapt to the new pressure points. The culture is stressed. In effect, the fabric of the organization expands in places, opening the weave and exposing holes that are the results of obsolete practices. These gaps must be rewoven if the organization is to survive. One of two results is likely to follow.

First, as business conditions in general become more difficult and competitive, lower profits will translate into less income to invest in staff services. The personnel and training departments have always been among the first to suffer when business turns down. As Robert Townsend noted, changing the name from personnel to human resources did not change managers' perceptions of the value of the function or the practice of cutting it back during troubled times. The cyclical pattern of riffing and rebuilding human resources comes to be accepted as a natural process. And, as discontinuity becomes a way of life, the human resources department has to struggle even harder to justify its existence and to win support for its services.

The other, happier result will be that the company comes to view the gaps in its corporate fabric as opportunities. But while management sees that its needs are abundant, it has few solutions to offer. This is where the human resources department can intervene by becoming a midwife of change.

If human resources is to take up the opportunity afforded

it, the energy must come from within. Not long ago I was addressing the American Bankers Association graduate school of human resource management. I was asked how one changes a human resources function from a reactive to a proactive role. My answer was, You just do it! You don't wait for anyone's permission. Instead, you find a target of opportunity and attack it. Having reached your goal, you show management what you have done and then on to the next target. You will find that no one stands in the way of a winner.

Human resources can fill today's needs. All it requires is an open mind and a willingness to take on new challenges. At South Seas Plantation Resort off the west coast of Florida, the human resources function is playing a central and unusual role in the resort's management. Len Myers, who heads HR, brought responsibility for the quality assurance program to human resources because he saw it was a central issue and a key success point for the resort. His people provide the training and communications necessary to keep the program vital. They monitor the reports. As a member of the executive committee, Len ensures that the program gets top-level attention. The moral is obvious: Len saw a need and filled it. No one got in his way.

On the other side of the world, South Africa is struggling with a shortage of supervisory personnel. Human resources managers from a number of corporations are working with Nasser Associates on a national program to, as Martin Nasser puts it, "equip our people of color for upward mobility." The objective is to bring promising young people into business and give them the technical and interpersonal skills they need to move into management positions. Once a new employee has been hired, Nasser's mentor program works with the human resources department to train him and provides a mentor from management who can help him learn how to succeed and rise through the ranks. This is one of the best examples I have seen of how human resources is working systematically to alleviate a nationwide problem.

Human Resources' Chance

Never in its history has the human resources department had such an opportunity to affect organizational change. Many of the new problems that management must confront have to do with how to restructure their organizations, redesign jobs and work flow, stimulate increased productivity, improve quality, control benefit costs, train managers in new supervisory techniques, overcome labor shortages through remedial education, prepare employees for global market jobs, involve employees at all levels in decision making, and measure and pay for performance. Robotization will not solve these problems. These are human matters.

In my discussions with human resources professionals across the United States I found a near consensus as to the three most critical human resources issues: (1) finding, attracting, and retaining qualified people; (2) containing the cost of employee benefits—particularly health care costs; and (3) developing an effective method to pay for performance. The ability to compete on the global market is also tied to human issues. Substandard worker education, the lack of qualified supervisory personnel, the demand for better living standards, and rising expectations in regard to entitlements and civil rights are the most common problems. It will take a holistic approach to the human condition for businesses and governments to solve these problems.

Undeniably, many of management's dilemmas represent opportunities from the point of view of human resources. The forces of change cannot be ignored. They are too deeply embedded in the new world economy. Someone must address them. Someone will have to guide the organization's attempts to adjust to the new market forces that are rendering the old ways of managing human beings obsolete. That someone would logically be the human resources department. In this view it is not a luxury for an organization to have a fully functioning human resource management function. It is rather one of the prerequisites of long-term organizational health and financial growth.

Pat Aburdene, coauthor of *Reinventing the Corporation*, claims that "the [human resource] function is becoming so critical, so important, that if your people don't assert a real leadership capability in matters pertaining to people, other people in the organization will do so and almost usurp the purpose of having an individual whose job it is to develop and sustain that important people element" (Naisbitt and Aburdene, 1985, p. 3).

Human resources practitioners can take this statement as a threat or as an opportunity. But if they are going to be of any consequence in the twenty-first century, they have one last chance to change their strategy and show a new face to the market.

Human resources departments are learning to address the business objectives of their organizations. Many of them no longer run routine "personnel" programs with limited objectives. Managers everywhere are faced with the demand to be more productive and to turn out higher-quality products. Human resources, in some organizations, is supporting this imperative by providing only those services that show value.

When the requirement for greater productivity first surfaced in the United States in the late 1970s, we had the chance to step in and take on the human side of productivity management. Unfortunately, we were too busy administering programs. We blew our chance to make a contribution to the number one management problem of the 1980s. As a result, other people picked up our opportunity and ran with it. We can't afford to let our chance get away again.

Management is searching, often frantically, for new solutions to its new problems. Human resources probably has the answers to many of them. If you choose to step forward and take on the human side of these current business dilemmas, you can become a valued member of your organization's management team. The way that you help management from the top down recognize the need for a stronger human resources function is by fixing problems. If you can show that you have both identified the significant problems and come up with solutions for them, you will seldom find people standing in your way. The human resources profession's problem has been that it lacked sufficient self-confidence to make the changes it can make—changes that most line managements welcome.

The Starting Point

Caroline Jackson, who was formerly on the national personnel staff of the American Red Cross, underlined the posture that will mark successful human resource practitioners in the next decade:

> We must not simply be messengers, but advocates and creators of change.

Sometimes today's challenges look like a worktable covered with old correspondence, reports, telephone message slips, dirty coffee cups, dried-up ballpoint pens, and dozens of paper clips of assorted sizes. Office flotsam and jetsam have a way of building up until we can't get anything done because we can't find what we need. If you are feeling that way, remember what Wally Amos, founder of the Famous Amos cookie company, said:

> It is important to start—start from right where you are.

I can't emphasize this point enough: just start! Take a risk and don't worry about making a mistake. If you have prepared your strategy, you will survive the occasional mistake and learn from it.

There are fundamental problems that human resources must overcome if it is to take up the challenges ahead. One is the negative perception of human resources that I described in Chapter One. This image problem hit me smack in the face recently while I was walking through the exhibit hall at a marketing convention. One of our client companies was showing its products. I approached the young lady staffing the booth and started talking with her about the company. She said she had been with the firm for only a few months. She then volunteered that she was lucky because she had gotten her job "without having to go through the personnel department." She had never met anyone from human resources, yet she had picked up a negative stereotype about the function. That image absolutely must be shattered, now and forever.

Negative stereotypes will be overcome only if we are willing to redirect some of our attention away from administrative trivia and instead focus our efforts on the important needs of the employees and management of the organizations that we serve. Refocused action, not new labels, will be our solution.

The other change we have to make is within ourselves. We have to reposition human resources within the organization by repositioning the function within our own value system. Before we can reconnect our function to the organization, we have to do some soul searching about why we entered this profession in the first place. This requires time and it can't be done on the run. It is going to take a strategic reexamination of our role and some degree of change in our operations.

Leadership for Change

The factors I have described provide ample reason for changing the human resources function. There are five classic signals for changing the culture and operation of an organization:

- When traditional values are no longer functional
- When the market for a product or service changes quickly and substantially
- When organizational performance is substandard
- When there are major increases or decreases in the size of the organization
- When the organization passes certain threshold points

Numerous human resources managers around the world have become aware that they are faced with several of these phenomena. Many have found that old "personnel" values no longer serve their customers' needs. Most markets are moving rapidly. Even such formerly stable industries as banking, insurance, medical care, and electric power are finding themselves in rapidly, significantly changing markets. Past performance, which was perhaps barely satisfactory under more stable conditions, is falling below an acceptable level in the new environment. Downsizings and decentralization of human resources departments have been the rule since the early 1980s. Mergers and acquisitions have created megacorporations, and this in turn has created the need to integrate diverse cultures under a new vision. One or more of these forces have hit just about every human resources department. Traveling internationally, you discover that many of the same changes are taking place in markets worldwide. We are all feeling the effects of fundamental shifts in social, technical, political, and economic sectors.

There are periods in the history of any system, whether it be a nation or an organization, when there is a critical need for leadership. Now is such a time for almost all organizations, whether they be established public agencies or private start-ups, nonprofit charitable groups or companies totally committed to the bottom line.

Leadership is not the exclusive province of the chief executive officer. Organizations need leaders in all functional areas. The chief executive provides the vision for the total enterprise, but the human resources manager should be the herald of that vision. The leader of each function must translate the overall vision for his or her segment of the organization. Large systems are nothing more than an integrated collection of smaller systems. Or, to more accurately reflect organizational realities, I should say that many large organizations are a collection of smaller systems that have the potential of being integrated. For it is clear that many departments do not work together well internally and do not function as an integrated part of the larger organization. This is the other need for leadership. By communicating an organization's vision and showing their commitment to it, leaders provide the glue of integration.

The twenty-first century will be a time of intense competition among complex multinational organizations, all of them struggling for shares of a one-market world in an era of rapid technological development. It will be a marketplace where rigid minds and bureaucratic structures will be counterproductive. Survival in the twenty-first century will require people who have the vision, energy, and courage to change today's systems so that tomorrow's results will satisfy the demands of the new global market.

Even the most successful organizations have to stay alert. Merck is one of the most admired companies in the United

States. Its earnings in the late 1980s were exemplary. When I questioned executives there about the reasons for their success, I came away with a consistent story. Dick Parker, for example, emphasized that Merck is very self-analytical and self-critical. It takes nothing for granted. The company continually audits its systems and policies to make sure they are adding value, not becoming roadblocks. A few years ago, Steve Darien, president of employee relations, led a task force of managers and human resources people that spent six months reviewing all human resources activities. Their conclusion was that Merck had all the programs it needed. But it needed to take them more seriously and make them more than paper exercises.

Unfortunately, not all companies are as aware of the danger of complacency. I will never forget the case of Visicorp. Although many readers may have forgotten the name of this company, it once had the hottest computerized spreadsheet program on the market, VisiCalc. At the apex of Visicorp's fame I was talking with one of its recruiting managers. His attitude was that the company was so good that it didn't need help from anyone. However, it wasn't twelve months later that he was laid off, the company was sliding rapidly into oblivion, and he was "my friend" looking for a job.

The basic task of leadership is to move the performance of the organization from the level it is at today, no matter where it is, to higher levels tomorrow. This is the mandate of human resources. First, make the changes in your area that will allow it to function successfully within the larger organization. Then, help the organization make the changes it needs to survive and grow in the new marketplace. Many students of leadership agree that leadership involves creating new visions of positive change and stirring people's imaginations to pursue these visions. Rosabeth Kanter (1983) defines "change masters" as the right people in the right place at the right time. The right people are those who have ideas that can be formed into visions. The right places are the environments that support innovation. The right times are those unique moments in the flow of events when it is possible to reshape an organization for a more productive and successful future.

Resistance to Change

As you know, most people don't like change unless they are the ones directing it. When change is forced upon them, it has much less appeal. One of the most insightful examples of the uneasiness that change causes human beings is also one of the simplest. Eric Hoffer, the longshoreman-philosopher, opened his book, *The Ordeal of Change*, with this story:

"Back in 1936 I spent a good part of the year picking peas. I started out early in January in the Imperial Valley and drifted northward, picking peas as they ripened, until I picked the last peas of the season, in June, around Tracy. Then I shifted all the way to Lake County, where for the first time I was going to pick string beans. And I still remember how hesitant I was that first morning as I was about to address myself to the string bean vines. Would I be able to pick string beans? Even the change from peas to string beans had in it elements of fear" (Hoffer, 1963, p. 3).

If a man as intelligent and insightful as Hoffer could be frightened by a switch from picking peas to string beans, we can perhaps be forgiven for being uneasy about changing how we manage our job or function. Fearful or not, however, we have no choice but to face up to the changes impacting us and learn how to cope with them. Otherwise they will surely bury us. This applies to our personal lives and it applies to our careers.

A great deal has been written about the reasons why people resist change. In fact, this resistance probably has both personal and organizational sources. At the personal level, people resist change for several reasons:

Homeostasis. As you learned in high school biology, organisms have a natural tendency to maintain stability and consistency. People need a feeling of security and safety, and they will go out of their way to avoid threatening situations.

Habit. We all prefer the familiar. When you ask people to change where or how they work, you are instantly stripping them of their competence. Hoffer's story is a perfect example. Some people have a greater spirit of adventure than others. But many don't like change, period!

Selective Perception. Our senses are constantly bombarded by so many stimuli every second of our lives that we have to be selective in what we take in or we would go insane. But this protective process can go to the extreme where we shut out all new ideas and maintain fixed attitudes toward people and work. You hear this expressed in cliches such as "you can't teach an old dog new tricks" or "there is nothing new under the sun." One chief executive I know consistently refuses to accept data that conflict with his preconceptions.

Dependence. This refers to reliance on and preference for past values as being appropriate for all current or future circumstances. The hymn, "Give me that old-time religion, it's good enough for me," says it well. Acceptance of the past saves us from having to think and from possibly finding out that our "tried-and-true" ways of conducing business have become liabilities.

Regression. This is a search for psychological security in the past. It is a desire to return to safer or more peaceful ways. Preschoolers who want a baby bottle are looking back to a better, safer time. Adults who reject computers in favor of manual systems are also seeking simpler, less stressful ways.

Within an organization there are also forces that make it difficult to bring about change. The principal blocks are as follows:

Norms. These include consensual agreement on the proper ways to dress, speak, work, and socialize. People are rewarded for conforming and punished for not conforming. In 1970, I grew a mustache while working at Wells Fargo Bank. I was told that I should consider the impact that this nonconformist behavior might have on my career. In regard to work, a veneration of norms prevents us from questioning why "we've always done it that way."

Vested Interests. People build fiefdoms in organizations that then become sources of power and prestige. There is a natural reluctance to give up power. The true source of resistance to change is sometimes shrouded by statements that sound righteous but hide the true reason behind the reluctance.

Rituals and Taboos. Procedures usually are established for valid reasons. Over time, however, they may develop into rigid, obsolete, or even irrational systems. After a while they take on a sacrosanct aura. The continued existence of these sacred cows depends on people's preference for the familiar.

Rejection of Outsiders. The "not-invented-here" syndrome ossifies some organizations. Detroit's refusal to see the market for small cars is a classic example of this kind of thinking. People naturally cling to old relationships as being more trustworthy and comfortable than new ones.

Change requires the communication of relevant information that can be personalized. People will resist change less if they are fully informed and involved in the change process. There are a mountain of studies going back to the famous Hawthorne experiments conducted at the General Electric plant in Hawthorne, Illinois, in the 1920s that prove that employee involvement produces positive responses. In its eagerness to get on with a new plan, management often gives too little time to winning its people over. A communique goes out regarding the change. Some discussion takes place, but not enough to enable employees to absorb the information and grasp what the change will mean to them. Because they have been left in the dark about the change, their predictable result is resistance.

Employees need to be told all the reasons for a change and what implications it may have for them. They need a chance to fully question the change and time to consider and accept the rationale for it. They must be convinced that the change has a chance to be successful. They must come to accept that, in the long run, the results will be beneficial to them as well as the organization.

Hewlett-Packard provides an example of how one company dealt with the expected resistance to organizational change. Two manufacturing operations were to be consolidated for the sake of achieving greater efficiencies. The question of how to best accomplish that restructuring was answered by involving employees in shaping the change itself. Task forces covering everything from compensation to process engineering went to work to meld the two operations into one. Human resources supported the negotiations between the groups involved in the change process.

The objective of the reorganization was not to solve a quality or productivity problem but to achieve even greater improvements in manufacturing processes. In addition to this focus on process improvement, Hewlett-Packard was trying to generate greater flexibility among employees. Overall, the idea was to implement the Factory of the Future with teams taking responsibility for managing the manufacturing process. Supervisors were being asked to design the future—a significant change from the traditional day-to-day supervisory responsibilities to which they had become accustomed. Teamwork, communication, and selling and presenting ideas were emphasized in training. Initially, the supervisors did not want to accept responsibility for designing and managing the process, and the concept of complete accountability was difficult for them to internalize. Thus, they were not at first too happy with the reorganization, but on seeing the results they began to make comments such as, "I can see what you are trying to do and it makes sense."

Hewlett-Packard understood that employees do not put their work lives and their personal lives into separate compartments. Change at work affects personal and family life. So, the company encouraged the families of employees to become involved in the reorganization. In this way, they would better understand what the change involved and the effect it might have on home life for a while.

In the end the changes were accomplished at record speeds, and attitude surveys showed positive response and understanding on the part of workers. Through job redesign, change process facilitation, and the resettling of employees, human resources was able to contribute directly to the success of the reorganization.

As a result of that success, in May 1989, when Hewlett-Packard announced another factory consolidation, this time involving a move to Roseville, California, human resources was intimately involved in the decision and in driving many of the consolidation activities. For example:

- The human resources manager was a member of the team that analyzed the data and made the recommendation to consolidate certain operations in Roseville.
- Human resources led the team in developing strategies for anticipating both acceptance of and resistance to the change by employees and customers.
- Human resources also led the team in defining the business rationale for the decision and in developing the communication plans.
- Human resources involved employees at all levels early on and defined their role in the Factory of the Future.

Hewlett-Packard recognizes the depth and complexity of organizational change. The human resources function has become the focal point of change management at the company. Karen Scussel, who led the change process, can point directly to the improvements her team has made on the operating efficiency of Hewlett-Packard.

Successful Culture Change

Deal and Kennedy (1982) have given us the seven ingredients of a successful culture change:

- *Put a hero in charge of the change.* Big changes call for people with big hearts, big visions, the tenacity of bull terriers, and an acceptance of the possible need to make personal sacrifices.
- *Recognize the real threats outside.* Change efforts fail when managers underestimate the power required to overcome

the existing culture. They will not be successful in ridding their company of its obsolete culture unless they are able to demonstrate that the external threat affects everyone's survival.

- *Involve people in transition rituals.* If the employees are involved in the transition process, they will find ways to mourn the passing of the old and learn first hand the values of the new. Transition rituals become a temporary culture. This prevents people from backsliding into the old patterns or rushing ahead thoughtlessly.

- *Provide training in new values and behavior patterns.* The best training is on-the-job training. Work on the new processes provides opportunities for training employees in the new values, behavior, and language that they will need to function in the new culture.

- *Bring in outside shamans.* Outsiders can wield a magic of their own. They are better at defusing conflicts because they are not emotionally involved in them. They can provide different insights and different perspectives. Most importantly, they can provide examples of how others have successfully brought about change.

- *Build tangible symbols of the new directions.* Structural changes — such as new titles, new reporting relationships, and new responsibilities — signal that a unit will soon move in new directions. They confirm that management is serious about the change. Also, they are like road signs pointing the way for people.

- *Deal with the question of job security immediately.* If it is true that no one will lose his or her job, say it. If it isn't true, don't say it. People can't manage a major shift if they are feeling vulnerable. If job security will be jeopardized, deal with that issue first.

Change is a human problem. Machines don't get anxious, and organization charts are infinitely adjustable. Hence, human malleability is the dependent variable.

Supporting Behavior Change

Let's personalize the issue. How can we facilitate change within our function? George Odiorne (1984) suggests five steps that will encourage change within the human resources department:

1. Ask the staff for innovation and expect to get it.
2. Train people in methods of creativity and innovation.
3. Let people know that the status quo is not good enough and that standing still will not be rewarded.
4. Do not promote stodgy, anti-innovative people.
5. Reward innovation and creativity in tangible and intangible ways.

One of life's tried and tested truisms is that you get back what you put out. People will follow your lead if they can see that the system you have put in place truly rewards them for the expected behavior. If you are direct and unequivocal in your actions you will inspire the changes you would like to see.

By far the most frequent excuse I hear from people when I tell them that it is time to rethink their mission is, "I don't have the time to think. I'm short staffed and working ten hours a day as it is." Yet, the result of an inappropriate mission and strategy is that you have to work harder to achieve less. It seems to me that if you have time to be inefficient, you have time to think about ways of becoming more efficient.

The second most frequent excuse for not strategizing is, "I don't get paid to plan. I get paid to act." It is probably true that no one ever got a performance bonus because he or she planned well. At the same time, it is unlikely that people ever get bonuses just because they acted. People aren't paid simply to get results. They are paid to get the right results. This is a common human resources department problem. You and your staff work hard. You go out of your way to be understanding, accommodating, and what do you get for it . . . usually condescension. The reason is that the results you are achieving are neither very visible nor of prime importance in the mind of the observer.

Unplanned actions seldom produce positive results in key success areas. How can you obtain practical results if you don't have an up-to-date, focused strategy? If you don't know where you're headed, how are you going to know which road to take? Operating without an appropriate strategy is like jumping into a car and driving off to a party without knowing exactly where it is. You might find it eventually, but it is certain that you will waste a lot of gas getting there — only to find, perhaps, that the party is already over.

The real, unstated reason why so many human resource professionals refuse to think strategically is that they have lost heart. They love their profession, but they have given up hope of ever making it really work the way it should.

Some time ago, at a national convention of health care human resource managers, I met a woman who was the human resources manager at a hospital in Florida. As we chatted, she began to describe her unhappy situation. She was woefully understaffed by any standard. There were about 1,100 employees that she was struggling vainly to service with a three-person department. I tried to suggest a few small things that she could do to demonstrate some effectiveness and thereby gain extra resources, but she simply refused to listen. She was married to her plight and would not hear of the possibility that she might be able to change it. Finally, she wandered away, glancing half-heartedly at exhibits, seemingly in a daze. Why is she here, I wondered, if she isn't looking for help? The answer must have been that she just needed a week out of the pressure cooker.

As sad as I felt for her, I felt even worse for the 1,100 employees of that hospital who were undoubtedly poorly served by its puny human resources department. I was also concerned about what she was doing to the image of the human resources profession. She was imprinting in the minds of those 1,100 people the idea that the human resources department has little to offer employees.

I found a similar staffing shortage at a company in Los Angeles. When I pointed it out to the manager, she said bravely, "And we don't mind it a bit." Some people spend their careers as self-flagellating martyrs. That may yield a perverse sense of satisfaction. But giving in to an unacceptable situation is a disservice to the employees of the institution.

Contrast that attitude with the approach that Bob Lang and his human resources staff are taking at the Greyhound Corporation. There probably aren't many tougher managers to work for than Greyhound's chief executive officer, John Teets. Mr. Teets is not one to hand out resources unless their would-be recipients can prove that they will invest them in a way that improves Greyhound's bottom line. Bob is developing a human resources management information system covering the four very diverse business segments and the twenty-seven operating companies within Greyhound. His strategy is to position human resources as a value-adding partner in management with the line general managers. The human resources committee meets regularly to review how its operations are contributing to Mr. Teets's stated objective of a 15 percent return on equity. When human resources finds a need that is not being met, it goes to management with a business-based proposal. If the plan makes sense in terms of servicing a corporate imperative, it is funded. The result is that management and employees can count on support where and when it is warranted.

Finding Time to Strategize

I understand that human resources staffs are busy. They have many groups to service, and they don't have a lot of extra time on their hands to think strategically. Such thinking is usually relegated to an annual offsite meeting of no more than three days. Then, it is back to work and running out to fight the next fire. Without some kind of support mechanism back at the workplace, this mode of strategizing simply will not be effective.

Wanting to strategize but never having time for it is like wanting to be proactive but never having time for that. Either you are going to commit yourself to acting strategically or you aren't. I'm not suggesting that you spend 20 or 30 percent of your time strategizing, but what about one hour each week? If you work a 50-hour week, as do so many human resources practitioners, it is only 2 percent of your workweek. Now, you are probably asking yourself, What can I do in an hour? It won't be worth anything. I am willing to gamble that if you get into the habit, you will find that this one hour yields so many ideas that you will think of ways to expand the time you spend strategizing.

You are not alone in being busy. I have not met an effective manager anywhere in any function who had much time to spare. You know the old saying, "If you want to get something done, give it to someone who is busy." There is always time to do the necessary task. And strategizing is more than a necessity, it is an imperative.

I face the same time problems that you do. I run a growing consulting and research business that cranks out a large number of national and international surveys each year. We also consult and design systems all around the country and internationally as well. At least 50 percent of my time is spent out of the office traveling and consulting. Time is at a premium for me too. But I find that if I don't devote regular periods to strategizing, our company wastes time and money on programs and processes that are no longer productive or profitable. I have to strategize to keep my business alive. And do you know what? You also have to strategize to keep your business alive.

In the following chapters I will provide a model and a set of processes that will help you make the changes that will in all likelihood be required by the future demands of the marketplace. Comments, examples, and cases from human resources professionals around the world will illustrate how they are applying this model in dealing with today's dynamic markets. The goal is to show you actual examples of how the change is already under way from the old personnel administration approach to the new, more practical, human value management system.

Conclusion

The marketplace is changing and we have to change with it. We are faced with evolutionary changes that are moving at revolutionary speed. The 1990s will be a period of opportunity such as the human resources function has not seen since the productivity issue first surfaced in the late 1970s. This is our chance to make a contribution to the evolution of organizational structures and operations.

With so much happening at so many levels and at such high speed, a person can start to feel overwhelmed and powerless. He might want to throw up his hands and scream, "I can't do anything about it!" But my dad told me something once that I never forgot. During a particularly trying episode in my life when I was struggling painfully, I finally cried out to him, "Dad, I can't do it!" He said to me, "Son, there is no such word as *can't*."

There is a truism of nature that I learned long ago. It can be expressed like this:

> The magnitude of the result is directly proportional to the force of the effort.

The way you make changes in the face of seemingly overwhelming obstacles is by taking one step at a time. No one has the power to overthrow the old order all at once. Even if you were the CEO you could not change your company overnight. As individuals, we usually have to proceed at evolutionary speed even in the face of revolutionary change. I recommend the water torture method: drip . . . drip . . . drip. If you keep at it, eventually the rock will crack. If you consistently achieve small victories, you will gradually find an army of supporters flocking to your side. Everyone likes to associate with a winner.

When the San Francisco Forty-Niners won the National Football Conference championship in January 1989, Bay Area people who never follow football in a normal year became wildly excited about the team. They bought Forty-Niner jackets, caps, blankets, beer mugs, and anything else that a logo could be put on. They wanted to participate in the thrill of winning. If you can consistently make positive changes in your organization, no matter how small, you will be seen as a winner. People will get behind you, they will add their strength and resources to yours, and your power will grow. But you must take the first step yourself.

The twentieth-century industrial organizational model is

rapidly becoming obsolete. Organizations are looking for products and services that will help them adopt the informational model that will very probably dominate the twenty-first century. A value-adding marketing strategy versus an administration-oriented product approach will help us reposition ourselves to contribute to the redefinition of organizational effectiveness.

But to make the shift from the old to the new market, we need to review our strategies on a regular basis. A profoundly changing, constantly moving marketplace must be continually watched and responded to. The value of operating strategically is that you can then clearly demonstrate how you are contributing to the organization's key objectives. When you are able to do that, you seldom have problems obtaining the resources that you need. The HVM, customer-focused system of human resources management by its very nature shows you and management what you need to serve the market, the managers, and the employees of your organization.

Management is not stupid. If you can show them that a dollar invested with you will earn them two dollars in return, it will be in their best interest to back you. So, let's stop making excuses and simply get on with it.

> What can a little man effect in the face of the formidable power of great corporations? The individual can take the initiative without anybody's permission.
>
> Buckminster Fuller

References

ASPA Resource, Mar. 1986, p. 3.

Deal, T. E., and Kennedy, A. A. *Culture Change*. Reading, Mass.: Addison-Wesley, 1982.

"The Happiness Barometer." Starch INRA Hooper, Mamaroneck, N.Y., 1988.

Hoffer, E. *The Ordeal of Change*. New York: Harper & Row, 1963.

Kanter, R. M. *The Change Masters*. New York: Simon & Schuster, 1983.

Naisbitt, J., and Aburdene, P. *Reinventing the Corporation*. New York: Warner Books, 1985.

Odiorne, G. S. *Strategic Management of Human Resources: A Portfolio Approach*. San Francisco: Jossey-Bass, 1984.

Strassman, P. A. *Information Payoff*. New York: Free Press, 1985.

Tichy, N. M. "Setting the Global Human Resource Management Agenda for the 1990s." *Human Resource Management*, Spring 1988, pp. 1–18.

Zuboff, S. *In the Age of the Smart Machine*. New York: Basic Books, 1988.

Case Studies — Chapter Two

Bell Helicopter Textron
Dallas, Texas
*(From discussions with Roger Williams, director of personnel and
equal employment opportunity)*

When the oil market went into a tailspin in the early
1980s, Bell Helicopter, which is based in Dallas, Texas, had to
adapt itself to vastly different conditions. A company that had
for years been used to a stable, lucrative market suddenly found
itself playing a game for which it was not suited. Before the oil
jolt, Bell got 80 percent of its revenues from the commercial
market. Today, it is 80 percent dependent on the government. In
the commercial market Bell worked in a demand-driven environment. It could afford to pay the high wages that made it the
best-paying firm in the Dallas/Fort Worth metropolitan area. But
the drop in oil prices changed all that. Bell now has to bid for
fixed-price contracts. Furthermore, the company has to work
under the scrutiny of government contract administrators. As a
result, Bell finds itself struggling to lower both its fixed and
variable operating costs.

If economic change wasn't enough, Bell has also had to
simultaneously deal with technological change. Ever since the
1930s, aircraft were basically constructed of metal. Aluminum
stringers and sheet aluminum outer skins were standard. Now,
however, such synthetic materials as composites and epoxies are
being used to build the aircraft of the 1990s. Bell had a genera-
tion of loyal employees who were very skilled at metal bending
but didn't yet know how to handle the new materials. Furthermore, for the most part this labor force was very senior. That
meant that an inordinate number of workers were at the high
end of a very high pay program. In addition, the benefits and
work rules that they had won in collective bargaining over the
years made Bell a very expensive operator. If the company was
going to survive in the new environment, it would have to
substantially change the way it managed people. Every function from recruiting through compensation and benefits to

labor relations and training would have to play new roles. Not only did workers have to address technical innovations in their specialties, they had to work with supervisors and managers who were struggling with the turmoil of market changes.

Credit goes to Ed Szol, now senior vice-president at Bell, who was determined that human resources should play a major role in orchestrating the changes at the company. He knew that the only way that human resources could get its foot in the door was by demonstrating its ability to make a quantifiable, value-adding contribution to the business. He also knew that his audience, the top operating and corporate echelon of the company, managed by numbers. The aircraft business is not a Sunday social. It is a blood and guts, very high stakes game. If you want to play on the team, you have to be able to do more than keep the bench warm.

The staffing area provides one of the best examples of the changes that human resources accomplished at Bell. Under the direction of Roger Williams, staffing soon began to operate like a business. In 1987, for example, staffing received 27,000 resumes. To effectively handle that awesome load, Roger put in place an automated applicant control system. His staff uses it to retrieve past qualified applicants from the pool. Of course, just about every company with any degree of sensitivity to job applicants will send out replies to applicants telling them that, although the company doesn't have an opening that suits their qualifications at the moment, it will keep their applications active and call them should a suitable opening arise. The applications are then tossed into a bottomless storage device seldom surfacing again. At Bell, however, staff members really do access that device and hire people from it. In fact, they used this pool so often in the past two years that Bell was able to cut almost $1 million out of its advertising budget.

By applying data on cost per hire, the time needed to fill jobs, and employee turnover, human resources was able to focus attention and company resources on a growing turnover problem. Human resources staff members have shown that they are business people who have the numbers to back up their opinions about how to manage, solve problems, and exploit people opportunities.

A litany of program savings at Bell could be described, such as the one about a new work rule that streamlined the "bumping" system. This new process shortened the time for the layoff process to filter through the organization. Normally, in a layoff, people who are to be let go choose to bump a junior person, who in turn bumps a still more junior worker, and so on. "Bumping" can take a long time to work its way through the organization and in the process cause tremendous loss of productivity. Under Bell's new system, a process that used to take up to forty-nine days now can be completed in one week. There are also tales to be told about how pay was restructured and starting rates for entry-level positions lowered.

The reader, however, may have gotten the impression that the only issue on management's mind is to cut costs at the expense of employees. That is an erroneous view. Management's intent is to increase the value it receives for the money it pays for its labor.

In 1988, a major consulting firm persuaded Bell's management to initiate a competitiveness study. The alleged purpose of this program was to identify redundancies that could be eliminated, thereby saving the company millions of dollars in employee operating expenses.

In time, the study team reached the human resources department, and thought that this would be easy pickings. In fact, however, this was one department that was prepared to deal with facts and figures instead of impressions and conjecture. In preparation, Roger Williams had purchased a copy of the 1986 American Society for Personnel Administration/Saratoga Institute *Human Resources Effectiveness Report*. That document contained comparative data on human resources budgets and head counts. It also included information on thirty measures of human resources activities and results covering staffing, compensation and benefits, training, turnover and absence, and other items. Roger annotated several pages of the report with Bell's position vis-à-vis the norms for its industry.

Roger took the data into a meeting that was convened to determine how deeply human resources should be cut, and he walked out with his department's budget untouched. He showed that pay and benefits at Bell were higher than in the rest of the industry and argued that his staff could continue to reduce this disparity as long as it had the necessary resources. He was able to demonstrate that not only was human resources not overfed, it was understaffed for its tasks. For example, expenses and staffing for human resources management at Bell were lower than in the industry as a whole. To make a long story short, not only did human resources get the budget that it needed then, it still does—consistently.

Author's comment: The story of how the human resources function at Bell responded to a changing marketplace is truly remarkable. It demonstrates that human resources professionals can play a major role in helping an organization weather a difficult period. No one gave them a signal to proceed. No one threw resources at them before they had proved that they could use them to help business. They got what they needed because they earned it.

Top management was so impressed with the job that human resources did that Ed Szol was promoted to senior vice-president and given responsibility for the Management Information Systems department.

TRICORP
(From material furnished by and discussions with the vice-president of human resources)

This company, which we will call TRICORP (it prefers to remain anonymous), went through a major restructuring in the late 1980s. It was a classic case of organizational change brought on by shifting market conditions and corporate objectives. At the heart of the reorganization was the human resources manager. Working with the chief executive, he developed an incentive compensation plan aimed at stimulating a quick turnaround of the corporation. It was a high-risk move. The following description of events, in the words of the human resources manager, tells what happened:

> It all started in early 1986. We were then working under a long-term incentive plan based on preferred stock. For a variety of reasons, we concluded that it would be better to let that plan lapse and develop a new long-term plan.
>
> As we began to consider items for this new plan, it soon become obvious that it would have to be based on performance objectives. It also became obvious that major changes were needed at TRICORP. We are a world-class, very capital-intensive company in a cyclical market subject to wide swings in profitability because of supply-and-demand forces over which we have little control. In addition, some of our businesses no longer fit our strategic plan. And as in the case of any business, we needed to tighten our belts. All this told us that our problems were very immediate and pressing and that a new long-term incentive plan might not focus our energies soon enough and in the right places. We eventually concluded that a special incentive plan tied to our restructuring objectives was necessary. We needed to significantly improve our cash flow, divest certain assets, including a major portion of one of our product lines, and cut our expenses. We developed an eighteen-month incentive that would run from January 1, 1987, to June 30, 1988, and would pay off at approximately twice the level of a standard normal long-term incentive plan. In other words, the numbers were very generous.
>
> For example, even if the chief executive officer earned as much as $1.5 million for the eighteen-month period, the total pool for the entire corporation would still be $15 million. That is a great deal of money to be spread over sixty-five participants, but we thought there had to be sufficient money to get their attention. If we were successful in our plans, we would be able to divest a portion of a business line, improve profitability, and increase cash flow by some $300 million. When considered in those terms, the $15 million seemed like a rela-

tively small amount of money. As a result, we developed profitability and cash-flow objectives for the eighteen-month period for the corporation and each of its businesses. The objectives included net ordinary earnings and capital recovery, with threshold and maximum objectives. These were then used to determine the percentage of the total incentive fund that was disbursed.

The net effect was that we paid $11 million in incentives, divested a major portion of one line, recaptured more than $300 million in cash, and significantly improved our earnings. The plan focused TRICORP's earnings in the right places and helped prepare the company to enter a new stage in its history.

Author's comment: Flexibility and the willingness to take risks are two key traits of successful organizations. In TRICORP's case, the incentive plan that the chief executive officer and human resources manager devised was just the stimulant needed to make the reorganization succeed. Now that the company has passed through the first phase of its reorganization, it has developed a new set of goals, a new time frame, and a new incentive plan to meet those goals. There is no question about the value added by the human resources manager.

3

Human Value Management:
The Strategy for
the Next Decade

THE SIMPLE TRUTH is that we have no tried-and-true
organizational models—or management practices—to
fit an age in which volatility is the norm.
                                        Tom Peters

Human value management can be described in one short
phrase:

Create value through and with people.

Managing in today's economy is a very different game
from what it used to be. The fundamental issue that every
manager and every professional has to face is how to operate in
the new, volatile marketplace. When everything is changing, a
fixed model will not work. When uncertainty and discontinuity
are the norm, where will we find any rules to apply? As we will
see many times throughout our discussion of the human value
management model, the solution lies within the question. If
there is no certainty on the surface, then we must look for it
beneath the surface. We must dig through the distracting layers
of daily activity until we reach the bedrock on which driving
assumptions can be safely anchored.

Let me emphasize at the start that I am not going to
suggest yet another Japanese solution to American problems.
This is not a me-too model under a new label. Nevertheless, we
do have something to learn from the analytical processes that
the Japanese used to solve product quality problems during the
two decades after World War II.

45

On the surface, it would appear that the Japanese found the solution to the inferiority of their manufactured goods in quality control. That is the tool they used. But the really important matter here is the thought process that brought them to the quality-control solution.

Japan's business leaders recognized that their products were not competitive in the postwar world market. Exercising the principle of looking for the solution within the problem, they asked themselves why they were turning out inferior products. Any end result is dependent on both the inputs and the throughput process. The classic inputs are capital, material, equipment, and people. The throughput process includes the methods used to produce given results, as well as the performance of the workers.

Japan had access to capital for plant and equipment purchases through loans and grants-in-aid. It could buy whatever raw materials it needed on the open market. That left only the employees or the throughput process as the problem.

The Japanese therefore concluded that there were two steps to the solution. One was to develop a process that would naturally generate the desired result, namely, high-quality products at competitive prices. The second was to train employees to run this new process. Significantly, Japanese executives had great faith in their workers. Imai (1986) quotes one of these executives as saying that Japan's principal natural resource is the brains of its people. At any rate, subsequent events show that the Japanese did an extremely good job in implementing both of these steps.

The lesson is that Japan's leaders had the wisdom to forgo external gimmicks. They believed that they could, and indeed that they had to, rely on their people. So, they built their monumental success on the bedrock of their belief in *people*, the commitment to seek *constant improvement*, and a standard of the highest possible *quality*.

In the early postwar years, Japan was unable to consistently manufacture functional and dependable products. But its leaders made a decision to commit the nation to product quality. Initially the Japanese were introduced to quality principles by the U.S. Army Engineers. In 1950, they began to adopt the concept of statistical process control developed by W. Edwards Deming. In 1954, they expanded their approach to encompass management activities, making use of Joseph Juran's quality control management system. Eventually, they came to refer to this system as total quality control (TQC). TQC took ten years to develop. Along the way, it worked well enough to vault the Japanese into the forefront of every world market they chose to enter. Today, it is a formidable tool that others have adopted in self-defense.

A Lesson Learned

A growing wave of human resources professionals world-wide are employing that same thought process in reference to quality control. In the early 1980s these professionals acknowledged the negative image of their function and added to that the uncertainty of the changing, highly competitive world economy. The question became obvious: What changes did they have to make in their approach and, once having made these changes, how could they demonstrate that the human resources department was making a contribution of value? The answer was to adopt an uncompromising style of management that seeks to eliminate waste motion, waste activities, and waste programs in favor of a value-adding strategy. Could it be done? Of course it could, if there was a commitment to it, along with the perseverance to see it through.

That decision generated the process model that I call human value management. The principles of this model were hammered out during the 1980s. Trial and error has allowed us to learn where the true value of human resources work lies. HVM has forced us to define very specifically what we are trying to become, how we will act toward our customers, and what products and services we are capable of providing. It has helped us identify our key success points and focus our resources on achieving results. It has taught us how to generate relevant, challenging objectives. It has shown us how to measure our internal efficiency and our external contribution to the enterprise. Finally, it has given us a method for connecting the outcomes of human resources to the organization's goals. As a result, we can demonstrate to our satisfaction, and to that of top management, the many subjective and objective values that we create for our institutions.

This sounds like a major achievement, and it is. It's all true, but the model and the methods did not emerge overnight. Many people helped build the model throughout the past decade. My objective with this book is to pull together their work and put it into a recognizable form. This does not mean that the process is complete and perfect. No process ever is. It is simply now available for others like yourself to continue to improve on. The best thing about human value management is that it works. HVM principles and methods change the position of the human resources function within the organization. And HVM expands the contribution that human resources can make.

Principles of Human Value Management

Every model operates on a set of principles or beliefs. These principles or beliefs are the result of questioning, formulating, applying, testing, discarding, and adopting various ideas and approaches. Over the past ten years I have worked with hundreds of companies and thousands of human resources people from perhaps fifteen countries. Some of this work was done in the United States and some in other nations. We tried many different tactics and methods. We observed and discussed the results from different organizations, industries, and countries. Eventually, we developed a data base of operating results and norms that we could use to measure how well we were doing.

In the beginning, all we knew was that we wanted to upgrade the position of human resources within institutions. For some time we didn't think very strategically. Our focus was on tactics and methods. There was no one, single great revelation. Instead, the model grew from many small insights. Finally I came to the realization in the early 1980s that there was a recognizable, describable, and cohesive strategy being formed. Discussions, experiments, observations, and more discussions finally coalesced into what I have come to call human value management, or HVM. The driving belief behind this model is that human resources is a value-adding process.

This assumption is supported by many managers and executives. Perhaps best known among them is Roy Vagelos, chief executive officer of Merck & Co. Speaking to the worldwide meeting of Merck's human resources managers in Montreal in 1988, Vagelos (1988) challenged his audience: "Human resources is charged with helping make our vision a reality. If you do this [carry out the vision], Merck will continue to prosper, and I'm looking to you in human resources to bring this about. Each of us must ask ourselves daily, How can I add value to what I'm doing today?" The principles of human value management are dynamic, not fixed. They are all critical, but priorities will shift depending on the conditions extant at their time of application. Circumstances change and actions must be chosen accordingly. There are times when any one or two of the principles can mean the difference between survival and failure. But in the long term, all of them make the difference.

Please note, however, that value management principles are not patent medicines that will instantaneously cure all the management and operating ills of a company. Diagnosis before dosing is a good idea. Managers need to develop the energy and wisdom to constantly focus on these key principles and selectively emphasize the ones that are most important at a given time.

1. Create value at all times, everywhere, and with everyone. Values are of three kinds: human, financial, and production. Values are subjective, but they are usually easy to recognize. Pat Brown, a human resources manager at First Tennessee Bank in Memphis, lays it right on the line: "We have a maximum performance philosophy here. It stems from the ultimate goal of increasing shareholder wealth. We do that by increasing income through products, services, and people. Human resources adds value first at the selection stage where we make an extra effort to hire the right person. We truly analyze jobs and apply selection instruments specifically designed for each job group. This approach can be seen again in our employee development prac-

tices. When someone wants a training program, we ask whether it will develop people in skill areas that the bank needs in order to compete or if it will just make people feel better. We don't do things if we can't see the value in them."

Contrast that attitude with the fact that only a very small percentage of business training in the United States is ever assessed for its effectiveness. Based on three years of surveying the activities and results of corporate training departments, it has been commonly estimated that 95 percent of the more than $30 billion that America spends on training has never been evaluated. IBM knows that it spent $900 million on training in 1988. What it does not know is what it got for its money. Now, it has launched a major program to measure costs and value received.

Successful managers learn how to locate value in the interplay of people, things, processes, outputs, and impacts. At Systematics, Inc., a data-processing operations management company, the human resources department carries out the company's strategy of increasing the unit value of employees. Systematics believes that it makes good economic sense to invest in people as assets. The employees at Systematics are trained and paid above the mean for their industry. But the care and attention that go into supporting these employees yield a very low turnover rate and a very high productivity factor. Systematics thinks that it can afford to spend 5 percent more on pay and a lot more than the national average of 75 cents per employee per day on training, because the company is consistently able to run data-processing operations centers with about 25 percent fewer employees than other companies use.

Staff departments have been allowed to wallow in the subjectivity myth that says you can't measure (find objective value) in their type of work. This is simply not true, as thousands of managers and professionals have proven over the past dozen years. Every staff function from accounting through human resources and information systems to marketing and planning is subject to being strategized, operated, and measured along cost, time, quantity, quality, and human reaction indexes. A manager's primary responsibility is not, as in the traditional textbook definition, "to get work done through other people." Instead, it is, "with the employees, to jointly create value in and for the enterprise."

2. Focus on the customer. According to most accounts John Sculley fired Steve Jobs, cofounder of Apple Computer, because Steve became product obsessed and ignored customer demands for changes in Apple's products. There are internal and external customers. Everyone, staff included, has a customer. Everyone who is touched by your processes, products, and services is a customer. According to Japanese quality consultant Kaoru Ishikawa, "the next process is the customer" (Imai, 1986, p. 51). Ultimately, it is the customer who defines value.

Atsushi "Ako" Ue, general manager of personnel and labor relations at Seiko Instruments, puts it this way: "I want my staff to understand that employees are their customers. I want them to realize who the customer is for their services and what the customer needs. I expect them to focus on improving the abilities of employees and helping them effectively use those abilities."

Unlike sales and production, staff functions have seldom been customer focused and market tested. Until recently, line managers had to requisition services from staff departments. The staffs could act arbitrarily. They had a monopoly and, like all monopolies, became disdainful of their customers. This has begun to change, however. We will see later some examples of the death of the captive market in services.

3. Communicate your vision. Whenever people find themselves up to their elbows in alligators, they have a tendency to lose sight of why they are in business. When the stress becomes particularly heavy, the driving vision can get lost.

Everyone needs a vision to live and work by. Daisy Systems in Silicon Valley keeps its vision alive and vigorous by distributing a copy of its management credo (Exhibit 1) to each employee and posting a copy in every office.

Without a vision, an employee's purpose becomes blurred, and it is the responsibility of the top manager to provide that vision. Many organizations, however, have neglected this basic tenet of management. It is not uncommon for the chief

Exhibit 1. Daisy Systems' Management Credo.

MANAGEMENT'S RESPONSIBILITY
TO OUR EMPLOYEES

THE RESPONSIBILITY OF EACH MEMBER OF THE MANAGEMENT TEAM OF DAISY SYSTEMS, ASSISTED BY HUMAN RESOURCES STAFF, IS TO CREATE A BUSINESS ENVIRONMENT WHICH ENABLES OUR EMPLOYEES TO PURSUE POSITIVE CAREER GOALS IN A PARTICIPATIVE CLIMATE OF HIGH CORPORATE ACHIEVEMENT, FEATURING:

- Equal Employment Opportunity

- Open communication through a direct relationship between and among all levels of our organization.

- Human dignity and integrity by management example.

- High standards of individual and team performance and of ethical business conduct.

- Organization planning and personnel staffing with emphasis on our internal resources.

- Enhancement of career growth through technical, professional and educational opportunities.

- Equitable compensation and benefits.

- Recognition of achievement, contribution, and sustained superior performance.

- Concern for the safety and well-being of our employees.

Note: Reprinted by permission.

executive officer to fail to communicate the strategic vision that he or she has of the company. In our studies at Saratoga Institute we found that perhaps half of middle- and upper-level managers did not even know what their organizations' strategic imperatives were.

Clearly, if employees don't know where you want to take the organization, they will be unable to help you move it in the right direction. Conversely, those organizations that have communicated clear visions have performed better than average over the long term. A few of the most notable examples are IBM, McDonald's, Neiman-Marcus, Delta Air Lines, and Federal Express.

4. Empower the people. It is time to rewrite the psychological contract between the organization and the employee. That contract is not just a matter of trading a fair day's pay for a fair day's work. Instead, we are engaged in a joint venture with employees. Together we contract to create value for the individual, the organization, and the customer. It is no longer possible for an organization to operate on a We versus They basis. Now, it is Us or Nothing.

Human resources people are known for their support of the employee. They consistently try to convince supervisors to act in a participative manner. Human resources employees need to be involved in the development and implementation of the value management system. The three legs of the empowerment stool are involvement, training, and accountability. If you involve employees in formulating strategy and tactics and train them adequately to perform their new tasks, then you can hold them accountable for their actions and results. In fact, if you carry out the first two steps you will find that your people want to be evaluated. People always want to know how they are doing. In a study conducted on 4,000 employees in a dozen companies over a four-year period, we found that the two topics employees most wanted information on were job performance and career opportunities. People are not afraid of being evaluated. They are afraid of arbitrary and unfair methods of evaluation. Once you involve them in designing the measurement system, you will find them to be very supportive of it.

Managers also have to be empowered. Transamerica Insurance empowers its managers by giving them access to employee data. Human resources has developed the first phases of
a data base that helps managers make better selection decisions.
In today's high-risk environment one mistake in hiring can not
only saddle a company with a substandard employee but can
also land it in court. Timely, relevant data also help Transamerica's managers work on other human operational problems, such as excessive absenteeism and avoidable turnover.

The vice-president of personnel for a major Wall Street
brokerage house talks about involvement and empowerment
from the standpoint of risk avoidance. He sees juries assessing
penalties on the basis of the organization's ability to pay rather
than on that of any legal precedents. The average citizen looks
upon highly visible, apparently wealthy corporations as having
very deep pockets. This attitude makes it imperative that managers be trained and empowered though data to make the right
decisions regarding delicate employee problems.

5. Control fixed costs. Staff departments have always
been the first target when expenses need to be reduced. Much of
what human resources departments do is of dubious value in the
eyes of our organizations. Our survival depends on changing
this perception. Now is the time for a proactive strategy. Remember that any task, process, or job that does not clearly add
value must be viewed as waste. Waste is expensive. Few companies can afford much of it today and hope to remain
competitive.

At Secor Bank in Birmingham, Alabama, Jack Phillips has
institutionalized the "no waste" philosophy. He has published an
action agenda that contains eight processes aimed at keeping
costs low at the bank. This approach must be working because
Secor has more assets per employee than any of its competitors
in the South. In some cases, it is ahead by a margin of more than
two to one. This philosophy allows Secor to employ fewer people both to attract and to retain assets.

Review all your activities and outputs. Try to change any
expense-based operation to a value-adding function. If you find
that the operation contributes some value, teach your people to

plan and run it with that in mind. If you can't find value in it, drop it. Someone will let you know if you have stopped providing them with some valuable product or service.

There is an organizational truism relating to value:

Distance consumes value.

Move all your processes as close as possible to the customer. Although it may mean decentralizing some human resources functions from corporate headquarters to line divisions, it is imperative that you assign the job to the position that is closest to the customer. In more profitable times, staff managers often built functional empires as a way of increasing their power. Today, in the information age, power goes to those who add value at the least expense. Staff departments add value by providing timely information, not by building large staffs and commanding large budgets.

Decentralization of human resources staffs has been a trend since the mid 1980s. Downsizing and reorganization programs began to transform corporate staffs into line divisions. In some cases, this has almost eliminated the central staff. But I find that the total number of human resources people is often larger under a decentralized system. I understand this is the case at McDonnell-Douglas, which spent over a year downsizing its corporate human resources staff. Although there was no reduction in total human resources personnel in the corporation, these personnel are now closer to the customer.

About once a month I come across a company that has moved almost all human resource administrative functions out to the line departments. In fact, there seems to be a slowly gathering movement in some areas to dissolve the corporate human resources department or at least shrink it to the smallest possible cadre. The surviving human resources people are being changed from personnel administrators to organizational analysts. As John Stapleton at International Minerals and Chemicals says, "Now we're dealing with the strategic issues, which is a lot more rewarding."

It appears there are two ways to be successful in an environment that emphasizes low fixed costs:

1. Become a broker of services from outside vendors. If business turns down, it is easier and less painful to terminate a vendor than an employee.
2. Cross-train your staff so that ad hoc teams can be formed to meet customer needs. This will earn you a reputation as a responsive problem solver.

Flexibility will be the hallmark of survival in the 1990s. The successful staff manager will not have to personally produce services. Rather, his or her responsibility will be to see that a quality service is delivered to the right place at the right time.

6. Reward value-adding performance. Pay practices are undergoing their most significant change in decades. There is an accelerating shift away from fixed, nondifferentiating annual increases in base pay. Many new types of incentive pay programs are being tried. Pay for skill development and pay for measurable achievement are the two most in favor at the moment. The only constraint that keeps management from going fully to pay for performance is that it hasn't yet figured out satisfactory ways to measure performance. That situation won't last long. New techniques are coming on the market and, sooner rather than later, organizations will find ones that work.

Some research suggests that the key criteria for successful pay plans include the following (Wallace, 1988):

- A clear vision of the business strategy
- Focus on jobs having high discretionary content
- Clarity on what is wanted, along with the skill to measure it
- Direct ties to the business plan
- Clear distinctions between incentives and base pay

Practically every company is looking for new forms of compensation today. A larger percentage of pay in the near future will be at risk, dependent on performance. As a human resources manager, you have a choice. You can allow someone else to show you how you should reward your people. Or you can learn what works best for you before the expert is brought in by an impatient management. If you adopt HVM as your operating system, you will be able to identify value in the work of your staff and reward it accordingly. Chapter Ten will show you how to connect human resources work to organizational objectives in ways that are measurable.

The other side of the reward system is the nonmonetary. Companies are achieving significant improvements in productivity and quality without monetary gain sharing. People love what I call "carnival prizes." They cost so little and achieve so much. Coffee cups, T-shirts, caps, and so on seem to mean a lot to employees if they are presented in the right manner. They can be a more personal form of recognition than a pay raise. You should be the expert on reward systems, particularly in this area. So, I am not going to suggest anything specific. Just remember to think the system through, keep it simple and easy to understand, and make sure that it stimulates the kind of behavior you want.

7. Persevere. Human value management is not a panacea that can be selectively applied, worked for a while, and abandoned in favor of a new fad. Perseverance is mandatory.

On a trip to Australia in 1987 I was told a story about a Japanese management expert who was invited down under to lecture on Japanese quality improvement methods. At the conclusion of his talk, someone in the audience asked him two questions:

1. Are you telling the whole story about these processes?
2. If you are, why are you giving away your competitive secrets?

The Japanese gentleman allegedly said, "I am telling you everything I know about this process. I can safely do so because we do not believe that the Western nations have the commitment or the discipline to do the things that are necessary to compete with us."

The secret to survival will not be found in some exotic management formula. There are no easy answers. The only solution is that old-fashioned notion of hard work that adds value. I don't think we have the luxury to make a mistake in this direction. Pat Aburdene (Naisbitt and Aburdene, 1985) has warned us that we must step forward and take up the challenge. It took American businesses thirty years to accept Deming's notion of statistical process control and Juran's quality management principles. Human resources doesn't have thirty years to respond to its market's demands.

I am intrigued by the speed with which people flock to buy oversimplified management books. Perhaps these books are so much in demand because they eliminate the need to think. But most of them are fairy tales. We know that the combination of television-engendered values and an educational system that graduates illiterates has given birth to a nation of people who want instant gratification. I'm not acting holier than thou. In varying degrees we are all products of our time.

Nevertheless, it seems to me that the deluge of simplistic One-Minute Anything books are to American business what Professor Harold Hill was to River City. Just as he won over the citizenry of that mythical village with his simple solution to juvenile delinquency, so too does the one-minute formula convince managers that there are simple solutions to complex new problems. The result is the same in both cases. Angry citizens threatened to tar and feather the professor. Angry investors are becoming fed up with executives who are not willing to carry out the basic principles of organizational management.

Make no mistake. It is tough to be a good manager. A vice-president of sales for a national building products company put it plainly: "Sales isn't all that difficult. Products, pricing, goals, incentives are not especially mysterious. But managing people is the hardest part of the job." This is from a man who has a wealth of experience and a natural talent for managing. How difficult must it be for the average manager?

The Heart of Human Value Management

The mechanics of managing for value can be demystified if we focus on three phenomena of organizational work: processes, outputs, and impacts. In order to evaluate them we need two conditions: a value goal and the opportunity to observe more than one occurrence of an action. If we know what we want and are able to observe an activity several times, we can make supportable statements about whether or not we have reached the value goal that we set for ourselves. Also, we can determine whether the results improved or not over the several observations.

People work with one another, and they also work with things, equipment, and materials. Person-to-person processes include interviewing, coaching, disciplining, training, and paying. An observer can evaluate two or more people as they carry out an identifiable action. By contrast, leading and communicating are more abstract, more complex constructs. I can't see a person "lead," but I can see him writing out a plan, speaking to his staff, giving encouragement, and performing dozens of other acts that I may interpret as partial examples of leading. Leading is a composite, not a single discrete act. As you will see below, it is a waste of time to try to measure "leading." The result of leadership is the point on which to focus our attention.

People-to-thing processes include programming, analyzing financial statements, drafting, and evaluating jobs. For professionals, the people-to-thing process usually requires more than eye-hand coordination. It is often an intellectual activity that demands analytical and expressive capabilities.

Processes are subject to evaluation if we know what their objective is. Whether we are conducting an interview or a counseling session, providing on-the-job training, processing a form, or analyzing a document, we have to know what our specific process goal is. For instance, the process goal of an interview is not to hire someone. Rather, the objective is to obtain information on which to make a selection decision, and that would be the criterion to apply in judging the value of an interview.

A process such as an interview can be evaluated in two ways:

1. How did the process work this time compared to the last time? Was it faster, cheaper, and easier to carry out? Did it produce the kind of information that you wanted to acquire? How satisfied were the participants—interviewer and appli-

cant—when it was finished? Exemplified here are the five common indexes of measurement: cost, time, quantity, quality, and human reaction.

2. What did the process yield or cause to happen? That is, what was its output? Did you get more data or more useful information? Was it an applicant screened or a decision made to hire? Outputs from other processes could be a better document, a more productive employee, or the settling of an argument.

A process can thus be evaluated in terms of the intrinsic improvement that it produces or in terms of its effect on some output. An output is a result of a process and is assessed in relation to the value goal. Once again, the measures of value are changes in cost, time, quantity, quality, and human reactions. Did the output cost more or less than it usually does? Did it take a longer or shorter period of time to produce the output? Did you get more or less from the process compared to the last time you carried it out? Was the quality higher or lower? Did it make the participants or the customer happier and more satisfied or not?

Within human resources operations, specific examples of output measures are cost per hire, the time needed to fill jobs, the quality of hires, recruiter effectiveness, number of jobs leveled, percentage of salary actions submitted on time, benefit claims and employee records processed, process error rates, number of employees trained, cost per trainee hour, and percentage of HRIS jobs completed on time and within cost projections. The old idea that we can't measure human resources work has long been shattered. That was simply a defense mechanism based on fear, ignorance, or laziness.

Many human resources professionals will agree that the processes and outputs of their function can be measured, but they are unable to bridge the apparent gap between the outputs of human resources and organizational effects, which is the true value measure. This brings us to the third and most important value arena: impact. I call it the "so what?" factor.

By continually improving our processes we can increase efficiency. By constantly obtaining more outputs from the same processes without increasing inputs we can increase productivity. The last step is to see if we can locate an impact that the process or output had on an organizational objective. At that point, we are talking about effectiveness. Effectiveness is a matter of applying the right process, in the right way, with the right people, at the right time, to yield the right output, which in turn generates a meaningful impact. Your task is to demonstrate, with objective and perhaps even subjective data, that a particular result (an impact) added human, financial, or production value to your organization. You can make that connection if you learn what the customer's goals and objectives are. I will show you later how to connect a human resources process and output to an organizational objective. When your unit is consistently making these kinds of connections, it is engaged in human value management.

The Meaning of Value Added

When we talk about adding value in business, we usually mean financial or economic value. Value added can be calculated in several ways. To me the simplest is: Value added equals sales minus purchased goods and services. Figure 1 provides a graphic example of what value added looks like.

The objective in business is to spend funds in ways that will generate the best return on investment. Management hopes to add value when it spends money on research, manufacturing, technology, distribution, and/or marketing activities. If the organization can cut its cost of capital, it can increase pretax earnings — the bottom line on which value added is most easily seen. If funds can be invested in people or in equipment that helps people become more productive, then value can be added through greater human efficiency and effectiveness. The job of human resources is to help management make that investment wisely so that value is in fact added through human activity. Human resources practices this when it focuses its hiring, paying, training, and counseling programs on the objective of adding value through employee effectiveness. That is where the human value management system differs fundamentally from personnel administration.

Figure 1. Example of Value-Added Components.

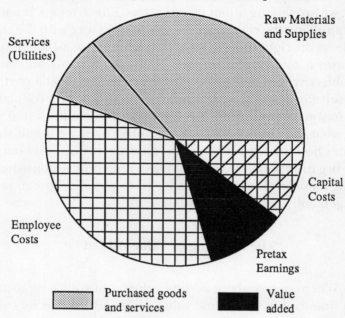

Services
(Utilities)

Raw Materials
and Supplies

Capital
Costs

Employee
Costs

Pretax
Earnings

☐ Purchased goods
and services

■ Value
added

Three Pitfalls

No system is without potential problems. HVM is not self-correcting and self-sustaining. I have touched on some of the potential pitfalls earlier. Essentially, there are three, and they are serious enough to deserve separate attention. Indeed, any single one of them is powerful enough to scuttle any management system.

The Activity Trap. Japan built an industrial juggernaut by adopting an activity focus. The Japanese principle of *kaizen*—gradual, unending improvement—looks to the process as the path to results. For the past thirty years, Japanese workers have doggedly worked at performing the myriad of tasks that make up a process a little bit better each time.

In America, staff departments also have an activity focus. However, in our case it has worked to our detriment because it has taken on the character of an excuse system. We talk about how hard we work, how many people we have seen, how many pieces of paper we have processed, how many employees we have counseled or trained, how many programs we have written, and so on ad infinitum. What we don't talk about is whether we have made something better, have achieved some worthwhile goal, or have truly added value. While the Japanese factory worker focuses on process improvement, the American white-collar worker focuses on activity counting.

I used to live next door to the "world's greatest computer salesman." I know he was because he used to tell me so all the time. Whenever I saw him he would hail me across the hedge with something like "Jac, I sold twenty-seven systems last week." He must have been good because he was always winning contests for sales performance. But in all the years he lived next door he never said to me, "Jac, last week I drove 897 miles, saw thirty-two prospects, and gave away twenty-two pounds of product brochures." He understood that he was rewarded for making sales, not working hard. It may be true that the value of human resources work is not as easy to measure as the value of sales. But throughout this book you will find dozens of examples of human resources people who are measuring value added, so it can't be all that difficult.

Keep in mind that no one gets paid simply for keeping busy. Everyone gets paid, or should get paid, for results: outputs and impacts. It is only these that are value adding.

The Quick Fix Trap. America is the land of the cowboy, and it shows in our management style. We are not prone to analysis. Instead, when confronted with a problem, we would sooner fire a few random shots at it and hope that takes care of everything. The gunfighter school of management looks for instant solutions to sometimes complex and sensitive problems. A quick fix is often preferred over dialogue and diagnosis.

If you look at the history of management solutions over the past forty years in America, you can see how willing we have been to accept the latest management fad. Table 2 is a tribute to the gunfighter school. The irony here is that all the ideas in Table

Table 2. Famous Fads and Fixes.

1950s	1960s
Theory Y	Matrix Management
Management by Objectives	Humanistic Management
Quantitative Methods	Managerial Grid
1970s	1980s
Zero-Based Budgeting	Theory Z
Participative Management	Intrapreneuring
Quality Circles	Culture Change

2 have merit. But we don't stay with them long enough to find out where and how and under what conditions they work. I showed this table to Bruce Roquet from the Bull Moose Tube Company. This company, which got its name from a character in the "Li'l Abner" comic strip, has steel tube manufacturing plants in Illinois, Georgia, and its home state of Missouri. Bruce pointed out that his organization had gone through several of these programs. When a process had done all that it could for Bull Moose, the company phased it out and went on to another that was more appropriate to its current condition. This is a lot different from the practice of running a program for a while and then getting bored with it. We will never find long-term solutions as long as we exhibit the attention span of a preschooler.

Complex problems require thorough analysis and a period of testing, trial and error, and learning. Conditions constantly change in the workplace. It is absurd to believe that because something worked in one case it will work in all cases. Quality circles, for example, are an excellent method for involving people in a manufacturing process, but they can't save an organization that is making the wrong product for its market. Intrapreneuring is a fine way to stimulate creativity, but it won't work in a company that rewards conformity. Participative management can be a marvelous system for running an organization, but it may take ten years to institutionalize it.

A study of quality improvement programs in the insurance industry in 1985 revealed the importance of management commitment ("Productivity Practices. . . ," 1985). In nearly every case where quality programs died, it was because top management withdrew its support. This was true even in the initially successful programs. If the executives pulled out before the process became institutionalized, it didn't last another year.

A story that illustrates the value of commitment is Motorola's success with participative management. In the early 1970s, Bob Galvin, chairman of Motorola, declared that the company would adopt participative management as its way of operating. But he did not try to jam it down the employees' throats. He said, in effect, "When you are ready we will provide you with the training and support to make the change." It took almost ten years to convert 90 percent of the company to participative methods, but Galvin never wavered. In 1988, Motorola, Inc., was voted the best-run company in its industry by Nomura Securities, the largest brokerage firm in the world. In 1989, Motorola became the first U.S. company to win the Malcolm Baldridge Award for excellence in quality management.

If you are thinking of adopting human value management, do yourself a favor. Don't give it six months and then throw it into the fads-and-fixes bin. It will take longer that that. Start small, work out your strategy, and introduce HVM into the system with a minimum of disruption. Follow the process outlined in this book and you will be successful if you are really committed to this new form of management.

The One-Way Communication Trap. Human value management is more than a way of managing. It is a strategy and perhaps even an ethic, a way of living. It requires that people understand and accept it, for they must execute it every day. It will become their way of operating. They must adopt your vision of human resources, come to understand their customers better, learn the key success points, and design the measures needed to monitor their work. Clearly, their involvement is a prerequisite of success.

To make HVM work you have to trade one-way, downward communication for a joint-venture methodology. There are six steps to introducing HVM, bringing it on line, and keeping it alive and useful:

Reduce perceived threats. Not everyone is going to jump on the bandwagon and beg to participate. If your staff members have been around organizations at all, they may view this as just another quick fix. Prepare yourself before you attempt to introduce HVM. Then, present it to your staff in a way that will elicit acceptance and willingness. Without knowing your people I can't tell you how to do it. But you know them; think it through.

Describe the payoffs. It is human nature to want to know "what's in it for me?" Use the list of payoffs described in Chapter Five. When you personalize benefits, you will find that people are more willing to change.

Train your staff. There is a model and a process that people need to learn when implementing human value management. To the extent that they understand the methodology, they will be less resistant to the new system as well as more effective. Make them competent through training.

Involve all your staff members. You will see evidence throughout this book that the success of HVM depends on the degree to which the entire human resources unit becomes involved. HVM is more than a tool. It is a way of operating. Unless you are going to carry the whole unit by yourself, you had better involve your people in HVM at the beginning and make it their process.

Persevere. Keep your staff focused on value versus activity. If you don't have the energy to continuously support this method, forget it. For at least a year or two you will be tested for your sincerity. It takes a long time to unlock an existing culture and to institutionalize a new one. Show the staff the payoffs for the value orientation on a regular basis. Personally model the behavior you want. If the system is working, they will gradually take the process away from you and it will become theirs.

Recognize achievements. The truest statement in organizational life is that you get what you pay for. If you recognize and reward value-adding performance, that is what you will get. If you start to pay for activities that produce nothing, you can have that again too.

Conclusion

Human value management is a strategy that a growing number of human resources professionals in many countries are now practicing. Its underlying theme is to create value through and with people. HVM views employees as assets, something of value. This is a concept that I wrote about some ten years ago (Fitz-enz, 1981). It has since been validated by a Harvard Business School group led by Michael Beer, who developed a curriculum around this construct. Beer and others (1984) described the model in *Managing Human Assets*. Human resources professionals have taken the idea a step farther by using it as the reference on which they are building a management system.

The principles of HVM are to create value at all times, focus on the customer, communicate your vision, empower your people, eliminate waste and control fixed costs, reward value-adding performance, and persevere. Value is the driving concept. It recognizes that organizations do not pay for activity but for results.

Chief executive officers such as Merck's Roy Vagelos are charging human resources with carrying management's vision into the organization. That means that human resources must become an integral part of the business. It demands a mind-set and a type of behavior that can propel human resources out of its traditional expense center position into a new value-adding role. To play this part, human resources needed a new model. HVM is the evolving model that human resources professionals are shaping.

Of course, there are traps that await anyone who ventures along this new route. The first is the activity trap. HVM constantly warns the practitioner that the objective is to eliminate waste and focus on results. The second, the quick fix trap, is an American hallmark. HVM acknowledges that today's problems are complex. Their solution requires analysis before action and persistence until results are obtained. The third trap is one-way communication. HVM is a joint venture between management and staff. It can only be optimized if the people are involved to the limit of their interest and abilities.

Finally, human value management is an action-oriented model. It says have confidence in yourself, share your vision with your staff, position yourself for maximum effect, analyze your market and assess your capabilities, select your key success points, act, and then objectively evaluate your performance so that you can continuously improve it.

> The human race is divided into two classes, those who go ahead and do something, and those who sit and inquire why wasn't it done the other way.
>   Oliver Wendell Holmes

References

ASPA/Saratoga Institute. *Human Resources Effectiveness Report.* Saratoga, Calif.: Saratoga Institute, 1987.

Beer, M., and others. *Managing Human Assets.* New York: Free Press, 1984.

Fitz-enz, J. "Human Resources: A Different Perspective." *Personnel Journal,* Feb. 1981, pp. 118–120.

Imai, M. *Kaizen.* New York: Random House, 1986.

Naisbitt, J., and Aburdene, P. *Reinventing the Corporation.* New York: Warner Books, 1985.

"Productivity Practices in the Insurance Industry." Life Office Management Association (LOMA), Dec. 1985, p. 8.

Vagelos, P. R. "The Future Vision and Direction of Merck." Summary report of Human Resources Conference, Montreal, Oct. 1988.

Wallace, M. J. "Closing the Gap in Compensation." *MR Reporter,* Nov. 1988, pp. 2–3.

Case Studies — Chapter Three

Daisy Systems Corporation
Mountain View, California
(From discussions with Bob Coon, vice-president of human
resources)

Based in Mountain View, California, Daisy Systems manufactures computer-aided engineering workstations. The company has had a checkered history. At one time it had a very strong market position. However, like a lot of other high-tech companies, Daisy encountered some problems and went through a change in management. Now, it has recovered and seems to be regaining a prominent market presence. The company recently made an acquisition that brought its total number of employees to over 1,000.

Before Bob Coon accepted the position of vice-president of human resources in 1988, he discussed with chief executive officer Norman Friedmann his view that human resources should be described as a "department of the environment." Bob's view is that the management of the human resources function is best exercised if it is approached from a broad perspective — a perspective that might be described as "human value." Thus, the employee cannot be treated as though he or she is untouched by the working environment. All functions, factors, and influences that "surround" an employee (whether environmental or hygienic, motivational or productive) must be reviewed and managed by a single organizational entity. The more traditional approach subjects the employee to multiple managers of the environment. This approach not only is inefficient, but at times leads to conflict. When the environment is governed from a single standpoint, the end product is an improved workplace.

The head of the human resources function should be a business person who happens to be assigned personnel and other services functions. In this way, the needed balance is achieved through an integrated approach, and a parochial view dominated by either personnel or facilities management perspectives is avoided. The question is, What is best for the employee and what is the best business way of achieving that desired result?

Let us first examine the drawbacks of the parochial view. On the one hand, most facilities and services responsibilities are placed under operations directors or finance and administration vice-presidents, who tend to look principally at only two bottom-line numbers when considering building improvements: initial installation costs and ongoing maintenance expenditures. On the other hand, placing facilities or services with a traditional personnel director may result in a narrow focus on employee relations concerns and a disregard of financial considerations. Only a consolidated business-employee, cost-benefit approach really works.

The probability is high that your organization is spending money on things that do not matter, that have no positive effect on the environment, and that have no cost-benefit value. You should concentrate only on those things that improve working conditions, that increase employee productivity, and that contribute to the corporate culture you are trying to create. When you have clearly identified the key environmental products and services needed, realign the organization to service those functions, reassign your staff to perform those services, and rebid all external support contracts.

Let me give you an example. At Daisy Systems, employee benefit costs were negotiated with an insurance company by the finance department and then audited on the basis of budgeted versus actual monthly expenses as a percentage of payroll. When the responsibility for benefits planning was transferred to human resources, the basic environmental question was posed, What do our employees really want out of this benefit plan? It was found, for example, that the current long-term disability plan included a number of features that employees never used but that the company routinely paid for every month. At one location, it was found that the majority of long-term disability claims were not being offset by the companion short-term disability plan. At another site, which had almost 420 employees, *not one* long-term disability claim was filed for the year because these employees were covered under extended paid sick-leave provisions. By redesigning both the short- and the long-term disability plans, the human resources staff was able to increase employees' understanding of their disability coverage, streamline administrative procedures for all plans, and cut monthly company-paid premiums by almost 55 percent. The moral is that you can make employees happier and save money simultaneously.

Every time that the $120,000 video-conferencing system between two research and development locations was proposed by the engineering department, it was turned down by both the operations director and the finance vice-president as just "another expensive toy for engineers." When subsequently submitted by the environmental manager (also known as the human resources manager), the proposal was accepted because it had been revised to relate business costs and environmental and operational effects. The new proposal demonstrated, for example, that the system would pay for itself in less than one year simply by saving the cost of twelve business trips per month between sites (the average number of trips at that time was sixty-eight per month). This made the system very attractive to those in finance. By showing that individual productivity would be increased by the eight hours lost in airports per trip, the proposal appealed to the people in operations. The new technology solved a productivity problem, and thus improved the work environment of the engineers. By making sure that a sound business solution was developed, the human resources department gained recognition and respect throughout the company.

It is by applying this dual focus, one looking at business needs and the other at the employee's environment, that human resources can often find a balanced solution. This style of operation should allow human resources to play a significant role in strategic business planning and implementation.

For example, in the recent merger of Daisy and two other software development companies, human resources was a key member of the acquisition team. Senior management realized that the *employees* were the only important asset being acquired since software development is people created and people dependent. The success of this merger was going to be based on the retention, utilization, and motivation of these employees. Such mergers are not a matter of technology, buildings, or even financing. They are made or missed by how successfully people work together.

A proactive, environmentally tuned manager also must have the ability to foresee social change and impending workplace legislation. She or he must be aware of emerging social currents that may soon develop into employee-perceived "entitlements" and develop longer-range plans to get employee programs in place ahead of formal legislative enactment.

For example, a number of California companies used proactive planning to prepare for the issue of maternity leave. Recognizing the social forces that supported maternity leave, many personnel managers began to change their leave-of-absence policies in the mid 1980s to allow for up to four, six, or even twelve months of unpaid maternity leave, depending on the specific circumstances. Some time later, when the state legislature finally got around to passing a law requiring four months of mandatory maternity leave, it was a nonevent in these companies. These personnel managers showed employees that they were valued by their companies, which were leading the way in discharging their social responsibilities.

Author's comment: I've known Bob for almost ten years. He has a great deal of insight and common sense. When he got his chance to apply human value management principles, he was able to catapult the human resources function into the inner circle of decision making at his company. Concurrently, he established a working environment that showed that the company valued its people. And he didn't do this with a magic wand. He did it day by day, case by case, chance by chance. It isn't magic, and it isn't impossible.

Merck & Co.
Rahway, New Jersey
(From discussions with and material supplied by Steve Darien,
vice-president of employee relations, and Dick Parker of corporate
human resources administration)

Everyone must have heard of Merck & Co. by now. It was voted the most admired company in the United States by *Fortune* magazine for three years in a row. It is a giant in the pharmaceutical industry worldwide. Besides being extremely profitable, the company has a reputation of concern for its employees. As already noted, in October 1988, over 100 human resources managers from Merck facilities in twenty countries gathered in Montreal for the Human Resources Conference. This week-long meeting was centered on the theme "The Globalization of Management Issues: Toward the Year 2000." The program emphasized the role of human values in Merck's drive to excel in an era of intense global competition. Most of the top executives in the company journeyed to Montreal to address the conference. A number of outside speakers were also invited to present their views on a variety of related subjects. The following is a condensation of remarks on key issues.

Merck's chief executive officer, Roy Vagelos, began his talk by quoting from Proverbs: "Where there is no vision, the people perish." He went on to emphasize that Merck focuses on knowledge and the capabilities of its people. Its goal is to be the leader of innovation in the pharmaceutical industry. To do that, Vagelos told the attendees, all Merck employees must ask themselves, "How can I add value to what I'm doing today?" The role of human resources is to provide development programs for employees so that they can grow and be capable of competing in the global marketplace.

Stanley Fidelman, senior vice-president of Merck, Sharp, and Dohme Research Lab, pointed out that recruitment and retention of talented people are the cornerstones of Merck's plans. He said, "Recruiting is a key issue, and all senior executives must have recruiting as an objective."

Jerry Jackson, president of Merck, Sharp, and Dohme International, noted there is a crucial need to develop the organization's resources to meet the challenges of globalization. He stated that Merck must successfully address these key issues:

1. The growing complexity of the global market
2. The European Community in 1992
3. Emergence of Japan as a major global player
4. Global product availability

5.   Launching new products while maintaining current
     products

He concluded by stating, "You, human resources, will be our
partners in meeting these challenges [of globalization]."

John Zabriskie, president of Merck, Sharp, and Dohme,
talked about business strategies and globalization. He said,
"Global opportunity is founded on several management principles. Those that strongly impact human resources are: (1) employee strength, (2) cultural harmony, (3) shared objectives, (4)
training as renewal, (5) pervasive communication, (6) new value
measures, (7) focus on the outside, and (8) belief in human
dignity."

Edith Weiner, president of Weiner, Edrich, & Brown, Inc.,
focused on quality of life issues. She talked about how the rapid
changes that people constantly experience cause them to search
for intrinsic values. Morale is related to the amount of affiliation
that an employee feels toward the organization. As the environment becomes more difficult and threatening, personal relationships in the workplace will become more crucial. Her conclusion was that these developments will make human resources
a more complex function in successful organizations.

Noel Tichy, professor of business administration at the
University of Michigan, challenged the participants with the
question, "How can Merck continue to get executives with a
global mind-set who can cooperate cross culturally within the
company, and how can Merck ensure the ongoing development
of mechanisms to operate worldwide?" He told them that, "to
respond to your CEO's challenge, you need to mobilize. If
human resources doesn't take this window of opportunity, your
CEO will."

James Walker, managing director of the Walker Group,
said, "CEOs are looking for human resources professionals who
will bring objectivity, expertise, and knowledge of competitive
and innovative human resources practices to the company. In
terms of results, they want people to be accountable for prompt,
effective solutions to people problems." Jim's conclusion was
that the mission of human resources is to support managers in

their efforts to maximize the contribution of employees in achieving successful competitive performance.

When my turn came, I started by refuting the image that human resources is too expensive and doesn't add value. I talked about human value management and what that meant in terms of acquiring the human asset, maintaining it, and developing it. I described how work can be measured from a cost-avoidance or a revenue-contributing viewpoint. Finally, I described the personal values that arise from the practice of HVM. My conclusion was "Everything you do—every program, every product, every service you provide— is done for one reason only: because it serves the economic and human goals of Merck."

Vittorio Tesio, director of planning and management development at Fiat, in Turin, Italy, spoke at length about Fiat's Project for the Internationalization of Management. From the point of view of the HR function, Fiat developed three areas: people, organizational structures, and company values and goals. Tesio's main point was that being international means thinking internationally—having the cultural values of an international company.

John Kotter, professor of organization behavior at Harvard, described the leadership issues that will define the future. He suggested that organizations develop several leadership themes in their strategic human resources planning:

- Establishing direction and vision for the company's future
- Aligning employees with this vision
- Motivating and inspiring employees

The program focused on the idea that people are the key to success in a high-tech industry such as pharmaceuticals and emphasized that the role of human resources is absolutely critical. Again and again the theme was one of partnership between human resources and management. Vice-chairman John Lyons put it squarely on the participants' shoulders: "You are the builders who see the vision."

Walt Trosin, vice-president of human resources, chaired a final panel discussion. In his remarks at the conclusion of the conference he said, "This week in Montreal we have heard and learned a great deal about what will be expected of us in the coming years at Merck as the company works to achieve the stretch goals that Dr. Vagelos has defined for us. The 1990s will require personal growth and development for all of us. Our roles may change; certainly we will need to become more knowledgeable of the business problems facing our clients if we are to make a full contribution. We must continue to earn the partnership we share with Merck managers worldwide."

Author's comment: The conference speakers dwelt on strategic themes. No one talked about tactical matters such as employee testing, performance review programs, or training techniques. At Merck, they know that success is built on a common strategic focus. Tactics come after everyone understands the problems and opportunities.

Merck has developed a reputation for doing things right, and this shows in its products, in its relationships with its employees, and in its profits. The reason for going into detail on the Merck conference was to provide an example of effective human resources activities and to give you a glimpse of one way of practicing human value management.

4

A Strategic Plan
for Effective
Human Value Management

WHEN EVERYONE IS thinking alike, then no one is
thinking.
General George S. Patton

Strategic management transcends daily operating and
administrative tasks. It focuses on developing and executing the
objectives of the total enterprise. The strategy process sets the
tone and scope for the development of operational systems,
administrative procedures, and behavioral expectations. In one
sense, it serves to link the conceptual products and customers in
the business plan with the real products of the company and the
actual customers in the marketplace.

Human value management is a strategic management
concept and process. It is a model of how the organization will
acquire, maintain, develop, apply, and manage its human assets.
HVM's premise is that people are valuable. This strategic assumption underlies all decisions about the design, development, and delivery of human resources services.

While some people will claim that they don't have time to
strategize, the fact is that they can't afford not to strategize in
today's market. A good strategy is the greatest efficiency tool
available. Without a strategy all that you can do is react, and
reaction puts control in the hands of your environment. It's like
trying to lasso a dog's wagging tail. You stand at the south end of
that puppy following the lateral motion of its tail. Every time you
throw the rope you miss, because the tail moves faster than you
can react to it. A better strategy would be to position yourself
beside the dog. When the tail comes in your direction, along a

fairly constant plane, you can grab it. Without a strategy, you are just an extension of the dog's tail. Whichever direction he wags you must follow, spending a lot of your resources with very little chance of ever catching up.

At McGraw-Hill, Inc., human resources management takes a strategic look at its programs from a financial perspective. This information and publishing company has been a takeover target for some time. Top management is naturally concerned about positioning the company to ward off a hostile takeover. This means that the company must strengthen its financial ratios. One way to cut costs and conserve cash is simply to fire large numbers of people. However, history has shown the folly of that approach if a company wants to maintain a strong market position. Walt Whitt, head of staffing and development, explains that human resources at McGraw-Hill has adopted a proactive financial management strategy that not only controls costs but leaves the company in a strong operating position. Here are some of the issues that his department has concentrated on:

- Restructuring the employee medical insurance program to avoid a large increase in medical costs while continuing to provide employees with protection against financial disaster. This saved $2 million in 1989.
- Lobbying against legislation and regulations such as the FASB postretirement benefit-funding draft and developing postretirement benefit plan strategies for reducing the potential financial impact of FASB. This may allow McGraw-Hill to avoid a $50 million outlay in annual operating expenses.
- Changing the compensation plan in 1989 to put more emphasis on pay for performance and to lessen the amount of automatic raises in base salary. The financial impact of this approach is unknown at present, but it should stabilize fixed salary costs and link variable costs to performance.

The success of human resources in these areas is obviously having a huge impact on McGraw-Hill's profitability and competitiveness. The savings far exceed the cost of maintaining the human resources function.

Essential Elements

There are three legs to the strategy stool: (1) thinking and planning, (2) managing, and (3) effectiveness. So far, I have not mentioned strategic planning. I have avoided it on purpose. America does not suffer from a shortage of planners. Every M.B.A. program in the country regularly adds to their number each June. Our corporate headquarters are awash with bright young people and their statistical models, scenarios, and voluminous printouts, all illustrated with graphics that would do *Star Wars* proud. May God bless them. Who would we make jokes about if we didn't have economists and planners?

The greatest shortage in American business today is strategic managers. We need more people who have the insight and self-discipline to look beyond the immediate scene, the common sense to interpret clues to future developments, and the guts to act according to their instincts.

Strategic management depends on, but is not paralyzed by, plans. Strategic managers do a great deal of strategic thinking and planning but don't waste much time writing cumbersome plans. The hallmark of strategic management is action. That is the critical difference between planners and managers. Power, Gannon, McGinnis, and Schweiger (1986) describe strategic management as a future-oriented, proactive management system. Note that they call it a system, not a plan. Plans are static, systems are dynamic. Strategic management attempts to keep an organization aligned with its environment while capitalizing on its internal strengths and the environment's opportunities and simultaneously minimizing or neutralizing its inherent weaknesses and external threats.

One of the most successful banks in the U.S. is the Fifth Third Bank of Cincinnati, Ohio. This uniquely named bank is a model of profitability, but it does not have a formal strategic plan. When I asked senior vice-president Ward Withrow how the bank did it, he told me that it was principally a matter of dedication to hard work. But there had to be more to the bank's success than that, so I pressed him for details.

Fifth Third's profit objectives for the future are extremely ambitious. The bank's executives know they can't achieve those objectives by staying within the greater Cincinnati area that is their home base. So, they have opened a two-front campaign. First, much of the bank's growth will have to come through acquisition of banks in the Indiana, Kentucky, and Ohio markets surrounding Cincinnati. Fifth Third plans to expand through acquiring other banks and opening new branches along the interstate highways that traverse the tristate area. This is where consumer and commercial growth will take place. Second, since management wants to increase the rate of return on assets, which is currently running at 1.8 percent (1.0 percent is considered good), its strategy is to maximize fee income from as many sources as possible. The bank takes products that, as Ward puts it, "work well at home" and markets them in the East and Middle West. This strategy is obviously working since the bank now serves electronic cash register authorizations at Bloomingdale's and Lazarus department stores and supports ATMs from Chicago to Washington, D.C. Management is counting on the combination of these two strategic thrusts—expansion and fees from services—to bring the bank to its 1990 goal. Underlying this strategy is the ability to react extremely quickly.

I asked Ward how human resources is servicing this flexible, hyperspeed strategy. According to him, human resources is very attuned to the sense of urgency that exists throughout the bank. It also is aware that the costs of delivering services and the effects of programs are being closely monitored. The human resources staff knows where the bank is going in terms of its profit plan and how quickly it wants to get there. This awareness is the criterion on which all human resources decisions are made. Thus if someone in human resources comes across a person outside the bank who might fit a future need, the human resources person takes advantage of the discovery and builds a relationship that often results in a job offer later. This is just one small way that focusing on strategic management and not strategic plans can work and how the human resources function manages strategically.

Strategic Questions

Ries and Trout (1989) claim that a strategy is not a goal but a coherent marketing direction. A strategy is coherent in that all its elements are focused on the tactics that will be used. It is marketing oriented since it covers all activities related to getting a product or service into the hands of the customer. It has directional aspects since it calls for committing all resources in a given direction to exploit the opportunities provided by the market.

The strategic process is a planned way of answering the basic questions of organizational management from the formation of mission to the measurement of results. It is a structured guide that addresses the following questions:

1. Who are we?
2. What is our purpose?
3. On what will we focus?
4. What are we able to do?
5. What is absolutely necessary?
6. How will we operate?
7. What have we achieved?

As we work through the strategy system in this chapter, you will see how these questions are answered. The HVM model follows this line of questioning.

Strategic management is not an option for today's human resources professionals. It is an imperative. The issues facing these professionals go well beyond helping their staffs become more efficient or productive. In *Managing Human Resources Issues*, Heisler, Jones, and Benham (1988) divide the major human issues facing organizations today into four groups:

1. Health and safety (for example, substance abuse and AIDS)
2. Compensation and benefits (for example, health care costs and comparable worth policies)
3. Changing the employment environment (for example, organizational downsizing and employment at will)
4. Employee performance and productivity (for example, performance management methods and retraining).

The authors go on to suggest that there are still other emerging challenges for human resources managers. The list includes mergers and acquisitions, employment trends, and that still unfulfilled desire — linking human resource management to business strategy.

My experience suggests that the three main worries of American companies going into the 1990s will be (1) attracting and retaining people capable of functioning in changing organizations; (2) discovering effective ways to pay for performance; and (3) controlling benefit costs, particularly medical costs. None of these problems can be solved simply by working harder. You have to think and act differently, that is to say, strategically.

If that isn't a sufficient argument for the strategic approach, then consider all the implications of the word *technology*. The computerized workplace is changing the face as well as the inner workings of organizations. It would be difficult enough to deal with the issues outlined by Heisler, Jones, and Benham in a stable, known work environment. But technology is replacing people with robots and computers, redrawing communication channels, and restructuring organizational cultures. Not only can you not grow, advance, and succeed in organizations today without a strategy, you can't even survive.

To become a strategic manager, you must start thinking holistically. Effective strategic thinking deals with the total organization and the environment in which it operates. Each organization must deal with environmental forces that may be common to many organizations. It also has idiosyncratic problems, needs, and opportunities.

For an illustration we can turn to Gannett Co. Gannett is involved in several information businesses. It owns a number of community and metropolitan newspapers, publishes *USA Today*, has an outdoor advertising division, and operates several broadcasting properties. Many of the issues confronting Gannett are common to today's businesses. For example, the problems of controlling medical costs and fine-tuning pay plans to attract and retain good employees are not unusual. But beyond those, Gannett has some unique needs. As Madelyn Jennings, head of Gannett's human resources department, puts it, "We are in the business of words." This means that the low rate of literacy in the United States is of particular concern to Gannett. The media giant is looking for ways to get involved in helping solve that problem. Also, Gannett places a strong emphasis on "farm teams" and on developing its own employees. The question that human resources is addressing at Gannett is, How can one best manage a diverse work force composed of traditional families, career families, and single parents, given the numerous relocations that inevitably occur along the career path? Finally, since one-third of the employees work part time, where can the company go and what can it do to fill its employment needs in the 1990s? This is more than a recruitment problem, it is a question of Gannett's survival in the next decade. To be effective today, human resources must be able to see ahead and warn the organization about upcoming problems as well as opportunities. The human resources function of the 1990s must operate from a strategic frame of mind.

People who think strategically are able to visualize what lies ahead. They are usually creative and risk-taking people. Successful strategists are adaptable. While they often have strong egos, the successful ones are able to modify their views as circumstances shift or when they are proven wrong. They are intellectually ambitious. They want to understand not just what is happening but why it is happening. The difference between strategic planners or thinkers and strategic managers is that the latter act. Strategic thinkers who are also strategic managers translate their thoughts, plans, and insights into action.

To deal with the critical issues affecting the survival and growth of their organizations, strategic managers ask questions such as these:

- What are our most important organizational issues?
- How are things different today from what they were three to five years ago?
- How are things likely to be different three to five years from now?
- What types of external changes can we expect in the near future?
- What types of internal changes can we expect in the near future?
- How do we compare to our competition in critical areas?
- Is our technology state-of-the-art?
- What can we do to close the gap between what we are and what we must become?

Strategic Effectiveness

Rowe, Mason, and Dickel (1985) describe the characteristics of strategic effectiveness. They state that it (1) takes a systems approach, (2) is multidimensional, (3) incorporates change and adaptation as natural phenomena, (4) connects individual performance to organizational goals, and (5) objectively as well as subjectively demonstrates the value of the outcomes.

Strategic thinking and management are learnable skills. The results of exercising those skills are visible as strategic effectiveness. McGraw-Hill and Gannett provide just two cases of effective human resources strategies. Secor Bank in Birmingham, Alabama, offers still another example.

Secor is a fast-growing savings bank with branches in Alabama, Florida, Louisiana, and Tennessee. Three strategic imperatives drive it:

1. Growth through acquisitions. Human resources at Secor has prepared itself to constantly integrate employees from several acquired banks into the Secor system. They have worked out ten specific techniques to ease the adjustment process for the newly acquired employees. Within a few days after announcing an acquisition, Secor conducts a meeting with the employees of the acquired bank to discuss Secor's goals, mission,

and financial strength. Within the first week Secor staff reviews the benefits package with the new employees, places them on Secor's payroll, distributes and discusses the employee handbook, describes how their former salary system will merge with Secor's, and goes over the acquisition timetable. Beginning in the second week, Secor implements its open-door program, addresses the issues of work consolidation, conversion, and staff reassignment or reduction, carries out the reduction program if necessary, and holds a progress meeting to bring everyone up to date on the status of the acquisition and the schedule necessary to complete the acquisition process.

2. Remain a very lean organization. As noted earlier in this chapter, Secor has published a set of specific actions that cover both human resources and line management. It is monitored by the human resources department. The actions include:

- Formulate and communicate philosophy of lean organization.
- Require economic justification of additions to the payroll.
- Tighten controls for approving new employees.
- Monitor and communicate results by region.
- Develop innovative work-scheduling techniques.
- Provide mechanisms to remove ineffective employees.
- Use incentives to increase productivity.
- Redesign jobs to eliminate narrow specialization.

3. Reduce turnover. This imperative has been translated into several human resources programs. There is a twelve-point program covering initial selection procedures, orientation of new hires, communication of policies, pay and benefit analysis, training, and corporate culture programs.

There is no one way to strategize, and strategy is more than a matter of reacting to opportunity. I have a consultant friend who told me one day that his strategy for the coming year was to focus on working with dentists, sports teams, and real estate agencies. Coincidentally, he had told me just a few weeks before about how he had been approached by someone from the American Dental Association, the coach of a college basketball team, and the president of a chain of real estate offices. What he was doing was reacting to his opportunities. This is a great way to be successful, as long as the opportunities keep popping up. But in this case there is no evidence of a coherent marketing direction. It is hard to imagine three groups of people with less in common than dentists, athletes, and real estate agents. What happens when these three opportunities have been exploited? What is he doing to find others? That is where strategic thinking comes in.

It helps to have a strategic theory around which to build your system. Theories are attempts to explain the fundamental elements of a complex phenomenon. We find it so difficult to deal with the changes impacting today's marketplace mainly because our static, sequential model of organization does not work in the new, more dynamic, and nonlinear world. We need a new theory of organizational effectiveness to guide us. Unfortunately, such a theory is still in its formative stage, at best. We see flashes of it now and then in companies that value flexibility and speed of reaction or that focus on the customer and are concerned about cost effectiveness. Nevertheless, a validated and unified theory is not currently available.

Lacking that theory we have three choices: We can wait until a workable theory is discovered, we can stumble along and hope to come to some understanding of our new world, or we can quit. I don't think we have time to wait, and most of us probably do not want to quit. I suggest we struggle onward. At least, we have the comfort of knowing that no one else knows what's going on either.

Two Strategy Problems

Many people talk about strategizing as though it were a purely logical, objective process that always operates according to a plan. Both parts of this assumption are faulty.

Problem number one is the human element. Strategic thinking is done by people, not computers. Even if you use computer models, people will still have to select the inputs and interpret the outputs. You probably have noticed that people do not always operate from an unbiased, logical standpoint. Whenever we think or act, our physiological, emotional, and psychological filters come into play. Such matters as truth, justice, and the right way to run a business turn out to have very idiosyncratic definitions. But if we can't keep the nonlogical out of our strategizing process, at least we can prepare ourselves to deal with it by taking the following precautions:

Keep the discussion at a high level to avoid turf battles. Strategic thinking, planning, and managing should deal with the larger issues of organizational effectiveness. When they degenerate into internecine wars among factions and functions, you and your organization are in deep trouble.

Make the plans short and comprehensible. The more you put on paper, the more there is to misinterpret or argue over. One-page directives get more results than ten-page documents that try to cover all the possibilities.

Keep it flexible. Flexibility and responsiveness vary inversely with the weight of the document. Remember, a plan is meant to be only a map, not the road itself.

Anticipate the illogical. Envision the most wrong-headed, most ridiculous responses possible and be prepared for them. You are sure to encounter such responses from time to time.

Be alert. Watch for verbal and nonverbal actions that are tip-offs to some off-the-wall act. Don't become paranoid but do maintain an effective intelligence network.

Listen to everyone. There are many views of the world other than yours. Other people see, hear, and feel things that you might miss.

Don't be afraid to exercise the power of your office. I have found that many human resources managers fail to do what they know should be done because they are afraid to upset their staffs. But after all, who is running the show?

The second major strategy involves "immediate demands." An immediate demand is something that comes along and gets in the way of the strategic plan. It says, Whoa, forget what you had planned to do and deal with me now.

Immediate demands are of two kinds: scheduled and unscheduled. A scheduled demand is a routine break in the strategic process. Examples are stopping to close the books at month end, preparing quarterly reports, taking annual inventory. Employees know these are coming and seldom get upset when they have to stop and take care of the scheduled immediate demand. The unscheduled demand is the bump in the road. It is usually an event of some significance. An unexpected union-organizing drive or the actions of a competitor might divert you from your plan for a while. Sometimes the event is traumatic—for example, a fire or an accident that seriously injures or kills someone. The Tylenol tampering case is a dramatic example of an unscheduled immediate demand. Almost certainly that incident occupied the attention of Johnson & Johnson's senior executives for several weeks.

I encountered a somewhat less dramatic example when I was directing the human resources function for a company in Silicon Valley. One of my managers could not understand why we had to temporarily abandon our longer-term plans in order to deal with a downturn in the business. I had hired this young training manager and along with him had developed an ambitious plan for management training. Everything was fine for about nine months until business suddenly and drastically fell off. When I told him we would have to stop most of the formal classroom training and concentrate our efforts on internal consulting, he became irate. It took me a long time to convince him that I was not backing out on my commitment to the strategic training plan. I learned my lesson. Now, when I work with someone on a plan, I advise him or her that this is our preferred strategic direction but that we might have to alter course should conditions change.

A Strategic Management Model

Once we have decided to act strategically, the next tool that we use is a good model. A model is simply a way of converting words into a visible picture. It helps us to coalesce a multitude of perceptions about a dynamic environment into a systematic, cognitively consistent, and comprehensible picture. Some people think that theories or models are useless. However, there

Figure 2. A Strategic Management Model for Human Resources.

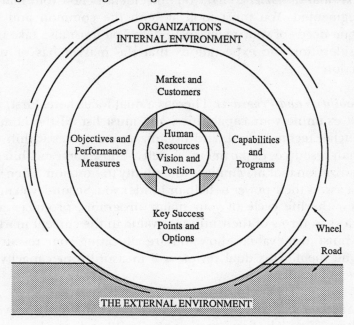

is nothing so practical as a sound theory. With such a theory we can make sense out of chaos.

Figure 2 presents a model I have used for several years with numerous clients. It gives a picture of the basic relationships between the major forces within the strategic organizational world.

There are seven components to the model. Collectively, they describe the major elements that a strategic manager must deal with.

Vision and Position. In the opening chapters we discussed the necessity and value of having a clear vision of what you, as a human resources practitioner, want to be and how you want to be seen by your customers within your organization. Basically, this covers your purpose and your customer relationships and includes factors such as mission and role.

Market and Customers. First, you must identify how your market is segmented. You must look at both the common and the unique needs of your many customers. You must also take into consideration the expectations that the market has of your function.

Capabilities and Programs. There is a dual focus here. First, you must examine your capabilities. You must list all the human, financial, technological, and organizational forces within the human resources department, as well as those forces within the organization that may impact your ability to function. Then you must assess their power to help or hinder you. Second, you must review the life cycle of your major programs, products, and services in terms of their utility or value in the current market. You must also evaluate how you are allocating your resources among them. This dual review will measure your capacity to serve the market.

Key Success Points and Options. This is a reality check and a review of alternatives. The first question here is, What do you have to do to be successful in each of eight key areas (described in Chapter Nine)? The next one is, Which of ten options or alternatives (also described in Chapter Nine) provides the most appropriate way to address the issues confronting you? Key success points tell you what needs to be done and options suggest how to do it.

Objectives and Performance Measures. The last internal human resources element deals with the types of values that you will attempt to contribute to the organization. What kind of human, financial, or production objectives will you set out to achieve? Then, how will you apply cost, time, quantity, quality, and human reaction measures to demonstrate where and how you have added value?

The Organization's Internal Environment. This is the immediate arena within which human resources operates. Here you review the human, financial, technological, and operational forces at work within your marketplace. What is the organization trying to achieve and how will those forces support or inhibit your attempts to contribute to its goals?

External Environment. Finally, what is going on in the outside world? What does the road that your strategic management wheel runs on look like? Again, you must examine the social, economic, political, ethical, and technological forces operating in the market that your organization is attempting to penetrate. A major data services company in England—Datastream International—found itself buffeted by changes coming from several directions at once. In response, the company identified nine strategic management issues, and human resources has become directly involved in this problem-solving process.

In the past two years Datastream has grown over 60 percent through expansion and acquisitions. Corporate strategic plans include growth in international markets in East Asia and, after 1992, in the twelve-nation European Community. In late 1988 the number of Datastream employees grew 20 percent overnight as the result of a merger. Simultaneously it has experienced increasing pressure from customers for more accurate and flexible data bases. There is also growing competition from in-house systems and bureaus. The company's growth is outstripping its current facilities, and a plan for relocating some operations must be worked out. There are skill shortages in programmers and analysts that can be remedied only through new recruiting and education programs. There is the question of how to manage a company twice the size of the old one. Finally, the company is grappling with the problem of how to measure performance in a service industry.

The human resources staff has worked out a strategy for dealing with these problems as four related groups. The issues break down like this: First, human resources needs to design an integrated system for acquiring, managing, and developing employees in a changing culture. Second, there must be a system and method for managing expansion that considers not only acquiring new facilities but doing business in new geographical areas. Third, customer demands and competitive pressures must be considered in relation to each other. Fourth, measures of effectiveness must be built by which processes, outputs, and impacts are related to operational objectives. This strategy will optimize resources and speed solutions as one problem flows over and affects an adjoining problem.

Strategic analysis prepares you to operate. You learn about yourself, your market, and the environment in which it exists. The wheel in Figure 2 is meant to suggest the dynamic measure of your world. There are many benefits that come from learning to manage strategically:

- You become future oriented, anticipative, and proactive.
- You learn to use systematic analyses and models to inform and persuade others.
- You discover how to allocate resources better, make more practical decisions, and act more decisively.
- You become skilled in using quantitative data to set objectives, evaluate performance, and operate more effectively.

The Strategic Process

Given a strategic management model, the next requirement is to put it into play. For that I have provided a process. The process in Figure 3 pictures the dynamic quality of strategic management.

This process also covers the last element in strategic thinking and management. The right-hand column in Figure 3 lists the issues that business strategists deal with. They are the operational definitions of the verbs in the left-hand column.

The remainder of this book takes you through the process of strategic management. It offers procedural guides or tools that will help you transform the imperatives of a model and a process into a doable task. It takes abstractions and concepts and converts them into concrete actions.

But putting a strategy in play means that YOU have to initiate it. You begin by just doing it. The first imperative in strategic action is to take the model and the process and start to implement them. Begin the process today. Develop your system. Try out your assumptions. Begin by doing the many little things

Figure 3. The Strategic Process Model.

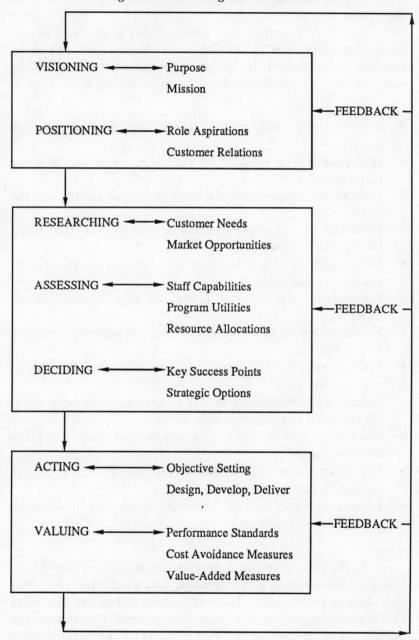

VISIONING ←——→ Purpose
                Mission

POSITIONING ←——→ Role Aspirations
                 Customer Relations

FEEDBACK

RESEARCHING ←——→ Customer Needs
                 Market Opportunities

ASSESSING ←——→ Staff Capabilities
               Program Utilities
               Resource Allocations

FEEDBACK

DECIDING ←——→ Key Success Points
              Strategic Options

ACTING ←——→ Objective Setting
            Design, Develop, Deliver

VALUING ←——→ Performance Standards
             Cost Avoidance Measures
             Value-Added Measures

FEEDBACK

that will prepare you to take advantage of new opportunities as they come along.

Kami (1988) argues that success today requires an adjustment in management style to meet the changes brought on by the new environment. In his strategic management audit, he suggests that organizations examine these questions:

- Talent: Are we able to hire, keep, and motivate talented people?
- Innovation: Are we able to encourage and create some innovation?
- Loyalty: Are we inspiring the same degree of loyalty as in the past?
- Rewards: Are we rewarding our people the way that really pleases them most?
- Delegation: Are we delegating and operating a more horizontal organization?
- Bureaucracy: Are we fighting and winning the battle of red tape?
- Entrepreneurship: Are we motivating our people to practice self-initiative?
- Productivity: Are we increasing overall productivity by 10 percent annually?
- Research and development: Are we getting the needed faster results from our development efforts?
- Marketing: Are we marketing solidly and really satisfying our customers?
- Export expertise: Are we knowledgeable about export opportunities and procedures?
- Long-term view: Are we balancing long-term needs with immediate necessities?

In the past, many human resources managers would have said that these are largely operating and marketing problems that do not come within their sphere of influence. But every business objective has a human component. I find that the human resources people who practice HVM principles jump right into the middle of business problems, and these are the people who make a difference.

The second action imperative is to constantly reinforce the plan through action in front of others. Words may inspire, but action generates belief. Whenever possible, show your people that you mean to operate according to the plan. Nothing is so reassuring and reinforcing as action. If your staff and other people see that you have a plan and that you are committed to using it, they will know that you mean business.

Finally, keep your strategic system alive by constantly modifying it to meet changing conditions. No one can foresee the future. The best of plans start to become obsolete the first day that they are put to work. While you must continually emphasize the importance of operating with a strategic direction, don't become blind or stubborn. Seek both formal and informal feedback. Feedback is to a strategy what blood is to a body. Blood serum carries life-sustaining and life-renewing nutrients throughout the body to keep it in balance with its environment. Feedback carries fresh new information throughout the system to keep it alive and responsive to *its* environment.

How to Communicate the System

The easiest and best way to communicate your strategy and system is to involve people in its creation. Your managerial and professional staff should be directly and intimately involved in all those aspects of the plan and process to which they can add value. Not only will you gain the benefit of their viewpoints and opinions, but they will obtain valuable training and insights into the process of management.

Let me contrast how two sections within one human resources department worked on the design and development of a strategic management and measurement system. In section A the manager's attitude was that the worker bees, mostly young women, would not be interested in the design and development process. His condescending opinion was that they did not have the interest, intelligence, experience, or background to contribute to the new system. In section B, by contrast, the manager communicated details of the process and offered opportunities to workers to ask questions and make suggestions. In both cases, the program was put in place and is currently operating effectively. The only difference is that in section A the workers are less motivated, and consequently require more supervision than those in section B. When I periodically visit the department, I find two distinctly different operating environments. In section A, the system represents just another set of tasks, and it belongs to management. In section B it is "our system."

Some people will not be able to contribute to a strategy. They may not have the training, experience, or position within the organization that will let them add value. Still, you should communicate the basics of the strategy even to those who are not directly a part of it. You certainly need to tell them where you are going if you expect to get any help from them along the way.

Most important of all is that your people are told and shown how your (their) system is linked to the overall corporate strategy. At PACCAR, Inc., in Bellevue, Washington, the corporate theme has always been "quality." As Ingrid Rasch, who directs planning and development, says, "Quality is key!" So, when the management of the human resources function worked out its strategic system, it used this quality theme as its foundation.

There are three rules for communicating a strategic system to staffers who weren't involved in its design. One, keep it simple. Two, use language that they will understand. Three, ask for their responses to it.

Simplicity. It is often difficult for a person to comprehend a strategy if he or she has not been involved in its development. This is especially true if the person has limited experience in planning. Therefore, when you describe the process and objectives, eliminate most of the details and just communicate the key issues and major intent. More than that probably won't be appreciated or necessary.

Language. Don't use jargon. There is no need to show how smart you are. Staff members know the truth. If you are bright, they know it. And if you aren't, jargon won't fool them. It often helps to use visual models. Concepts are easier to understand if your people can see the model as well as hear about it.

Feedback. You can learn how effective your communication was by asking your audience to talk with you about the system when you finish describing it. This should not look like a test. You can pose questions in nonthreatening ways. Ask for opinions that will help you understand whether or not staff members got the gist of your presentation. If they didn't, it isn't their fault. It is the responsibility of the communicator to make himself or herself understandable to each listener.

Whenever I put in a strategic management or measurement system, I strongly suggest to the department head that an all-staff meeting of one hour be held at the very beginning. I make a presentation to everyone about what changes are in store and the benefits that will accrue to them from operating the system. At the conclusion of the design phase I recommend that another meeting for all staff members be held to outline the new system. The few hours spent at the beginning and end of the design process make a difference so great that even I can't measure it.

Few managers understand the value of communication more than VeriFone's head of human resources, Karen Ventura. VeriFone is a 600-employee company that has become a leader in point-of-sale transaction terminals. From its inception in 1981, it has been a technological innovator with an international perspective. Headquartered in Hawaii, it supports systems throughout the United States, Asia, and Europe.

For Karen the purpose of human resources is to increase the productivity of people in this far-flung organization through communication. Her first thought about any new program is, How should we communicate this? Her staff spends a large amount of time on both employee and family communications. Since the company is so decentralized and thinly spread around the world, everyone has to take on extra responsibility. This impacts the family members at home because VeriFone employees work long hours. In order to ensure that the family is not neglected, human resources has started an employee publication that goes to the home. It covers general interest news about the company, as well as information on benefits and career growth opportunities. When you have to rely on managers thousands of miles away to describe new programs such as stock distributions to employees, your communications system must be well thought out, well organized, and timely. Human resources makes sure that managers learn about changes before the grapevine gets the word around.

Karen practices what she preaches with her own staff. When we designed a measurement program for VeriFone's administrative functions, almost everyone was directly involved in the design process. Other than those personnel needed to cover the phones, all professionals and many clerical staff members were involved in the discussions and design sessions. The support staffs at small field offices were informed immediately about what was going on and what it would mean to them. As a result, that system slipped on like an old glove and began to function smoothly from day one.

Tips on Implementation

Implementing and managing a strategic system are not easy jobs. However, it might be helpful if you keep a few basic principles in mind.

I suggest that you pick an easy target to start with. This is called the principle of low-hanging fruit. It is easier and less risky to pick an apple if you don't have to climb a twenty-foot ladder to do it. Take an important but simple task for openers. There are many things you will have to do to put your plan in play. Start with the issues that you know you can handle. Build up to the harder jobs. People who are consistently successful in organizations avoid being overmatched. Start simple. Gain experience. Learn and develop your skills. Then you will be ready to take on the tough situations.

One job at a time is enough. Pick an opportunity that is more or less independent of other issues. Although everything in a system is related to some degree, start with a task, problem, or opportunity that has as few extraneous or uncontrollable variables as possible. It is hard enough to solve simple problems. Complex problems increase the degree of difficulty geometrically.

Find a smooth track to run on. Pick an area where there is a supportive environment. Look for issues where you are unlikely to meet any resistance. Why ask for trouble? There is plenty of natural competition within organizations. Focus first on items where there are few obstacles. You can take on the hard problems later.

Conclusion

To be good managers, we must use both strategy and tactics. We use tactics for short-term problem solving and day-to-day administration. Strategy provides us with a frame of reference for operating and administrative systems, as well as for employee behavior. Strategic thinking requires a vision of what might be, creativity, risk taking, flexibility, and ambition. Effective strategists work with their staffs to set objectives and define priorities. They approach their function from a systems perspective. They acknowledge the inevitability of change as an antecedent of growth. Finally, they track progress and feed the data back into the system to optimize both efficiency and effectiveness.

Strategizing can be learned. The job is made easier if you have a starting theory. Absent that, you should at least have a model to give you a holistic picture of both the field in which you will be working and its environment. You can then start the process of visioning, positioning, researching, assessing, deciding, acting, and evaluating. A set of working guides and tools completes your kit. They help you through each of the process steps. But the most important step is to act: You will accomplish nothing unless you initiate your strategic system and continuously reinforce your intentions through action.

Words inspire hearts, actions direct hands.

Systems must be communicated if they are to be supported. You keep a strategy vital through observation, feedback, and modification. Many organizations never let anyone in on the key strategic imperatives. It is very difficult to service a program that staff members have neither seen nor heard about. The best way to communicate is through involvement. Even those who are not directly involved in the strategy system still have to learn its basics. Keep your description simple and jargon free. Use visual terms and aids. Check for comprehension by asking for responses that demonstrate understanding.

The easiest way to implement a system is to start with an important but achievable target. Save complex problems for later. The idea is to win, and the secret of success is to start with small goals and consistently achieve them. You greatly increase your chances of winning if you keep control of the game. Remember that people respect and follow winners. It is my experience that losers talk about how hard they worked. Winners talk about what they achieved. Today is the day to get started managing strategically.

> Opportunities should never be lost, because they can hardly ever be regained.
>
> William Penn

References

Heisler, W. J., Jones, W. D., and Benham, P. O., Jr. *Managing Human Resources Issues: Confronting Challenges and Choosing Options.* San Francisco: Jossey-Bass, 1988.

Kami, M. J. "Strategic Management Audit." From seminar on strategic management, periodically given by Kami.

Kami, M. J. *Trigger Points.* New York: McGraw-Hill, 1988.

Power, D. J., Gannon, M. J., McGinnis, M. A., and Schweiger, D. M. *Strategic Management Skills.* Reading, Mass.: Addison-Wesley, 1986.

Ries, A., and Trout, J. *Bottom-Up Marketing.* New York: McGraw-Hill, 1989.

Rowe, A. J., Mason, R. O., and Dickel, K. E. *Strategic Management and Business Policy.* Reading, Mass.: Addison-Wesley, 1985.

Case Studies—Chapter Four

Greyhound Corporation
Phoenix, Arizona
(From work and discussions with Bob Lang, vice-president of
human resources)

In the mid-1980s Greyhound sold its intercity bus service because it no longer met the income objectives of the corporation. Today, Greyhound is a holding company. It has four very diversified business segments that manage twenty-seven major operating companies. Each chief operating officer is given the authority and responsibility to make the decisions required for operating his division. There is as little direction from corporate headquarters as possible. This modus operandi holds true for the human resources function as well. Company human resources managers report directly to their chief operating officers and indirectly to Bob Lang at corporate headquarters in Phoenix, Arizona.

As the holding company was taking shape, however, it became clear to Bob that the human resources function was not prepared or positioned to play a meaningful role. The problem was threefold: First, the prior trend of increasingly centralized human resources direction from corporate headquarters had to be reversed. Second, the capabilities of the human resource professionals throughout the system had to be strengthened. Third, operational understanding of the future role of human resources management as it relates to the business objectives of Greyhound had to be increased significantly. The objective was to make the transition from a well-accepted "personnel" role to a state-of-the-art integrated human resources and business-planning function.

Bob initiated the transition in early 1987 with revisions of the vision, mission statement, and leadership within the corporate human resources function. The process began with complete revisions of Greyhound's human resources policies and procedures. This called for delegating control to the operating companies without abdicating the overall corporate control role through audit and monitoring procedures.

Next, a dedicated effort was made to strengthen the full range of professional human resource skills represented by the staffs of the subsidiary companies. The process started with the fundamentals at an intense three-day conference on measurement for the human resources staffs put on by Saratoga Institute. It was at this program that Bob introduced the "new" functional direction and began emphasizing it in daily interactions with the subsidiaries.

Later, the process continued with other seminars on a variety of subjects, including strategic business management. These provided human resources staff members with a solid foundation of skills and knowledge. During this period efforts also began to address the third concern. Discussions were held with operating managers to explain to them the changes that were taking place and to raise the standards of performance for the human resources staffs. The corporatewide strategic planning process was revised during 1988, and the 1989 annual plan included four distinct human resource requirements: (1) a review of statutory and policy requirements to determine areas that needed strengthening; (2) analysis of the environmental drives affecting human resources management within each industry; (3) identification of the critical business objectives as defined by each company's operating management team; and (4) analysis of their respective human resources implications.

From these, a fourth section was completed that identified the priority action items for 1989—the what, who, and when of what was going to be done by the human resources function during the year to enhance Greyhound's competitive advantages. The final section introduced a few quantitative measures relating to human resources management. This became the foundation for communicating the functions' effectiveness to operating management in a language that it would understand.

The Linkage. Annual plans had to be in writing, had to be endorsed by the chief operating officer, and had to be submitted as an integral part of the business plan. In addition, and most important to the success of the transition, the human resources executive in each operating company was required to accompany the chief operating officer to Phoenix for the meetings at which the plans were presented to the chairman of Greyhound, John Teets. Not only did they have to attend, but they were required to give an oral presentation of the plan they had developed. Also, a system was put in place to review the accomplishment of the human resources objectives during the quarterly operating review meetings with the chairman.

Have these changes been meaningful to the corporation? The evidence shows they have been very effective, even though they have been in place for only two years.

Each year since the chairman assumed his role, a presidents' retreat has been held to assess the corporation's direction and the strategic issues affecting its future. As part of this process, the presidents of Greyhound's operating companies discuss the strengths and weaknesses of the corporate staff and the degree to which staff support is suitable. During the first two years—1986 and 1987—that the new system was being put in place, the human resources staff's rating was the lowest of all the functions. In 1988, impressions began to change. The links that Bob and his local staffs were forging between human resources and the business plan were becoming visible. Most recently, at the 1989 presidents' meeting, the chief operating officers concluded that the function was the "most improved" department at corporate headquarters. No negatives were voiced, and comments such as "responsive," "helpful," "an asset," "necessary," and "is creating value" were used to describe the efforts of human resources.

Why did the presidents' perceptions change? Because human resources was able to integrate its programs with the business plan. The message that Bob continually preaches is that technological advances are rapidly eliminating the company's competitive advantages in operational, financial, and marketing areas. The one remaining opportunity for Greyhound appears to be in finding ways to create competitive advantages through its people.

Author's comment: There must be a thousand articles in business and personnel journals about how human resources and business plans should be and are being integrated. That is the good news. The bad news is that there are only a handful of companies that are successful in achieving this goal. Greyhound is one of them.

Bob Lang sums up the link by pointing out that there is no business objective that does not have a human resources component. I hope to see the day when the human resources plan becomes a direct, automated descendant of the business plan. There exists a method for doing that. Someday someone will pick it up and make it work in his or her company.

Manufacturers Life Insurance Company
Toronto, Ontario
(Prepared by Rose Patten, senior vice-president, human resources and organization development)

Manufacturers Life is the largest insurance company in Canada, with over $20 billion in assets. It is a prestigious, 100-year-old firm, headquartered in Toronto with operations throughout Canada and in international markets. In the past, it was highly centralized, it concentrated on sales, and its culture was built on consensus. Despite its strengths, however, it needed modernizing to maintain its market position.

When a new chief executive officer was elected in early 1988, he brought in Rose Patten to head human resources and to work with him on organization development. The chief executive's experience was in the investment area rather than the traditional insurance/actuarial background. Seeing things differently from previous chief executives, he decided that a reorganization was in order. His objective was to build on strengths and restructure the company to eliminate its perceived vulnerabilities.

During the next year he began a program of decentralization and downsizing, and he also initiated a shift in corporate culture. As one would expect, a change of such magnitude produced a certain amount of turmoil in the company. It was the task of human resources to orchestrate the reorganization from the "people" side.

Rose brought with her a vision of human resources management as an infrastructure of people involvement, commitment, competence, and focus, anchored to business strategy, goals, and priorities of the company. Her mandate was to work with the chief executive to establish strategies that would initiate a cultural shift toward a stronger sense of business issues, a stronger profit orientation, and performance accountability among management and employees at large. She built her strategy on the following initiatives:

- Start by putting in place a strategic organization structure designed to achieve the goals outlined above.
- Create an environment in which current practices can be reassessed and regrouped and values can be reassessed in line with the chief executive's business objectives.
- Put in place a team of top executives capable of pushing the needed changes through the organization.
- Establish the understanding that human resources programs will be driven by business strategies. Each program would be a response to a specific initiative and would involve employees in its design. This would be done without significant additional expenditures.
- Use compensation as a strategic tool to redirect behavior and focus attention on priorities and expectations.
- Provide the means for learning required leadership skills and for empowering managers to be part of designing and implementing their own strategies.

The reorganization of Manufacturers Life began at the top with a reduction of twelve senior positions to five. The old and new top organizational charts are shown in Figures 4 and 5. At the same time, the rebuilding of the human resources and organizational structure of Manufacturers Life was initiated with the following set of activities:

1. The annual bonus incentive plans were redesigned to focus greater attention on appropriate business goals and mea-

Figure 4. Inherited Organizational Structure at Manufacturers Life.

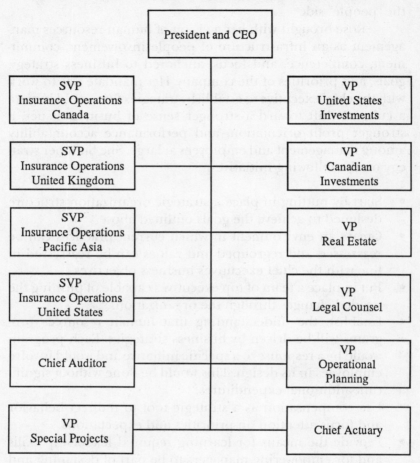

surements. The bonus plans were meant to provide an increased incentive to meet these goals.

2. The long-term incentive plan was redesigned to focus attention on long-range planning for profitability.

3. An organizational survey was conducted to solicit employee views on operating practices and their consistency with stated priorities, management style and skills, and human resources policies and practices.

4. A worldwide Executive Forum of top sixty officers was

Figure 5. New Organizational Structure at Manufacturers Life.

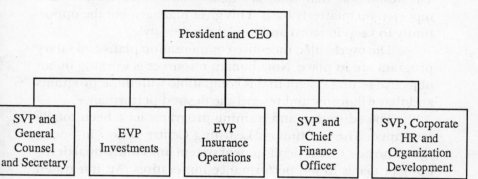

designed that empowered top divisional managers to present issues, strategies, and plans.

5. This forum was used to introduce the reorganization, the new company vision, company strategies for the next three years, and the success factors and leadership qualities that would be rewarded.

6. The human resources division was reorganized, and its mandate and operating philosophy and plans were articulated. Existing employees and/or newly hired people were selected to implement vision and strategies in various human resources departments.

7. The role of the Corporate HR Committee was redefined to show the relationship between divisional human resources and corporate human resources. This was done to ensure understanding of the importance of divisional involvement and representation in policy development.

8. Human resources worked directly with the chief executive officer in each major division worldwide to analyze its operations, issues, and unique needs.

9. A new concept and focus for training called the Continuous Learning Centre was created.

As you might expect, there has been considerable improvement in communication and involvement of employees. For example, local meetings of employees were held to deal with the issues that surfaced in response to the organizational survey.

The result was that nine key actions are to be tracked and reported on quarterly basis. This gives management the opportunity to keep its word and model the new style.

The overhauled incentive compensation plans and salary program are in place. Now, human resources is working on an objective-setting system that is compatible with these programs and that will foster and reward the desired performance.

The education and training programs have been totally revamped. The Continuous Learning Centre is now in operation. The new career development system links individual development needs to job performance imperatives. An integrated curriculum is being developed that will carry an employee from supervisory level skills all the way to executive management capabilities.

The Executive Forum has become a learning experience as well as a strategic management session. The chief executive officer uses it as a forum for describing corporate strategy. Attendees make presentations on how their units are responding to the company's strategic imperatives. Rather than being a consensus body, the forum provides an opportunity for executives to gain and use leadership skills. It empowers executives, increases their commitment to the company, and energizes the reorganization.

Author's comment: Rose Patten is fortunate to have a chief executive officer who understands and appreciates the value-adding role that human resources can play in a successful restructuring. Fortunately for the company, Rose is capable of handling the assignment. Human resources managers talk constantly about being a part of the inner circle of executives. Yet, how many are prepared by training and able by temperament to hold their own in that arena?

5

Creating a New Vision
for Human Resources

WHEN YOU DO common things in life in an uncommon
way, you will command the attention of the world.
George Washington Carver

A 1986 survey of chief executive officers of seventy-one
major U.S. corporations showed how much the market for
human resources has changed already (American Productivity
Center, 1986). The chief executives interviewed said they have
given directions to their line managers to buy staff services in
the most cost-effective way. This means that an in-house department can be circumvented if its services can be purchased more
cheaply elsewhere.

Working with human resources departments in many
different industries and locations, I find increasing evidence
that chief executives are being taken at their word. More and
more, managers are willing to pay only for what they use. The
human resources department is being put on a fee-for-service
base rather than being given a budget allocation as in the past.
In response to that change, a movement has started among
human resources professionals that is based on a new vision of
the function. The focal point has shifted from programs to
customers and from expense to value added. For decades, many
personnel and human resources people acted as though they
were separate from the enterprise that they were serving. This
notion is now being challenged as more people are starting to
reexamine why human resources even exists in organizations
and what its true purpose is.

The Prime Question

The auditorium was filled with hospital administrators. I
posed a problem for them. They were to discuss with the person

109

next to them and reach a mutually satisfactory answer to the question, What is your business? Everyone jumped to the task and began exchanging ideas with his or her partner. That is, everyone except for two men who sat silently in the front row. After a few minutes of watching them out of the corner of my eye, I walked over and asked, "Do you have it figured out already?" One man looked up at me and smiled. Then, he said quite simply, "No."

Our conversation continued like this:

Me: You don't know what your business is?

Him: No.

Me: Do you care?

Him: No. [Still smiling.]

At the next break they thanked me and walked out. I was mystified by their attitude. If they don't know what their business is, how do they know what to do every morning when they arrive at work? How do they plan? The answer is that they will probably do the same thing tomorrow as they did yesterday and wait for the next fire to break out.

It is possible for people like those hospital administrators to be managers, at least in a bureaucratic sense. But it is impossible for them to be leaders. The trait that distinguishes leaders from managers is that leaders provide a vision. In fact, the primary responsibility of a leader is to provide a vision. To qualify as a leader, you must be able to communicate a vision that stirs the imagination of your people, excites them, and captures their commitment. Anything less is not leadership.

Managing is important. It is necessary. But it is not the same thing as leading. Management focuses on systems, the means to an end. Leadership focuses on the end, the goal. Management sets operating objectives and monitors the attainment of them. Leadership inspires people to perform up to and sometimes beyond their capabilities. Managers look at the current reporting periods. Leaders look forward, over the time horizons of operating objectives to a transcendent future goal. They have a clear picture of the direction they want their organizations to take. Successful leaders are those who effectively communicate their vision of the future to all those who have a stake in it.

In sports, coaches design strategies and game plans and, through their assistants, train the players. Throughout the season they monitor progress by means of process statistics such as number of hits, baskets, tackles, or goals. They track outcomes by their won-lost record. At the end of the season, if they are successful, their team wins the championship. That is managing for goal achievement.

Leading is the interpersonal communication of a vision of excellence. Coaches who are great leaders see to it that the mechanics of management are being attended to by themselves and their assistants. They then go beyond that by providing the ideal that inspires the players to give their best. When you examine the careers of great coaches, you find a common thread. Vince Lombardi of the Green Bay Packers dominated the National Football League by building intense personal pride and commitment in his players. John Wooden won so many National Collegiate Athletic Association basketball championships while coach at UCLA that each year the result seemed predestined. He was a teacher whose quiet leadership style was so natural that it was almost invisible. Al Davis, owner of the Oakland Raiders, compiled a highly successful professional football record over a twenty-year period on a three-word vision: Pride and Poise. People need a vision to give meaning to their work. Without one, work is simply labor. With one, work becomes fulfillment. Henry David Thoreau pointed out that, for the masses, work is drudgery. His famous claim that "most men lead lives of quiet desperation" applies, unfortunately, to many human resources practitioners. Without a vision, the most that anyone has is a job. There is no excitement and little sustained motivation.

Shaping a Vision

A vision is a mental picture of the future. Kouzes and Posner (1987) describe it as "an ideal, unique image of the future." Visions spring from a desire for change and a need to do something meaningful. You sense that things are not what they could be. This may start as a vague feeling of uneasiness or a sense that something is missing in your life or work. Gradually, as you play with the idea, your continuing experience confirms that some fundamental change is needed. In time, a mental image begins to form in your mind. You might discuss this image with others to confirm your feelings and test your thoughts. As the image begins to coalesce, you find that you can articulate it, at least to yourself. You can begin to see the end results, and it all becomes very exciting. You want to run out and proclaim it to the world. It is so right that you want everyone to see the beauty of your new model. Now, you truly have a vision.

In their work on strategic planning, Below, Morrisey, and Acomb (1987) talk about an organization's mission. They describe mission statements as conveying the nature and concept of the organization's future business. They offer four reasons for having a mission statement:

1. To ensure consistency and clarity of purpose
2. To provide a point of reference for all major decisions
3. To gain commitment from those within the organization
4. To gain understanding and support from those outside the organization who are important to its success (p. 27)

The vision is the antecedent of the mission statement. It is the inspiration around which the mission statement is articulated. It lays the foundation, in a very few words, for the more lengthy mission statement. In my opinion, vision statements have more utility than most mission statements. A vision should be describable in no more than five words. It can be elaborated on later. I have found that there is an inverse relationship between the number of words used and the truth of the vision statement. If you can express your vision in no more than five words, you don't need a mission statement. Mission statements are noteworthy for their length and immeasurable idealism. Most mission statements remind me of the standard reply of irreverent graduate students who have just critiqued a self-evident piece of research, "Borrrring."

The Human Value Management Vision

There is a striking similarity among the vision statements of those who advocate human value management. The size, type, or location of the organization makes no difference. The line of business has little effect. Vision does not depend on externals. I have watched some of these people go from one organization to another over the years, each time with no perceptible difference in their style of operation. And everywhere they go they are successful. Vision is an expression of their personal value and belief system as it relates to the practice of human resources management.

The following is a list of vision statements I have collected over the past few years from people in different countries and different industries:

U.S. (computers): "Help managers manage better."

Sweden (telecommunications): "Business support."

England (chemicals): "Create appropriate organizational culture."

Japan (electronic instruments): "Promote personal development/contribution to the organization."

U.S. (savings and loan): "Partnership with management in valuing human assets."

U.S. (construction materials): "Stimulate productive utilization of human resources."

South Africa (conglomerate): "Help accomplish the organization's business objectives."

U.S. (conglomerate): "Ensure human resource support parallels corporate strategic directions."

Australia (conglomerate): "Facilitate organization's capability to perform."

U.S. (social agency): "The driving creative force."

Canada (insurance): "Creators of a high-quality environment."

U.S. (pharmaceutical): "Strengthen individual and organizational performance."

Israel (research): "Cost effectively match employee and
company needs."

Brazil (chemicals): "Business partners with management."

France (heavy equipment): "Stimulate universal competence."

West Germany (gas transmission): "Add value."

U.S. (investment banking): "Help managers achieve business objectives."

The Netherlands (telecommunication/data systems):
"With management build an environment of success."

Denmark (insurance): "Assist management in running
the business."

U.S. (insurance): "Facilitate positive change."

New Zealand (bank): "Responsive, efficient consultants
who devolve personnel responsibility to line management."

U.S. (publishing): "Value-added contributors to profits."

Canada (telecommunications): "Support the company's
business vision."

U.S. (hospital): "Develop people as a competitive advantage."

Venezuela (petroleum): "Be business partners with
management."

U.S. (semiconductors): "Create an atmosphere where people can contribute to their fullest."

United Nations agency: "Improve the quality of our program worldwide."

Did you notice the common theme among these visions?
Not one of them mentioned hiring, paying, and training people.
Those are activities, not visions of a purpose. Rather, these
visions all expressed what human resources is in the mind of the
human resources manager. The people with these visions take
the vision with them wherever they go, and they seldom join an
organization where they cannot fulfill their vision.

In my vision, the human resources function is like a

company within a market. Its customers are the employees and management of the organization that it services. In other words, the organization is the marketplace for human resources. This idea is present in many of the vision statements listed above. You will find this view expressed repeatedly by human resources managers throughout this book.

Communicating the Vision

Creating a vision is the first step. But until you share it with others, it will be very difficult to bring the vision to fruition. Everyone has some image of his or her work and organization. We saw in the results of the work satisfaction study ("The Happiness Barometer," 1988) that the images that many employees carry of their jobs are not very exciting. Your challenge is to communicate your vision to those around you. To move the organization the way you want it to go, you have to help your people see what you see. Practically every great achievement has its roots in a vision communicated by a leader. The vision is what stirs people to see not only what could be but what should be.

Adoption of the leader's vision has positive practical effects as well as inspirational value. Rationalistic Western philosophies have traditionally treated the emotional and rational aspects of personality as separate domains. Eastern philosophies point out that the two are part of a whole and that these two parts frequently interact and thereby influence each other. When you capture the imagination of your people with your vision, you are appealing to their emotional side. This provides the energy that feeds the rational side. With the two sides harnessed together, people work more efficiently and effectively. Overall, their productivity goes up, they feel greater satisfaction from their jobs, their commitment to you and the organization increases, and loyalty and team spirit naturally follow. Moreover, people want to be excited about and involved in their work. No one goes to work each day for forty or more years with the goal of wasting time and turning out inferior work. Everyone has pride, and if you can connect your vision to the personal pride of your workers, you will have them on your side.

We can learn how to make these connections by observing the communications techniques of effective leaders. One of the most obvious sources to look to is the evening news broadcast. If you can watch without getting emotionally involved, you will see how politicians move people. Do they play on rational issues? It might sound as though they do, but there is always an emotional undertone that is designed to engage people. The totally rational speaker is boring. Political history is strewn with the carcasses of brilliant statesmen who could not excite people. Adlai Stevenson was one of the most articulate and intelligent men ever to run for the presidency. But he was trounced soundly two times by a man that people related to emotionally: Dwight Eisenhower. In retrospect we can all see that the statesman Stevenson was probably better suited to the office, but "Ike" was the people's choice.

Before you can win the support of people to work for your vision, you have to win their hearts. How can you communicate the emotion that will carry them along? Kouzes and Posner (1987) suggest that you build your communications on the following principles:

- *Know your audience:* You must know which communications to avoid and which to use; knowing the hopes, fears, and biases of your audience is critical.
- *Be graphic:* Use pictorial language; this helps your audience "see" your message.
- *Be visceral:* Use examples that your audience can relate to on a very personal level; find something that its members have experienced.
- *Appeal to values:* Values are the most central and enduring part of personality; they are deeply felt beliefs.
- *Be positive:* Stress the positive in what you say and do; shift from what is to what could and should be.
- *Focus on your audience:* Communicate the strength of your personal belief in the vision but move early on from "I" to "we"; share the passion.
- *Be consistent:* Tell them every day, in every way, about your vision; make it part of their life.

In 1978–1979, the Saratoga Institute studied productivity correlates on 1,355 employees at all levels in three companies. We looked at 150 variables and factor analyzed them to locate twenty-two factors (Fitz-enz, 1982). From that list we identified five factors that most closely correlated with high productivity and commitment. At about the same time, *Psychology Today* published a piece on what people's jobs meant to them and what aspects of their jobs they found most rewarding (Lawler and Renwick, 1978). The two studies uncovered similar items. Furthermore, several of the most critical issues carried emotional overtones and illustrated how important it is for employees to have an exciting vision of the purpose of their work. The key factors in the two studies were:

1. *Psychology Today (PT):* The chance to do something that makes you feel good about yourself as a person.

Saratoga Institute (SI): Self-esteem obtained from the job was the strongest correlate of high productivity. Everyone wants to spend his or her time doing something valuable.

2. *PT:* The chance to accomplish something worthwhile. Endless data entry, invoice processing, applicant interviews, report writing, and attending meetings do not inspire people; they need to achieve.

SI: People also need to relate to their co-workers. Matching people with appropriate jobs and co-workers ranked third in this study.

3. and 4. *PT:* The chance to learn new procedures and develop new skills. There are monotonous aspects to some jobs. Most people welcome the opportunity to do something new, as long as it is not threatening.

SI: A sense of capability based on the belief that you have the skills, aptitudes, and interests to do the job well.

5. *PT:* Freedom to do your job.

SI: Two aspects of responsibility are important here. One aspect is the inherent sense of responsibility that a person brings to work. The other is the responsibility delegated by the organization that allows the employee to make the job his or her own. Employees do not want total freedom. They want a vision they can follow and space to operate, and they will then be willing to take responsibility for the results.

People want more than security and money out of their jobs. They want fulfillment. A leader who provides a vision that people can relate to will have no problems in retaining them and stimulating them to extraordinary levels of performance.

Most people realize that complex organizations need a central vision articulated to the members. Since each person in an organization occupies a unique position, no two people have exactly the same view as anyone else. Managers do not see events the same way as employees. The vantage point of supervisors is different from that of executives, and vice versa. Although we all share some general perceptions, our interpretations of events and conditions are idiosyncratic. A vision provides a valuable reference point for discussing plans and strategies and for making decisions. When your people know what your vision is, they will support it. A vision gives them choices while simultaneously providing them with a focus. The vision is like a signpost that points them in the right direction.

In 1980, Bob Coon and I were working at Four-Phase Systems in Silicon Valley, a company that was later purchased by Motorola. We had a vision of the company as a total environment in which people could fulfill themselves. From an organizational standpoint, this called for putting all functions that affected the working environment under one controlling unit. We visualized a Department of the Environment.

Unfortunately, the company did not see it that way. The Personnel Department was seen as having five traditional functional roles: staffing, compensation, benefits, employee relations, and training. When Motorola bought the company, some environment-related functions were added, but these too had become conventional over time — health, safety, and security.

In 1988, when Bob was approached by Daisy Systems to take over its human resources function, he accepted the offer subject to implementation of the environmental management concept. His business card does not read Vice-President of the Environment, but that is the way he manages his department. Along with the basic personnel functions and the usual health, safety, and security areas, he also supervises real estate, facilities, space planning, maintenance, landscaping, janitorial services, heating/air conditioning, cafeterias, exercise rooms, telephones, telecommunications, video and data networks, mail, distribution and copy centers, office machines, and all administrative services. This is the environmental vision, with implementation on a grand scale.

People want and need an ideal to which they can commit themselves. It is human nature to seek a set of beliefs and values by which to live. This is what religion does for people. At a simpler level, loyalty to one's alma mater is based on adherence to the value system represented by the school. In business, people need a credo to which they can pledge their allegiance. Without it, all they have is a job. With it, they have something to which they can bind themselves. Vision also helps the employees of a company explain to others what is important to them. Dissemination of the vision through actions helps outsiders perceive what they stand for.

Kotter (1988) sums up the value of a vision by making it the cornerstone of what he calls "an agenda for change." Simply put, the agenda includes the following:

- A vision of what can and should be
- A vision that takes into account the legitimate long-term interests of the parties involved
- A strategy for achieving that vision
- A strategy that takes into account all relevant organizational and environmental forces

HR's Need for a New Vision

Given the changing marketplace, organizations both public and private are asking fundamental questions about themselves and their operations. They see the need to examine their vision of themselves so that they can reposition themselves to meet the needs of the new market, as well as take advantage of its opportunities. The human resources function must ask itself the same fundamental questions.

The marketplace of human resources is the organization within which it exists—and *for* which it exists. This market includes employees, management, and stockholders. Since the organization is changing in response to its new markets, human resources must change to stay in touch with its market. In short, the human resources function needs to reexamine its notion of its role and position within the organization. Human resource's vision, in many companies, has been that of an expense center. I am suggesting that we develop a new paradigm that is focused on adding value.

Quite often when I ask human resources people what their business is, they give me back a litany of activities. They list all the programs, products, and services that they provide for the organization. Unfortunately, that's not the point. Their lists describe their work, not their purpose, and focus on means, not on ends. If human resources people believe that their purpose is nothing more than to be responsible for administering a given function, such as hiring or training employees, they are cheating themselves out of an exciting and truly rewarding career. There is a bigger, broader, more satisfying vision of their purpose.

You might ask yourself a very basic question. Why does the organization that employs you allow the human resources function to exist at all? What mission is it supposed to fulfill? When you talk about your purpose or mission, your focus must change from the daily list of tasks to the more basic and longer-term issue of the potential value of human resources. The question shifts from What should we do? to Why are we doing this?

What benefits does the human resources department contribute to the organization it serves? For the most part, these benefits fall into three categories. There are human benefits such as helping people feel secure. There are production benefits such as helping employees become more efficient and turn out better-quality products. And there are monetary benefits, including helping the organization achieve its revenue and earnings goals. Human resources has a role in securing all these benefits for employees and their organization.

Your customers within the organization do not want programs for their own sake. They don't want to pay you simply for hiring and training employees. The employees don't want wages or salaries just to have money in their pocket. People want the benefits or values that those activities and products imply. Customers don't buy products. They buy benefits.

Think about it this way. If you go into a store to buy an article of clothing, what is it that you really want? Clearly, you are seeking something more than a piece of fabric to cover yourself. If all you wanted was protection from the elements, would you spend several hundred dollars for it? The goals of warmth or modesty are secondary to the need for self-expression. Don't you usually ask yourself if the clothes will attract favorable reactions from other people? If the suit will make you feel more confident or powerful? If the dress will speak of self-assurance or sexuality or both? Similarly, if you go to a doctor with a broken arm, you are not shopping for a cast and a bottle of pain killers. You're hoping to have that limb made strong and functional again.

Think about your job and the human resources function in the same way. What is it that your customers look to you for? I can assure you that it is not programs.

One View of Human Resources' Job

Let me suggest that the purpose of the human resources function is to help managers improve the productivity, quality, effectiveness, and quality of work life of their units. Table 3 gives several examples of the types of values that human resources can help managers achieve within the basic functions of an organization.

This perspective represents a total departure from the program orientation. The program-focused department looks at itself and the products and services that it thinks an organization should have and then tries to sell them to the organization. That is called the inside-out method.

I am suggesting the reverse. Instead of trying to sell them the traditional program mix, ask the many customers in your market what is it that they are trying to accomplish within their areas. When you learn that, you can apply your professional knowledge, working experience, and personal insights to figur-

Table 3. Human Resources Effects Matrix.

Functions	Productivity	Quality	Effectiveness	Quality of Work Life*
	Help Managers Improve Their — Objective:			
Operations				
Producing	Units built	Scrap rate	Ship on time	Safety
Designing	New products	Redraws	Acceptance	Stress
Maintaining	Repairs	Breakdowns	Accidents	Morale
Procuring	Purchase orders filled	Incorrect orders	Delivery on time	Absence
				Turnover
				Complaints
				Grievances
Marketing				Employee cooperation
Selling	Units sold	Margins	Repeat sales	Legal actions
Servicing	Calls handled	No recalls	Problem solved	Suggestion program use
Market Research	Responsiveness	Relevant data	Customer saved	Employee Assistance Program use
Advertising/PR	Ads designed and placed	Errors	Responses	Career development
				Benefits use
Administration				
Information Systems	Job cost	Reruns	Faster operations	
Human Resources	Cost per hire	New hires	Company met schedule	
Finance	Invoices processed	Billing error rate	Cash flow increase	
Planning	Plan on time	On specification	Predictive power	

* Quality of work life issues occur in all departments.

ing out how to service those objectives. This is the outside-in approach.

This notion is often misunderstood. I am not suggesting that you give the managers of your organization a list of products and services that you can provide and then ask them to pick what they want. In the first place, they usually don't know what they want. In the second place, they usually aren't interested in human resources programs as such. What they want is to achieve their operating objectives—the goals that they get paid to attain. That should be your focus. Talk to them about what they are trying to do. Then decide which of your capabilities and resources can help them accomplish their objectives.

Use Your Imagination. The approach I just described takes some imagination because it forces you to think not of what is but of what needs to be. You have imagination. All people have imagination. And, as Einstein said:

> Imagination is more important than knowledge.

Leaders make decisions and communicate their visions not on the basis of what happened yesterday or is happening today. They use their imagination to conjure up what can or should happen tomorrow.

Apply your imagination this way. Every function in an organization has certain goals and objectives. They are described, usually quantitatively, through indexes of production, finance, or human activity. Human resources provides programs, products, and services for the twofold purpose of helping its client managers achieve their goals while simultaneously advancing the growth of employees in their careers. Thus, you can see that the focus should not be on administering programs but rather on adding value to the organization by helping clients and customers attain their production, financial, and human objectives.

Have Confidence in Yourself. Some human resources practitioners feel that they cannot do more than what their job de-

scription calls for. They feel constrained by organizational labels, past history, or their own lack of key competencies. The
problem with this type of self-limiting view is that we tend to
become what we imagine ourselves to be. We are the ones who
create our world. If we think we are failures, we will fail. By
contrast, once we recognize that we all have inherent abilities, we
can begin to exercise them. So, teach your people to relax and
have some confidence in their ability to change things.

Recently, I was working on a measurement system for a
large utility. Some members of the staff were skeptical that they
could carry out some of the activities that I was suggesting.
Rather than confront their skepticism, I set them an exercise in
which they had to list all the people, things, processes, and
outputs in their environment. When they finally completed the
list, it turned out to be a massive one, and it gave the group a
completely new perspective on their work. Most important, it
became clear to the group that it had all kinds of room in which
to operate. One of the supervisors said to me, "This is the first
time I realized what we were all about. I feel good because now I
understand what I can do."

Franklin Roosevelt put it well in his first inaugural address. His famous saying, "The only thing we have to fear is fear
itself," told us that nothing can hold back someone who has a
dream and the courage to fulfill it. There are plenty of good
ideas floating around. What this world needs are people with
the insight to make those ideas work—people who will not let
themselves be limited. And the first step on the road to success is
believing in yourself.

Foundation of a New Vision

In an earlier chapter, we noted that "creating value is a
matter of waste management. Anything that does not add value
is waste." This is not a vision statement, but it could be the basis
for reviewing the human resources function in your organization and for formulating a vision appropriate to your
marketplace.

This unequivocal statement is the motto I live by. It isn't

easy. Probably everyone wastes time. At least I do. I spend time on things I shouldn't be doing. I avoid attending to things I should be handling. People waste time for many reasons, and you know what they are as well as I do. The point is that we can no longer afford waste if we are going to be competitive in domestic and global markets. I could cite you endless examples of human resources staffs that are wasting time and money on obsolete programs while simultaneously ignoring the critical needs of their organizations. That is career suicide.

Far too many human resources people are working from a vision that accepts waste. They have not faced up to the changes that must be made in their modus operandi if they are to survive and contribute to their organization in the new marketplace. The key word that must move to the top of every human resource department's lexicon is VALUE. We can't afford to run programs simply because we like to run them. We can't afford to support products whose usefulness is fading. We can't afford to ignore the need for new services that will satisfy today's market imperatives.

The old-time management question was, Is this the best use of my time right now? But this question must now be rephrased to ask, Is this the most valuable thing I can do for my customers right now? As we proceed through the value-adding strategy in the following chapters, you will see many examples of how you can answer the value question as it relates to your customers.

Choosing a Team

One of my most strongly held beliefs is that human resources people should be part of the mainstream of organizational decision making. I see no reason why the function that advises management on application of the critical human asset should be anything less than a respected, equal member of management. I call this vision of human resources operations being on the Value Team.

No one is invited to play on this team. You have to earn your position. Human resources people have the added problem of a negative image and history. Because of mistakes made by your predecessors or your own self-limiting view, it may take a special effort to win a place on the V Team. But I can tell you from experience that it probably is not as hard as you may imagine. I have worked with human resources professionals in companies where the negative view of the function was decades old. Once they made the decision and the commitment to change that view through value management, they were able to turn it around in a relatively short time. You see, people would like the human resources department to be a constructive force. Even in organizations where this has not been the case, the desire is still there, although it may be hidden under conde-scending, disbelieving, or even sarcastic attitudes. So, even though there may be a latent acceptance of the notion that human resources can be useful, it does take a planned, con-certed effort on the part of the staff to join the Value Team.

The alternative is to join the Expense Team. If you want to play on the E Team, you can have a lot of fun and a very satisfying career, but it will be at a different level. Playing on the Expense Team requires just as much effort as playing on the Value Team, but it is work of a different nature. On the E Team your concerns are principally tactical in nature. They deal with the design, development, and maintenance of activities such as recruitment campaigns, compensation and benefit plans, training pro-grams, and employee assistance services. Obviously, these are all necessary products and services that someone must provide. For this you will be viewed as a human resources specialist who spends the organization's resources to provide needed human systems.

Your focus will be on activities such as administering programs. Activity is expense. That is why I call this the Expense Team. A position on the E Team is honorable. It is right for some people, I suppose. To me, it is like saying that there is no disgrace in being poor. And I agree with that. But wanting to be poor is just plain dumb.

When people feel a need for your services, they will call on you. When they have reason to circumvent your policies, they will fight you. Someone else will tell you what you should be doing in regard to serving the needs of the business. The job will remain what it was in the past, that of a useful ancillary function. If you do your job well, human resources will be treated as an employee-related service to be called on in time of need. There is a place for people like this in organizations. They play a valuable role. If this role satisfies your career goals, then I suggest you pursue it with all the strength you have. The only admonition I would add is that if you decide to play on the Expense Team, don't complain that you are not being treated like a member of the Value Team.

If you decide to try out for the Value Team, however, you have to become more knowledgeable. It isn't enough to keep up-to-date on human resources technology. You also have to understand the basics of how businesses are organized and run. John Stapleton at International Minerals and Chemicals says that you get on the Value Team by demonstrating that you understand the business. You have to find out why the manager is asking certain questions or requesting specific services. What are the business needs? Once you understand that, as John puts it, "you can deliver on the order." This is how you add value to the business.

Basic business skills are also critical to Vic Buzachero, former head of human resources at Baptist Medical Center in Birmingham, Alabama. He trained his management staff in basic financial analysis. He said that you don't have to become an accountant but that it helps to know the difference between an income statement and a balance sheet. Businesses depend on accounting systems to describe the state of their financial assets. Human resources people have to be able to understand the basics of finance since it is the language of business.

You don't have to know the intricacies of marketing, but it adds to your ability to contribute if you understand something about market segmentation, positioning, and pricing.

At MCI Communications, Bob Levit focuses many of his training activities on marketing issues. For example, MCI strives to be number one in customer service in telecommunications. To support that, Bob has his people actually in the field meeting customers, not simply waiting for customers to come in to talk about their needs and problems.

At Canada's Northern Telecom, Harry Garner, a long-time advocate of value management, urges his human resources staff to get into joint ventures with managers in line functions. "This way," he tells them, "you will learn what is important to making the product. You can talk about the qualitative and quantitative aspects of the work. When you learn to speak their language," as Harry puts it, "business people invite you back to the table."

Recently, a personnel manager asked the Saratoga Institute to develop a charting system that would demonstrate the impact of her programs on the company's profits. When we showed her one that we had already prepared, she pointed to a bar that was labeled "G & A" and asked what that stood for. One of the more common terms in business was not part of her vocabulary. It was hard to believe that she would be able to function as part of the management team.

The reason that you need to be able to talk the language of business is that as a member of the Value Team you are principally a business person who uses human resources technology along with a healthy dose of common sense to solve business problems. Throughout our conversations with HVM practitioners, the term *business partner* led off nearly every description of the modern human resources function. To play on the E Team you only have to know human resources programs. But the V Team is composed of members of line management from functions such as sales and production. Its objective is to get the organization's products or services into the hands of the customer within a profitable cost range. If you are going to be a contributing player, you have to understand business language.

This brings us to the last prerequisite of V Team membership. You need to know the products and services that your organization makes and sells. You might be surprised to learn that many human resources practitioners have only a surface knowledge of their company's products or the nature and condition of their marketplace. We continuously run into human resources staff who have never read the annual report or a product brochure of their company. On the V Team you must have current knowledge about your company and its market-place because you are directly involved with the strategic plan-ning process and the day-to-day problems of the company.

At Eckerd Drug Company, Bill Silberman and Wayne Saunders are deeply involved in a project to increase the prof-itability of the retail pharmacies. When the pharmacy services department said that it needed a major increase in management staffing to support the pharmacies, Bill and Wayne suggested that that assumption ought to be examined. We'll see later what they did to solve the problem. For now, the point is they didn't approach the situation from a traditional personnel view. They asked some business questions instead and found that the solu-tion to the problem did not require the company to add many new employees.

Some might say that V Team work isn't personnel work. And they would be correct if they believe that personnel issues are something apart from an organization's basic business pur-pose. I myself believe that there is nothing so fundamental to an organization as people. When you get down to the nuts-and-bolts level, organizations are composed of equally important parts of capital, technology, and people. It is only a historical error that has caused top management to continue to view people as nothing more than cogs in the corporate machine. It is that misperception that has placed the personnel function on the same level as other staff support or service departments.

Getting Rid of the Expense Center Image

Staff departments have always been treated as expenses to be controlled as much as possible. For this reason, whenever there is a cutback, the staff departments are the first to be hit. When personnel, training, public relations, advertising, plan-ning, and other staff functions are viewed as sources of expense, it is right and logical to eliminate them during tough times. A primary rule of business survival is to preserve capital at all costs. So long as that rule prevails, the personnel function as an expense center will be vulnerable.

To overcome the expense image of the human resources

department, you have to move it onto the Value Team. By definition, the V Team is a collection of human, financial, and technical managers whose job it is to get the organization's product or service into the market on a timely basis and at a profitable level. Anyone who is able to show that his or her function is critical to meeting production and financial objectives can apply for a position on the V Team. This book aims to give you the information and processes by which you can demonstrate that the human resources management function is vital to the financial success of your organization.

Changing the Modus Operandi. Although the human resources department has acquired new responsibilities since the 1960s, it has not, unfortunately, obtained the power to play its new roles. In many cases, the human resources department has one foot in the past as it steps tentatively into the future. Your people know the latest technologies for employment, compensation, benefits administration, and training. But a human resources staff needs more than new techniques. It needs an up-to-date vision of its current mission, its role, and what it can contribute to its organization. The new vision recognizes that adding value is the key prerequisite to survival. There are new rules and new requirements for human resources. They cannot be ignored. Human resources must have a plan and a set of operating processes that will help it synchronize its management of people with the changes being installed by line managers. Simply stated, many human resources departments are struggling to apply an outdated strategic model to the new marketplace.

Taking the Pledge. The first step in changing the image of human resources is to trade in the expense center label. To date, I have had over 5,000 human resources managers take the pledge to get rid of the expense center image. Here it is. I suggest you read it to your staff:

> I solemnly promise that I will never again think of or talk about the human resources department as an expense

center. Nor will I let any other bozo call it an expense
center, so help me Dr. Jac.

In place of the expense center label, we must substitute
the image of the human resources practitioner who is a professional counselor, a business problem solver, and a profit enhancer—in effect, a human asset investment adviser in a value-
adding operation.

Before your staff will be able to play that new role, it must
decide that it wants to. After all, there are some advantages to
being an auxiliary function. The pressure to contribute is limited to responding to requests. There is little call to be creative
or proactive. For many human resources people there is much
satisfaction to be drawn from the nurturing of other employees,
who are the real producers in the organization.

The Value Team image, which I described above, is not
meant in any way to denigrate the humanitarian side of our
profession. I am not suggesting that we become automatons or
treat people as though they were machines. Valuing employees
as human beings is as important now as it has ever been. With all
the changes that are impacting business organizations, the
human issues cannot be ignored. We simply must strive for a
balance between human and organizational needs. Human
needs are best served when we design policies and programs
that advance the security and growth of employees in their
profession while at the same time contributing to the organization's financial and operating objectives. In my view the two
needs are inseparable.

The critical factor in making this change is commitment.
This is where leadership and vision play key roles. The staff
person must commit himself or herself to the new strategy. This
will be difficult. People don't like to change. Most of them prefer
the security of the known over the uncertainty of the unknown.
Many human resources people are not high-risk individuals. I
find that they consistently look for the negative side of a new
plan or proposal before they will consider its possible value.
Many are not naturally assertive and self-confident. To persuade
them to change, you have to convince them that the new behav-

ior actually will be safer and eventually more satisfying than the old. In actuality, the value strategy is an absolute requirement for long-term employment at anything above the servant level.

The Payoffs. On the positive side, the new strategy has much to offer. Human beings are goal oriented. We always have in mind some payoff for what we do. It may be maintaining a comfortable position, avoiding some form of pain or punishment, or gaining some form of reward. To persuade people to change their roles, their styles, their methods, their very purpose for being in the organization, we must give them a different goal with a new and better payoff. The rewards of the new approach to human resources will be acceptance, involvement, equality, respect, power, and a chance to make a difference.

The payoffs to the staff for changing to the more appropriate and effective value-adding method include the following:

1. A clear sense of direction and purpose
2. Specific knowledge of the results of your efforts
3. Job satisfaction that comes from seeing how much you have contributed
4. Better relations with your customers because your services will be positively impacting their operating goals
5. Undeniable proof of your performance through the use of numbers
6. Defense against unfounded criticisms of your work or staff
7. Data to identify negative trends before they become major problems
8. Data to obtain the resources you need to do your job well
9. A stronger position in your organization
10. More respect for your professionalism
11. The money that comes with the recognition that you are making a vital contribution

I assume you are open to joining the Value Team. This book describes in detail a system of strategies and tactics that will help the human resources function evolve rapidly from an accepted expense function to a respected profit-enhancing partner of line management. You will learn how to exercise more leverage in the competitive struggle for scarce corporate resources. The methods suggested are designed to help you play a strong value-adding role within your organization.

Conclusion

Given the radical changes in today's marketplace, all organizations are reexamining the nature of their business. Since your market—the organization—is reconsidering where it is headed, you must do the same. You need to answer the prime question: What is the business of human resources?

Most human resources functions need a new vision of themselves, one that adds value and is in tune with the demands of their market. The most pragmatic view that human resources can have of itself is that it is in business to help management and employees achieve their goals. If its programs don't serve those ends, then they are a waste of resources.

The time has come to choose between playing on the Value Team or the Expense Team. You can have a career on either one. To be on the V Team you must learn the basics of your organization's business. Even more important, you need to put to rest forever the notion that the human resources department is an expense center and to substitute for that image a vision of human resources as a value-adding member of the team. The days of the captive market are over. The human resources staff must win the support of its customers by demonstrating that it is the most cost-effective source of human resource services in the marketplace. Success and even survival in the marketplace of the 1990s will require a new vision of the organization. It is up to you to provide the value-adding vision around which the people can rally.

Without a vision, the people perish.
                                    Proverbs 29:18

References

American Productivity Center and Cresap, McCormack, and Paget. "Positioning Corporate Staff for the 1990s." Towers, Perrin, Forster, and Crosby, 1986.

Below, P. J., Morrisey, G. L., and Acomb, B. L. *The Executive Guide to Strategic Planning.* San Francisco: Jossey-Bass, 1987.

Fitz-enz, J. "Sources of Human Productivity." Proceedings of Conference on Productivity: The American Way, Chicago, June 1982.

"The Happiness Barometer." Starch INRA Hooper, Mamaroneck, N.Y., 1988.

Kotter, J. P. *The Leadership Factor.* New York: Free Press, 1988.

Kouzes, J. M., and Posner, B. Z. *The Leadership Challenge: How to Get Extraordinary Things Done in Organizations.* San Francisco: Jossey-Bass, 1987.

Lawler, E. E., and Renwick, P. A. "What You Really Want from Your Job." *Psychology Today,* 1978, *12,* 56.

Case Studies—Chapter Five

Datastream International
London, England
(From information supplied by the human resources manager and
by Craig McCoy, senior training executive)

Datastream International is a subsidiary of Dun & Brad-street Corporation, the international publisher of financial information. It provides information services out of its London office. Although Datastream is a relatively small company, with less than 700 employees, it is expanding through acquisitions and internally fueled growth. Its growth has produced a strain on all functions, including the human resources group that must find the skills necessary to support this growth.

The human resources manager's vision of her function is that it should be operated as a profit center rather than as an expense center. This does not necessarily mean that she advocates that human resources sell its products and services to the outside market. Rather, in its internal operation, it should focus on how its efforts are contributing directly or indirectly to Datastream's profitability.

When I asked her what image of human resources she was trying to convey to the management and employees of Datastream, she gave me a list of words that constituted her message: "effective," "can do," "innovative," "customer focused," "business focused," "versatile," and "experts."

She told me that there were two very direct and simple ways by which this message was being communicated. First, of course, was by doing a good job. That means more than working hard. It means that the work being done is of value. Second, her department makes a point of publishing its achievements. Some might think that it is immodest to talk about oneself. Consider, however, the competition for resources within organizations. Simply doing a good job is usually not enough unless you have someone else doing your public relations for you. It is necessary to periodically point out what you have contributed to your organization.

Performance Pay System. The human resources manager and her associates have made a number of moves at Datastream International that have helped the company meet its growth goals. One program is a performance bonus system aimed at retaining and motivating good staff or encouraging poor staff to seek work elsewhere. To date, the results have been mixed, but more positive than negative. The plan's positive effects have been as follows:

- All directors agreed that the new bonus system is better than its predecessors.
- The exercise of determining how the system should be applied improved communications between managers within divisions.
- The system highlighted the need for better ways to set and publish objectives at the beginning of the year.

But there were also some aspects of the plan that needed improvement:

- In some areas, there was a tendency to overrate the performance of employees.
- Some opportunities to "deliver a message" were missed.
- Cross-divisional comparisons proved to be difficult to make.

Overall, improvements had been made in incentive compensation, but there was a need to institute certain training and counselling programs and to restructure the system in some ways to yield more value.

One of the more interesting aspects of the program is its tracking system. A small grid was prepared within each functional group — development, finance and administration, operations, production, sales, and so on. It is shown below:

		Performance Rating and Bonus %		
Group	*Level*	TARGET	ACTUAL	VARIANCE
Development	Managers	___	___	___
	Staff	___	___	___
	Total	___	___	___

Table 4. Spread of Performance Ratings.

				Ratings		
Division		1	2	3	4	5
Finance and	No.	3	10	21	2	0
Administration	%	8	28	58	6	0
Sales and	No.	4	9	45	1	1
Marketing	%	7	15	75	2	2
Production	No.	5	31	59	10	3
	%	4	29	55	9	3
Development	No.	2	35	68	12	5
	%	1	29	56	10	16
Operations	No.	5	25	54	8	2
	%	5	26	57	9	2

This grid allows top management to track how operating managers are using the program. It shows the money spent versus the target.

Two other reports give different views of the program's utilization. One indicates the spread of performance rating scores by division, and the other the average ratings by level within a division.

The spread chart is shown in Table 4 (the data in the table do not represent actual results). This table compares how the various division managers rated their people. The management of Datastream did not think this part of the system had much cross-comparison value. However, I reminded them that it can be used, within a division, to compare ratings versus results. For example, does the profile of ratings reflect the type of performance that the division is displaying? It can also be useful to head off the kinds of internal problems that occur when one division always gives very high ratings to its people. This can cause discontent in other divisions; in fact, it can even produce a line of people at the human resources office looking for a transfer to the high-rating division.

Table 5 shows the average ratings by level within divisions. (Again, the data shown are only a sample, not the actual ratings.)

Table 5. Average Ratings.

	Managers	Assistant Managers	Supervisor	Staff
Finance and Administration	2.3	2.0	2.5	2.7
Sales and Marketing	2.7	2.8	3.0	2.9
Production	2.2	2.8	2.7	2.9
Development	2.6	2.9	3.0	2.8
Operations	3.2	2.5	2.3	2.8

This table shows any potential discrimination across levels. If the management of one group consciously or unconsciously gives much higher ratings than another, someone has a chance to review that and make sure it is not going to create a problem.

The Quality Issue. At one point Datastream was having a problem in its Production Division regarding the quality of the data base being made available to its customers. This is not an uncommon problem in the information industry. The acceleration of technology, shortages of qualified staff, and other problems can throw off a sensitive system that has many intersecting operations. Since computers do their work behind panels at very high speeds, production problems are much harder to see and prevent than in other types of production work where the process is more visible and moves more slowly.

In this case human resources worked with the production director to solve the problem. First, weekly meetings were held with employees to obtain their ideas, and they were then asked to explore the ideas that seemed most promising. Then, two initiatives were tackled: fault recording and process-flow analysis. The purpose of the fault recorder was to capture and analyze problems reported by customers or staff and to monitor whether or not improvements were being made. The technique of process-flow analysis was taught to employees so that they could produce flow charts in their departments to identify productivity problems and improvements.

The key results were that data quality improved along with teamwork.

Author's comment: There was a great deal of work done in other human resources areas at Datastream. For example, Craig McCoy transformed the virtually nonexistent training function into a vital force in the organization. But the bottom line was that the human resources manager had a vision of her function as a profit-enhancing operation and was determined to run it that way. No one gave her permission. No one invited her to the table. She just demonstrated objectively that she had a right to be there and that her department had something of value to contribute. Management is often in such dire need of help on the people side that when a human resources manager shows that she or he has something of concrete value to add to the organization, that person is always invited to join the team.

Sun Microsystems
Mountain View, California
(As told by Peter Smith, director of human resources planning and development)

Sun Microsystems of Mountain View, California, is a very successful manufacturer of electronic workstations. Founded in 1982, it is one of the fastest-growing and most profitable public companies in the United States.

In the spring of 1988, when Sun's senior management was asked to identify potential concerns for the survival and success of the company, a number of human resources issues surfaced. The senior human resources staff ran a session with management to clarify those issues and to develop action plans. A wide range of activities were discussed and eventually reduced to four key areas: (1) hiring, (2) retention, (3) avoiding burnout, and (4) management development.

The challenge for the human resources department was to develop programs and services that would become a part of the mainstream management processes at Sun. A model of this "melding" process is given in Figure 6.

Four ideal future states were articulated. They identified the processes and practices for which the human resources department was responsible and the processes and practices

Figure 6. Integration of Human Resources and Management Processes.

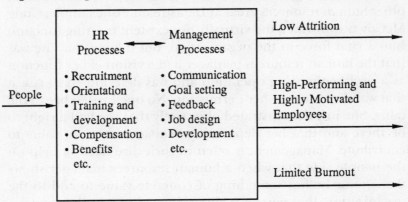

that were the responsibility of managers. For each process/ practice, a measure of performance was created. Examples of each are given in Exhibit 2.

In October 1988, the outline of a Quality of Life Plan was published. The objective was to develop approaches to quality of life at Sun Microsystems that would be built into the mainstream management process of the company. A general outline was provided by human resources, along with consultation support for line management. Each manager was free to construct a plan to suit his or her unit within the limits of the outline and the overall objective.

Managers were encouraged to start the process with some type of employee survey. This would help them identify the quality of life issues important to their people. Various topics emerged from these surveys:

1. A need for clearer understanding and communication of the charter and strategy of the company and of individual units.
2. An apparent discrepancy between Sun's aggressive goals and the resources available to carry out the tasks that employees had been given.
3. A concern about the company's commitment to training and career development.

These topics became avenues for managers and employees to explore in developing plans. A goal of having a first set of plans to review by January 1, 1989, was established.

Forms such as the examples in Exhibits 3 and 4 were distributed as worksheets and review documents. They list the process or practice, the result and its measurement, the current status, and the activities needed to fulfill the objective.

In order to assess the company's progress along its Quality of Life Plan, a maturity grid was developed by the human resources staff. It was based on the company's approach to product quality. The grid (Exhibit 5) lists six categories: management, organizational status, quality of life sensing, education, metrics, and quality of life plan. It then describes the state of maturity in each topic from the lowest (uncertainty) to the highest (maturity).

Author's comment: At the time of this writing, quality of life plans exist in all business units at Sun. The vice-presidents are required to do regular quality of life updates at the Joint Operating Committee meetings. Their plans will be "scored" twice yearly on the grid.

This program is an example of how a human resources function has given life to its vision of its role in a company. Sun's human resources function is involved in the design of the central management system of the company. Its vision clearly transcends administrative management.

Some might say that this is easy to do when you have a top management group like that at Sun. But keep in mind that no one came to the human resources department with the basic issue that started this process. Peter Smith and his associates brought up the subject of building for the future. Once they got senior management to identify potential concerns, human resources came up with solutions and sold them. It worked because they had a vision of themselves as codesigners of the future at Sun.

Exhibit 2. Four Ideal Future States for Human Resources.

Hiring Processes/Practices	Metric/Measurement Process	Processes/Practices That Avoid Burnout	Metric/Measurement Process
Human Resources		*Human Resources*	
• Has a data base and continuing flow of applicants, based on history and longer-term plans rather than just reqs	• Quality of data base, #s, job types, etc.	• Provides sensing categories and processes that identify potential burnout issues	• Sensing of x percent of population per year
• Optimizes lower-cost sourcing strategies, such as referral, and continually tracks these, stimulating and renewing as appropriate	• Source analysis and cost per hire from each source	• Provides sensing and other organization development processes that identify and correct organizational blockages	
• Has a process that takes resumes from multiple sources and input points and allows access to these by all recruiters		• Ensures that there is an individual goal-setting process in place for employees	• Informal sensing of a sample of employees regularly to check that goals exist
• Is able to fill most requisitions in x weeks	• Time to fill req by job type	• Offers stress management programs as part of Training and Development curriculum	
Managers		*Managers*	
• Take opportunities to add to potential employee data base, through own networking and encouragements of his/her people to do the same	• Referral analysis by Div/Dept.	• Monitor work patterns in their departments in order to identify and correct potential burnout problems	• Number of open requisitions, with emphasis on length of time they have been open
• Are aware of the sourcing costs for their Divs/Depts and support the stimulation/renewal of low-cost strategies	• Cost per hire and referral analysis	• Maintain a reasonable balance between plans/goals and resources, particularly staffing	
• Ensure that time is devoted to quality recruiting and that they and their staff have appropriate skills	• Attendance at "Hiring Process" workshop	• Should understand and explain rationale for organizational structures and processes and their relationship to specific roles and responsibilities	
• Involve themselves in final hiring interviews of all their second-level staff, i.e., people who report to his/her direct reports		• Should monitor the level and nature of organizational "ignorance" and/or blockages that contribute to frustration	• Part of Quality Plans process analysis?

Processes/Practices That Facilitate Retention	Metric/Measurement Process	Management Development Processes/Practices	Metric/Measurement Process
Human Resources		*Human Resources*	
• Tracks attrition trends via exit interview data and proposes solutions	• Attrition levels plus reasons	• Provides a management development curriculum covering newly hired, newly promoted, and established managers	• Curriculum model plus T & D schedule
• Monitors current "golden handcuff" situations and develops alternatives when necessary	• Stock vesting—time/price plus attrition by length of service and stock awards	• Encourages/ensures all appropriate managers are aware of curriculum and schedule	• Quarterly reports, by Div, on who could and has attended relevant programs
• Provides sensing categories and processes that identify potential attrition issues	• Sensing of x percent of population per year	• Works with division/function management teams to agree on development plans for all managers and supervisors	• Existence of plans
• Ensures that job-posting policy is adhered to and internal candidates are adequately considered	• Length of time reqs are open		• Promotion/hiring ratios for managers
	• Internal promotion versus hire statistics		
	• Internal movement patterns		
• Provides a range of career development programs			
Managers		*Managers*	
• Understand attrition trends in order to identify and act on possible solutions	• Attrition levels plus reasons	• Provide newly hired and promoted managers with coaching plan, as per "Management Orientation" plans	• Quarterly reports, by Div, on who could and has attended relevant programs
• Perform x # of skip-level interviews per quarter in order to sense any emerging concerns	• Quarterly report on # and issues	• Encourage/ensure relevant managers attend relevant programs in curriculum and allow time for this	• T & D records
• Hold regular one-on-ones with direct reports		• Have attended development event(s) of at least x days in last year	• Existence of posttraining plans
• Ensure that all performance review interviews are completed by __	• Performance review documentation in HR by __	• Engage in pretraining and posttraining program discussions and plans, in order to assist in the transfer of training	
• Give proper consideration to internal candidates; also champion own people for positions, where appropriate	• Length of time reqs are open		
	• Internal promotion versus hire statistics		
• Support career development programs and processes	• Promotion patterns by Dept.		
	• Career development plans for employees		

Exhibit 3. Quality of Life Plan Worksheet.

Div/Group _____   Date _____

Processes/Practices	Metric/Deliverable	Current Status	Progression Activities: What, Who, and When
Suggested Subheadings			
• Hiring			
• Training and Development			
• Organization Development			
• Managing and Optimizing Performance			
• Managing the Quality of Work Life			

Exhibit 4. Quality of Life Processes and Practices.

Examples in the Area of "Hiring the Right People"

Minimum Requirements	Developed	Advanced
• Well-completed requisitions that facilitate source and candidate matching • Having processes that ensure applicants are kept appropriately informed • Interview schedules that include appropriate "customers" and interfaces • Reference checking, with security checks for certain positions • Active consideration of minority and women candidates • All relevant jobs posted and meaningful consideration of internal candidates • Following agreed protocol for inter-division competitive hiring situations	• Interview/employment training for all managers • Proactive HR and hiring plans that optimize sourcing strategies • Management involvement in all final hiring interviews of second-level staff • Security checking • Use of unit's "best" interviewer in key hiring decisions • Goals for minority and women candidates, with active sourcing of them • Goals for number of positions filled by internal candidates	• Strategic HR planning is well integrated into the business plan • Skill-bank data that facilitate the matching of internal candidates to open positions

Exhibit 5. Quality of Life (QoL) Maturity Grid.

	Uncertainty	Awakening	Enlightenment	Wisdom	Maturity
Management	Little attention to QoL processes and practices; inconsistent in application of co. wide QoL processes	Some attention to QoL prompted mainly by co. wide programs or immediate issues	QoL improvement plan but main focus on applying corp. driven processes	Specific processes and practices in place related to division or group QoL issues	Strong championship of processes and practices, both within and without their boundary
Organizational status	HR mainly seen as a hiring and employee-relations department	HR has role wider than hiring and employee relations, but often as a "fire-fighter"	HR seen as key dept. and QoL an accepted management team agenda item	HR encouraged to be involved in business issues and integrate QoL into business plan	HR seen as a key business partner and QoL a key business element
Quality of Life Sensing	Little knowledge of employee feelings about QoL	Starting to recognize areas of concern but limited knowledge of feelings and issues	Some awareness of employee feelings but limited to certain groups or issues	Regular monitoring of employee feelings, via sensing and other processes	Formal and informal sensing of employee feelings is a management way of life
Education	Little involvement in QoL-type programs	Some managers attending QoL-type programs	Most managers attend corp. driven, QoL-type programs	Specific programs in QoL area developed for division/group	Specific programs developed plus attendance at "leading edge" QoL programs
Metrics	Very limited	Recognizing need but with measures more focused on immediate issues	Various measures, but not yet comprehensive	HR and QoL metrics a regular management agenda item	Emphasis on div/group specific data with comprehensive analysis when necessary
Quality of Life Plan	Irregular and incomplete	Main focus is on immediate issues, with limited breadth	Main focus is on meeting min. requirements across all QoL areas	Emphasis on div/group aspects with clear link to business/org. issues	Totally integrated into business planning and management way of life

6

Repositioning
Human Resources

To SUCCEED, YOU are going to have to redefine the nature
of your job. In addition to your other duties, you're going
to have to be part educator, part public policy expert,
part sociologist, part futurist, and part consultant to
senior management.

> Ann McLaughlin, former
> Secretary of Labor

Once your people have adopted the value-adding vision
of your function's purpose, you need to communicate it to your
marketplace, that is, the management and employees of your
organization. This action is called positioning.

Vision deals with the function's purpose. Positioning
deals with relationships between the seller (human resources)
and the customer (the organization). What you are trying to do
is connect your products with your market through positioning.
Positioning looks one way at the market and the other way at the
products and tries to tie them together. This process is shown in
Figure 7.

All marketing springs from a position. Ries and Trout
(1981) describe positioning as what you do to the mind of your
prospect. The result of your actions is your position, the place
you occupy in the mind of potential and existing customers. The
current perception of your department is based on the past
actions of yourself or your predecessors. Your current and future
acts will reinforce or revise that perception. Positions can
change overnight or over decades. Performance creates positions. Planned performance creates the position you desire.

It is a truism that perception is reality in the mind of the
perceiver. No one knows objective reality. We only know subjective reality, that is, the truth as we see it. Often, when you think

Figure 7. The Connection of Position, Products, and Market.

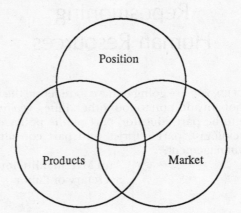

you know something that is empirically verifiable, new data become available, and you have to reset your thinking to the new truth.

Perception plays a major role in the repositioning of the human resources function within an organization. The woman in my earlier example who was glad that she didn't have to go through personnel to get a job clearly had a negative perception of the department even though she had never had any dealings with it. This is an example of a prejudice. She prejudged the personnel department without having had any first-hand experience of it. Why did she adopt that prejudice? Someone must have told her negative stories about personnel. She accepted them because she had no other image of personnel. Her attitude will change only if she has one or more positive contacts with personnel administration.

Employees and managers have positioned the human resources function in their minds either positively or negatively. The example given above notwithstanding, perceptions of the human resources department are most often based on experiences resulting from personal contact with the human resources staff. This was the basis of the negative attitudes of the 1,200 managers that I described in Chapter One. Their perceptions were built up over years of experience with human resources staffs, often in more than one company. Thus, to change the position of the human resources department within your company, you have to change the perceptions that managers and employees have of your function.

If you have to make major changes in the way human resources operates, you may find that the managers and employees in your marketplace become uncertain as to how they should relate to you. They have seen the function in one light for some time. If you try to change their perceptions and reposition the function, you can expect a bit of confusion. Social scientists describe perceptual confusion as *cognitive dissonance*. It is mental noise or agitation. People don't like that. They need consistency to maintain their psychological balance. If they see something one way, they want and need to relate to it that way. It may therefore take some time for them to come around to a new perception of the human resources department.

You see examples of cognitive dissonance all the time. In your personal life you know how difficult it is to be pleasant to someone that you heartily dislike. If you act other than how you feel, you experience dissonance. In organizations, cognitive dissonance is one reason why new programs such as management training often don't succeed in changing behavior. Managers' old values and attitudes sometimes clash with the expected new behavior. It takes time and consistent behavior to change perceptions.

People will relate to you in a way that matches their perception of you. If, for example, you are seen principally as an interference, it is unlikely that you will encounter cooperative attitudes. By contrast, if you are perceived as a problem-solving partner, you will experience little opposition when introducing new programs or services. Hence, if you want to be successful, you must occupy a position in the minds of your customers that is consistent with the role you want to play in the organization.

Strong positioning helps you establish relationships with strong allies. These, in turn, make your position even stronger. Power in organizations is built on relationships as well as on formal authority. So much of what makes organizations function occurs as a result of interpersonal relationships rather than rules and regulations. Everyone needs alliances in order to be effective. No one, including the chief executive, can move an organization for long solely on raw power. A staff function in particular needs strong allies since its power is purely advisory. If the powerful people in the organization see that you are strong in your resolve, they will work with you. If they see you as weak, they will run over you.

Begin at Home

Before you can change a perceptual position within your customer's mind, you have to change it within yourself. You have to want to create a new mental position. You have to know precisely what the new position looks like, and you have to learn what it takes to make the change. I'm sure you realize that all planned change starts with the initiator of the change. You and your staff have to determine exactly what position you want to occupy. It is, of course, not enough to simply have a picture of your new position. But without the picture it is even more unlikely that change will happen. This is why I said that position is a matter of perception plus action. One without the other usually doesn't work, but together they can make your strategy successful.

When Lisa Moriyama moved from computer manufacturer Digital Equipment Company to Transamerica Insurance, she knew the position that she wanted her Employee Relations/ EEO group to occupy in the minds of Transamerica's managers and employees. Her position message was "Employee Relations/ EEO is a group that simplifies and empowers." Rather than tell people what they can't do, Lisa expected her staff to show the client managers and employee customers how to solve their problems and achieve their goals in the most effective ways. She wanted to cut through bureaucracy and help people understand that they could take control of their destiny. Transamerica has been going through a massive change and downsizing. It sold off a major line of business and tried to turn the company around so that it could compete better in the highly volatile and cyclical insurance business. Lisa knew that the Employee Relations/EEO staff could play a value-adding role in the changes.

One of the early steps that she took was to develop a better information base. The company was "data deprived," as she put it. A lot of the information was in the computer, but people didn't know how to get it out and use it. But with her new database programs, they were able to identify the various factors that led to a selection of candidates for jobs created as a result of the restructuring. Through a job-matching project, the managers were able to make objective staffing decisions that previously had been done in a best-guess manner. By thinking proactively, uncovering a key need, and taking action, the Employee Relations/EEO staff members established themselves as people who could simplify problems and truly empower their customers.

The Position Message

I stated in the beginning that your basic objective is to occupy a unique, positive position in the minds of your customers. It is a goal that you must continuously strive to attain and maintain. Your vision is your idea of who you are. The position message that you put out, consciously or unconsciously, often turns into the vision that the customer has of you. Hence, your position message must be aimed at transmitting the vision that you have of your function to your customer. The goal is to align the vision with the position.

The more explicit your position message, the easier it will be for the customer to understand it. Complicated, equivocal position messages will create difficulties both for your customers and your staff. For this reason, the position message should be communicated in very few words. In fact, since most of the time you have to transmit the position message through other people, you *must* keep it simple.

An example of a position message that a human resources department might convey is that its functions are "necessary and cost effective." That carries a strong sense of purpose. Others could be "problem solvers," "change agents," "human asset advisers," "management partners," "value-adding consultants," or "human strategists." As you have probably noticed, there is very little difference between the vision and the position message. Obviously, they must be in harmony with each other. The only required difference is that they be phrased appropriately for each audience. Your staff members need to hear the vision expressed in terms that are meaningful and inspiring to them. Your customers need to have the vision communicated to them in terms that will cause them to position you in the perceptual slot that you seek.

Position messages and positions themselves are best when they are built on intangibles. Products come and go. If you are known and respected principally because of your skill and experience with a given product or process, you may quickly be forgotten when those needs fade. Being known for quality, responsiveness, reliability, discreetness, practicality, and utility is better because qualities such as these do not go out of style.

Let me suggest a short exercise that will help grasp what I am describing. Pick out a position idea from the list above or choose one of your own. If you put the book down and close your eyes, can you see yourself or your staff acting in a way that transmits this message to the customers in the organization? What do you see yourself doing to send your message as you interface with the customer? Isn't it a combination of words and actions? If you are having a problem visualizing that, pick out a reverse message. What would you do to convey the opposite position idea? Sometimes it is easier to visualize your message if you start from the negative side. A third way to visualize your position message is to imagine what you would want your customers to say about you. What words and ideas would you like them to use to describe you to other people? Write a short sentence of recommendation that you would like them to write about you. Does it make sense? If you have trouble doing this, you probably do not yet have a clear value-adding vision of your function. Take a minute now and try it. If you fail, don't worry. You are just starting. Remember what Helen Keller said:

> We can do anything we want to do if we stick with it long enough.

Whatever position message you choose it must be strong, positive, and easy to understand. It should be a direct extension of your vision. The message should create the picture that you want in the minds of your customers. The only difference between the vision and the position message is that the vision is a personally created self-image. It resides in your mind. The position is a result of interpersonal action and is held in the mind of your customer.

Here are sample position messages and their authors:

Miles Flannigan, Bridgestone Australia Ltd.: "Competent, flexible, and responsive."

Madelyn Jennings, Gannett Co.: "Objective and nonpartisan; you can count on HR, they have staying power and persistence."

Lise Bordeleau, Assurance-Vie, Desjardins (Canada): "Strategists, communicators, organizers for productivity."

Atsushi Ue, Seiko Instruments (Japan): "Improve employee abilities and help management make effective use of those abilities."

Pat Brown, First Tennessee Bank: "HR helps people succeed."

Denis Halliday, United Nations Development Program: "Responsive, transparent, involved with management."

Kath Rooney, Datastream International (England): "Effective, business and customer focused, can do, innovative, experts, versatile."

Dick Parker, Merck & Co.: "Enablers for employees and managers."

Ken Pritchett, Amatil Ltd. (Australia): "Strategic, professional, helpful."

Walt Whitt, McGraw-Hill, Inc.: "HR is an extension of the business."

Olle Alsen, Televerket (Sweden): "HR staff provides competent, professional business support."

Quinn Cramer, Hewlett-Packard: "They are helpmates,

not bureaucrats, part of the solution, not part of the problem."

Geert Rasmussen, Privatbanken A/S (Denmark): "Dynamic, serious, responsible."

Jack Phillips, Secor Bank: "HR is professional, helpful, experienced, and results oriented."

Len Myers, South Seas Plantation Resort: "Effective, competent, professional (technically and ethically)."

Des Tubridy, Bonlac Foods (Australia): "With management, developers of the human resource into a competitive edge."

Harry Garner, Northern Telecom (Canada): "A value-adding contributor."

Ed Kleinert, Memorial Sloan-Kettering Cancer Center: "HR means Quality."

Skeptics tell me that all this vision and position business is really unnecessary. They claim that they have gotten along very well without worrying about esoterica. I am willing to accept that they have operated for years without thinking about what they were doing for themselves and their companies. Can people function without a conscious vision or position? Of course. Although they may not be aware of their vision or the position that they occupy in the minds of their customers, that doesn't mean that the vision and positions don't exist. It is simply a matter of conscious realization. Even though at times it is more painful to be awake, it is also safer and personally more rewarding to be conscious rather than unconscious of what you are doing.

Prerequisites

There are four requisites to repositioning human resources as a value-adding function: vision, objectivity, simplicity, and patience.

Start with a New Vision. Positioning is concerned with the future, not the past. While you do have to take into consideration the past, because that is what generated your current position, the critical issue is the future. You want to position yourself to play a future role in the organization. There are two futures: short term and long term. The short term starts today and usually lasts no more than one year. The long term may be anywhere from one to five years from now. In some businesses the long term used to be a decade. Now, it is next year.

A major company provides a good example of how time lines change. Until the early eighties, this company enjoyed a strong position in a large market. It could set policies and know that the probability was very high that these policies would be implemented as planned. The human resources personnel group realized, however, that their reporting system was obsolete. For years they had tracked their volume of work but seldom its impact. They couldn't answer the "So what?" question. Now, in the new environment they needed to focus on the value that they could add to the competitive needs of the corporation. Their first response was to develop a system that tracked several employment activities. By focusing on the cost of external hires and internal placements and the time needed to fill jobs, they prepared themselves to talk with client managers about trends, reasonable expectations, and recruiting plans. This helped them change their position from administrative paper pushers to management partners.

If you are going to create a new position for yourself, you should know something about your organization's long-term strategy. You want to choose a position that parallels the long-term plans of your business. Many organizations are going through massive reorganizations now. They are repositioning themselves and their products in the new global marketplace. You must know what your top management has in mind, no matter how unfinished its plans may be. If they are planning to zig, you don't want to plan to zag.

Let's say, for example, that your senior management team has decided to branch out into new businesses. You need to know something about the nature of those businesses. Perhaps they are planning to begin retailing products that formerly were sold directly to corporate customers. Retailing is a very volatile business, and time cycles in that market are quite short. Whole product lines are born, live, and die in the space of two years. It is a very fast-paced, unpredictable business. If you wanted to create a useful position for your function within that type of business, you would not focus on the development of comprehensive, fixed programs. By the time you published a large policy manual most of it would be out of date. You wouldn't set yourself up to maintain and publish organization charts because you could never keep them current. Instead, your positioning strategy might be to assemble your resources into flexible, quick-hitting, problem-solving teams. These groups would have the authority, within limits, to make and execute policy decisions on the spot to help line management respond quickly to market problems and opportunities. This kind of strategic response would suit the retail environment.

This is exactly the strategy employed by Systematics, Inc. This Little Rock, Arkansas, company negotiates five-year contracts with banks to run their in-house data-processing systems. Because the staff is scattered in bank data centers all over the country, the company must decentralize authority or units would not be able to function efficiently. Human resources manager John Nichols says, "We expect line managers to be human resources managers." To make that happen, corporate management decentralized human resources decision making and, through training, provided the managers with the operating tools that they need to carry out their duties. These include the critical tasks of hiring employees and paying them properly. This approach must be working because Systematics expects that within eighteen months after signing a new contract with a bank, they will be operating the facility with only two-thirds as many employees as were needed before and with less computer hardware.

There is a subtle lesson to be learned here. Systematics has positioned its human resources system to enable managers to attract and develop people in the shortest possible time frames. Power does not always come from centralized control. John exercises a great deal of power within Systematics by delegating authority and providing support. In return, managers willingly follow his lead because they see that it works. That's the best kind of power.

Of course, I realize that top management is often unwilling to share its strategic vision of the company with anyone. There are many reasons for this and, for the purposes of our discussion, they are not important. But discovering the corporate vision is important. How do you do that? You talk and you listen. Talk to high-level executives whenever you have the opportunity. Ask them where the company is going. Urge them to be specific. Tell them that you need to have some idea of its strategic direction for you to be supportive and make a contribution. At the same time, listen to what middle managers talk about. Run a content analysis of official publications. Which topics appear most frequently? Soon all this will begin to coalesce into a fairly clear picture of the direction in which management is trying to take the organization.

Once you have the overall picture, fit your vision into it. This is how you turn a vision into a position. You may now see why I suggested that you build your vision on intangibles. It is because they are transportable. You can thus be a cost-effective problem solver in any organization. Nevertheless, the question still remains, What part do you want your unit to play within the larger organization that is your marketplace? Knowing the company's strategy and translating your vision into a position that parallels the company's direction will help you keep up with your market. Moreover, the odds are high that changes will occur in the external environment and that the corporation will have to make corresponding changes in its strategy if it is to survive. If you know what is happening and how you fit in, you will be ready to adapt and ride out the shock when the waves of change hit. The chances are that you will be able to anticipate most of the changes. You will be able to see them coming because surface conditions usually become unstable before the tidal wave hits. When a storm is on the way the color of the water changes and the wind ripples the surface. If you are watching the sky and see clouds forming, you don't have to wait to get wet to know that it's probably going to rain. You can set up your stand and start selling umbrellas.

Stay Objective. One of the hardest tasks for a human being is to face facts. This is particularly true when the facts contradict long and dearly held opinions. But you must set aside your prejudgments when dealing with the realities of the marketplace.

Every business person must do that if he or she is to survive. It is called being market focused. I would like to spend my time and resources running my business and turning out products and services that excite me. But if my customers aren't ready for one of my services, I can go broke trying to force it onto the market. Companies misread the market all the time. One of the more obvious examples of this in recent years was Federal Express's attempt to introduce Zap Mail service. This particular misreading cost one of the most innovative companies in America some $300 million in losses.

Most companies could not survive losses of that size. My own company must recognize where the market is at all times. The market is the value perceptions of my customer. I may decide to spend part of my resources educating my potential customers and trying to convince them that they do in fact need my product. But I had better spend most of my resources generating current sales or I could be out of business before my customers realize they need the other product.

The same principle applies to you. You need market research. Circulate through your organization and talk to people at all levels. Try out your ideas on them and listen to their opinions. You might find that there is no perceived need for, and even a resistance to, some part of the role that you want to play. Notice that I said "role." I didn't say "programs." Focus on the market, not on your services. Learn the market, then design programs to fill your customers' needs.

Russ Cunningham saw a need to change the supervisory style of Pacific Gas and Electric Company. The militaristic, highly directive style that had been in force since 1946 simply would not work in the environment of the 1980s. He wanted to start the change at the top by developing high-performance participative teams. But top management was preoccupied with a troubled nuclear power plant that was eating up millions of dollars daily. So, he took his idea and sold it to two regional vice-presidents. Russ and his organization development group put the program together. After the program started, one of the general managers was so impressed with the potential of the program that he personally took responsibility for running the program in his business unit. Now, the program is beginning to show great promise for the corporation. It succeeded because Russ correctly diagnosed a major problem and found a way to fix it.

Market resistance or indifference is often simply a matter of semantics—a matter of finding the correct way of phrasing your ideas. Listen carefully for the resistance arguments. Don't feel hurt and accuse your customers of being blind to their own good. That won't sell your idea. Talk to several people, listen carefully, and then implement what feels workable. Everyone has a truth spot in his or her body. You know what I mean. When something isn't right, you feel it in the pit of your stomach, the back of your neck, or some other place. That signal is never wrong, is it? Watch and wait for it. Then, go with it, because it is usually connected to the objective realities of your marketplace.

Keep It Simple. When an employee or manager thinks of your human resources function, you want them to have a clear, unequivocal idea of what your purpose is. Employees at the operating level obviously will not have the same expectations of your unit as top management or first-line supervisors. That's not a problem. The point is that you want everyone to know what your department is and why you are there.

Do you remember "the Uncola," "We Try Harder," "Great Tasting but Less Filling," "Have It Your Way"? These are positioning messages that left indelible pictures in our minds. They went beyond describing a product's market position and became part of our language. Hardly a day goes by that you don't hear someone use one of these phrases in a context totally different from its original one. We all know what they mean, and subconsciously we remember the product.

If you want someone who tries harder, you rent a car from Avis. If you want your hamburger prepared to suit your personal preference, you go to Burger King. But, as a human resources person, you aren't renting cars or selling hamburgers. What do you want people to think of when your name comes up? Or what type of problem or service do you want associated with your function? For example, how do you feel about these position ideas: "picnic planner," "advocate," "problem solver," "counselor," "time waster," "business partner," "friend," "confidant," "corporate cop?" Do you see what I mean? Each term brings a picture to your mind. What picture of human resources do you want in your customers' minds?

At Saratoga Institute we had a positioning problem in 1987. We had to try to differentiate ourselves from hundreds of other consulting, research, and software companies. We are not a general consultancy firm. We don't do headhunting, compensation or benefit planning, or general training. Our practice is very focused. We apply strategic thinking, an uncompromising value orientation, and quantitative methods to systematically measure and improve human effectiveness. We decided to position ourselves by using just four words: Human Resource Effectiveness Systems. We have named our product line to reinforce this picture. The newest software package is titled "HReffect$," and our survey reports are called Human Resource Effectiveness Reports. Our promotional slogans reinforce the quantitative image of our work. For example, "We've Got Your Number" and "You Can't Manage What You Can't Measure" are mottoes we used in 1988. Although we have been using this approach for only a short time, our backlog of consulting assignments and our rate of product sales have more than doubled in the past six months. Time will tell whether or not we have established a permanent, recognizable position in our marketplace. But at least for now, we have succeeded in conveying our specific identity to our customers.

Now, how about you? In one short, clear phrase, who are you?

Be Patient and Persevere. One night in the middle of a long, tiring trip I ran into Jim Spoor from Spectrum HR Systems at some long-forgotten airport. We went for a drink to wait out yet another flight delay. We sat commiserating over the difficulties of building a business from scratch without venture capital. At one point, Jim sat back, put his feet up on the coffee table, took a sip of his beer, and said ruefully, "Everything takes twice as long as you expected and costs twice as much as you figured." Jim and his wife, Nancy, who cofounded the company, are optimists, like most of us. We all like to think positively. We want to accomplish more than we probably can in any given period of time. And we get upset when things don't develop as quickly as we think they should. But we persist through the discouragements. Countless times over the past decade I have urged people to try some new process or apply a new method only to have them tell me later that it didn't work. In almost every case they simply did not persist. They gave it one try, often without proper preparation, and they failed. So, rather than learn from their failure and make the needed changes, they gave up.

You will probably find that the new position, the new method, the new service is not as well received as you dreamed it would be. This experience is common. It is called life. Don't let that stop you.

Carolyn Magura spent sixteen frustrating years working in government and then in private industry before she found an organization that would let her introduce her ideas about performance measurement. Finally, Tom Kelley, human resources director at Benj. Franklin Savings and Loan Association in Portland, Oregon, gave her a chance. Today, she runs one of the most efficient and harmonious compensation and benefit groups anywhere. Her story and her methods are described in one of the two case studies that follow Chapter Eight.

Recognize that there are a multitude of competing and conflicting forces at work in your marketplace. It is unreasonable to expect that you will be able to overcome all of them, all the time. You will come up against obstacles that you did not anticipate and plan for. Rework your ideas and keep at it. Persist. Nothing can take the place of perseverance. The president of one of our client companies has a succinct but powerful way of describing this attitude. He always tells his people, "Progress, not perfection."

Whenever my business is not going as well as I had hoped

it would, I repeat two of my favorite quotations. One is from Thomas Edison, who said, "In the early days there were times when I ached to give it all up. But I kept at it because I was too young to know it couldn't be done." What if Edison had given up? He had plenty of reasons to quit. There were accidents, failed experiments—he tried over 6,000 materials as filaments before the light bulb worked. Can you grasp the magnitude of frustration he must have felt? Critics who didn't have the courage to try ridiculed him. Does anyone remember their names? But Edison persisted and today his name is one of the most revered in America.

The other quotation is Winston Churchill's exhortation to a group of students during the Battle of Britain: "Never, never, never, never give up." As the battle raged in 1940 and the German Luftwaffe continued to pound England, Churchill became an iron-willed, jut-jawed symbol of determination for the British people. His courage and strength in the face of that national trauma inspired others to stay the course. As we all know, England and the Allies eventually prevailed over the Third Reich that was supposed to last a thousand years.

Six Basic Questions for Positioning

There is a natural temptation in American business to start throwing out solutions before the problem is clear. We are an action-oriented nation. Some people call it the shotgun approach; others call it shooting from the hip. These are good metaphors since they convey the destructive rather than the constructive nature of this approach to problem solving.

The quality of a solution is usually directly related to the quality of the problem-solving process. I will give you six questions that you can ask yourself and your staff that should lead you to a clear expression of your desired position.

What Needs to Be Changed? You aren't starting in a vacuum. There is a past that you must contend with no matter how good or bad it may have been. The first question has to do with how your customers see you now. Either you have a personal history with the organization that can be characterized in a few words, or you have just come into an organization and inherited the position of your predecessor.

In 1976, I joined a computer manufacturer in Silicon Valley as the head of the personnel function. My predecessor had been in the job just ninety days before he was dismissed. The department he left was a smoldering ruin. Not only was the staff in shock but middle and upper management would have almost nothing to do with the department. Why is not the issue. The point is that the function suffered from a very negative reputation. If I was going to be successful, I had to change the perception of the department in the minds of its customers.

I started in the most obvious place: I changed the name of the department. This partially put the old identity to rest. But that by itself would have achieved nothing. So, I set out to discover the single most important thing that we could do to make a positive impression. I talked to many people at all levels of the company. I was looking for one, universal issue that everyone thought was vitally important. It turned out to be ineffective first-line supervisors. The deficiency was due to the growth rate of this very young company—about 50 percent per year in revenues. There had been no time to develop employees. People were hired and promoted out of necessity, but much too rapidly to gain competence.

To make a long story short, we designed and delivered a training program for first-level supervisors. We gave short pretests and posttests on various topics. We kept track of test scores and proved that people were learning. We monitored the performance of supervisors as seen by the employees and reported positive results. Once these data were in the hands of middle and upper management, they saw that human resources could be effective. The position of the function changed from that of a leper colony to a place people came when they had a problem.

I hope that your current position is better than mine was. But I assume that it is not as good as you would like it to be or you wouldn't be reading this book. Whatever it is, define it accurately and accept it as your starting point. And don't worry about making a false start. Remember what Theodore Roosevelt said:

The only man who never makes a mistake is the man who never does anything.

What Do You Want Your Position to Be? In the beginning you need a very tightly defined position message. You can't be all things to all people. I've seen a number of one-person consulting companies fail because the individual projected too general an image. No one can solve all problems. If you present too broad a front, people will be unable to identify you with their problems. That's because there is no such thing as a general problem. All problems are specific. Unless you are taking on the total restructuring of a corporation, the problems that you will be asked to solve will usually be narrowly focused in a given arena.

In time, your function may be able to represent itself as a solver of a wide variety of problems. But in the beginning you will create less confusion in the minds of your customers and greater acceptance if you put forth a simple, very specific position message.

How do you know what target to aim at when there are so many things that need to be accomplished? Do your market research. Carefully record all the identifiable problems and opportunities in your organization. Study them. They will probably fall into recognizable and describable categories. Pick the one or two problems that most people in the organization agree are the important ones. Compose a position message around those choices. The position may fall into one of the five basic categories of human asset management shown in Table 6. We will go into those categories in depth in Chapter Ten, but for now, picture what your customers are trying to achieve. It may be increased efficiency, or greater productivity, or an improvement in the quality of work life. You have skills in the fields outlined in Table 6. How can you match what you have to offer with what your customers need?

The question for you to answer is, Where will I stake my claim? If you are a tactical unit such as the training function, what will you advertise as your reason for being? Are you trainers, skill builders, quality improvers, profit enhancers, or what?

Table 6. The Five Human Asset Management Factors.

Acquisition	— Staff and succession planning, recruitment, and hiring
Maintenance	— Pay and benefit programs, employee and labor relations, EEO and EAP programs, and the human resource information system
Development	— Career planning and development, skill training, and management and organizational development programs
Application	— Utilizing employees to get the work done and achieving organizational objectives measured in terms of productivity and quality
Management	— The cost of supervision and the effectiveness of managers

Are you support staff, fixers of "people" problems, productivity increasers, value adders, or a court of last resort?

PACCAR, Inc., is a manufacturing firm headquartered in Bellevue, Washington, just north of Seattle. With 14,000 employees spread across the world, it builds and sells Kenworth and Peterbilt trucks, pumps, winches, and mining equipment. Jack Quinlin and Ingrid Rasch have a very clear image of the position and the operating style that they want human resources to display. Jack describes it in two words: "internal consultant." Ingrid expanded on it to me this way: "You have to be providing support actively. As internal consultants we look ahead to what might be needed. We alert the general managers of our divisions to potential problems. Our job is to keep them aware — to lead management on the people side of the business."

An example of their forward-looking position occurred in 1988. Anticipating contract negotiations at two of PACCAR's unionized plants, the human resources department conducted an intensive study of the demographics of the plants. The employees at the two plants turned out to have quite different profiles. HR tailored a pay and benefits package that best suited the population of each plant. This analysis led to at least one early contract settlement. In the past, negotiations were a matter of responding to expected union demands. This anticipatory approach showed management that personnel issues can be managed in the same way as finance, marketing, or manufacturing issues. Jack and Ingrid have positioned human resources as a function that manages proactively. They can be counted on to lead.

What Do You Have to Overcome? Everything in your marketplace will not necessarily be on your side. Your challenge is to eventually win over the naysayers and overcome the barriers. In the words of Winston Churchill,

> It is no use saying we are doing our best. You have got to succeed in doing what is necessary.

There are several classic blocks to positioning or repositioning yourself. They are as follows:

- Change: Industries, products, and issues change. You must refocus on the new needs while you struggle to reposition yourself in the changing market.
- Resistance to change: People don't like to change. Customers may not want to open their minds and accept you in a different role.
- Customer knowledge: Education is required. Many people are ignorant of the potential of human resources. They may have only seen it operate as an expense center that wastes their time and interferes with their own initiatives.
- Past performance: It is necessary to overcome sins of the past. Either you or your predecessors may have been seen as nonprofessional, unresponsive, irrelevant, or not credible. This has to be changed through new behavior.
- Internal inconsistency: Teamwork may be lacking. All human resources sections may not be promoting the same vision. It then becomes critical to emphasize unity of effort.
- The unexpected: Prepare for the future. No matter how smart you are, you can't predict the future. No one knows what will happen tomorrow. Thus, flexibility should be part of your position message.
- You: Are you willing to change? Are you ready to change your behavior as well as your labels? You will have to give up your

sacred cows, let go of your prejudices, be willing to listen, and confront some hostility.

How Will You Make Repositioning Happen? One approach to making the changes required by your new positioning strategy is to analyze the field before you enter it. There may be some people out there who would simply like to be left alone. Some managers are mavericks. They like to do what they want to do, the way they want to do it, when they want to do it. For those people it's not just you who is in the way. They view the whole world as interfering with them.

The question is, How are you going to deal with them? Can you ignore them, at least for a while? Or, are they so central to your strategy that you have to convert them? If you can't convince them to accept your position and cooperate with you, can you neutralize them?

There is a classic change analysis process that you can use in circumstances such as this to help you decide the best way to swing the situation in your favor. It is called force field analysis (FFA). This is a fifty-year-old process developed by Kurt Lewin during his research in group dynamics. FFA is basically a process of listing all the positive, pushing forces that you have going for you and all the negative, restraining forces that you have working against you. In order to advance, you must either increase the "pushers" or decrease the "restrainers."

Restraining forces may be people, policies, structures, budgets, or other factors, and the same is true of pushing forces. You are in the equation too. As they used to say in the civil rights movement, you are either part of the solution or part of the problem. In any event, if you know what forces you are up against, you won't be blind sided. Your chances of successfully establishing and maintaining your position are better if you understand the arena in which you are going to compete.

Do You Have What It Takes? This is closely related to the previous question, but it has a broader applicability. It looks at all the factors both inside and outside your function and defines them as positive or negative (this point will be covered in detail in Chapter Eight).

There are four types of factors: (1) human—the people involved; (2) financial—the capital needed; (3) technological—the facilities, equipment, and type of business you are in; and (4) organizational—its structure, systems, and policies. What you need to do is identify and list the major factors in each category, both inside your department and outside in the organization and the external environment. After you have done this, classify the internal factors as either strengths or weaknesses and the external factors as either threats or opportunities. The differ-ence between the situation described above, where you apply FFA, and this case is one of scope. FFA is designed to diagnose an impasse in a specific situation. But this second process, which is sometimes called a capability analysis or a situation audit, looks at all forces in the entire field of operations. It is part of a strategy-planning process, while FFA usually looks to tactical actions.

The question of capability or capacity requires you to examine all relevant forces: your group's strengths and weak-nesses, along with the marketplace's threats and opportunities. After you identify a position that you want to occupy, you need to prepare yourself for the contest. You can seldom simply walk in and operate 100 percent of the way that you want to. You may need to shore up some weakly staffed area. Untrained or basi-cally incompetent people cannot carry out your vision.

One human resources manager arrived at her new com-pany and found people who had been on the same job for over twenty years. They were untouchable and seemingly untraina-ble. It took her almost two years to slowly turn those people around. She didn't do it with words. Instead, she let them sit on the sidelines and watch other people in the department experi-ence success and its rewards from using the new methods. She kept the door open and eventually one of them decided to try a new behavior. When he didn't get burned, he told his cronies and they tried it too. Eventually, they all became comfortable with the new methods.

As painful as it is, you may have to dismiss some people.

Or, in light of what you have in mind, you may need to make a case for more funds in a certain area. It could be that a re-organization or a realignment of functions is called for. You may need new equipment or a more favorable physical location.

On the other side of the field you need to look at the personnel, financial viability, technological level, structure, and systems of the organization, as well as the external environment. These factors will probably represent both threats and oppor-tunities for you. They can make or break your plan. You also don't want to forget the type of relationships that exist between these factors and your staff. Organizations are staffed with human beings who sometimes have conflicting styles and val-ues. Interpersonal relations are probably more important than any other single factor. When people want to make something work for you, they find ways to do so, no matter how tough it might be. When they don't like you they can be very unsuppor-tive, to say the least.

When one of our clients attempted to build a quantitative performance measurement system, he found himself thwarted by his own staff. Two of the managers laid down a smoke screen of resistance by arguing at length over minute differences in item definitions (they had lived for years without even noting the differences). However, the manager patiently answered every question over a period of two months until he wore them down. Eventually, they no longer had anything to hide behind and had no choice but to cooperate. He gave them a chance to maintain their pride and gradually accept the new vocabulary without coming to look incompetent in the eyes of the staff.

Finally, one of the worst mistakes anyone can make is to go into battle unprepared or lacking in resources. Take a good look at your situation. What are your capabilities and capacities? Do you have a good chance of seizing and holding the position that you have chosen? The only position for which there is no contest is the bottom one, and you scarcely want to end up there.

How Much Do You Want It? The final thing needed is desire. How badly do you want this position? What price are you willing to pay for it? What risks are you ready to accept? Do you have the personal and organizational resources to last through tough times?

Many small businesses that get off to a running start fail because they do not have the resources to sustain themselves when business slows down. The resource that is most lacking is not capital, it is the wisdom to read the signs and the courage to stay the course no matter how tough it gets. Many people think it will be fun to open their own business and deal in products and services that interest them. What they don't realize is that they may have to spend most of their time and energy sustaining the organization that they have built. Remember this: The bigger your goal, the harder you will have to work to win it and hold it.

To maintain a position in a competitive organization you have to choose your ground and defend it. Once you have committed yourself to a position you have to stick with it. People may fight with you just to test your resolve. If you roll over easily you are done for. They will know that you are weak and indecisive. In contrast, everyone respects persistence. So, you must show your commitment to your position. There may be times when you fear for your job, the security of your family, your reputation, or even your physical safety. These are the times that sort out the winners from the losers. Battle scars may not be pretty, but they are badges of honor. If you have courage, stamina, and the guts to hang in there, eventually you will gain all the respect and support you need to hold your position. In the words of W. Somerset Maugham,

> It's a funny thing about life. If you refuse to accept anything but the best you very often get it.

Conclusion

Visions don't convert automatically into new positions. You have to make them happen through action. Once you have a clear vision of yourself and your function, will you be able to translate that into a position message?

The position message describes the place that you want to occupy in your customer's mind. When your customers think of you, they should have a clear view of who and what you are. Your message should be objective, simple, and unequivocal.

Turning your vision into a message that customers will comprehend and accept requires patience, perseverance, and courage. It won't come easy, but if your performance is consistent with your vision and position message, sooner or later customers will grant you a place on the Value Team.

Positioning is critical because it facilitates later action. When people know what you stand for, they know what to expect from you. Given that, you will find it easier to gain access, establish a dialogue, obtain cooperation, and attain your goal of helping them achieve their objectives.

> At the heart of every good marketing strategy is a good positioning strategy.
> Regis McKenna

Reference

Ries, A., and Trout, J. *Positioning: The Battle for Your Mind.* New York: McGraw-Hill, 1981.

Case Studies—Chapter Six

Bonlac Foods, Ltd.
Melbourne, Australia
*(Prepared by Desmond Tubridy, corporate manager of human
resources)*

Bonlac Foods of Melbourne, Australia, is engaged in processing, marketing, and distributing dairy and tomato products
throughout the world. Bonlac resulted from a 1986 merger of
four independent dairy companies owned by farmer-producers.
After making two acquisitions in 1988, the group has become
Australia's largest manufacturer of dairy products. It has 2,250
employees in Australia and a small contingent in Singapore.

The company is now going through a consolidation period as it tries to absorb the aftershocks of the merger and
acquisitions. The key objective in the near term is to increase
productivity and profitability for the 4,000 farmers who own it.
The human resources group has positioned itself as one of the
functions that will carry out this imperative. There are both
external and internal aspects to its work.

External. Top management saw an opportunity to encourage
and develop greater levels of productivity among managers and
thus gave human resources the task of implementing a performance management program in 1988.

The first step involved the preparation of position de-
scriptions by the managers in conjunction with their supervisors. It was recommended that, to manage effectively, a specific
goal agreement should be prepared by each manager to cover a
six-month period, at the end of which it would be reviewed with
his or her supervisor. This detailed discussion would culminate
in a performance rating on a 1 to 9 grid. If goals were not
satisfactorily achieved, obstacles to performance would be identified and a plan to remedy the deficiencies would be drafted.

During the start-up phase the corporate manager of
human resources held training seminars throughout the group
to familiarize managers with the process and content of the

performance management program. Documentation, selection of effectiveness areas, interviewing, and role playing were the topics. Compensation guidelines were also discussed. Although it was risky, with typical Aussie confidence the company decided to link pay to performance from the beginning. This demonstrated how serious top management was about improving performance.

Generally, there would be two goal agreements per year, each lasting six months, and compensation reviews would be linked to them. The human resources department developed a preappraisal worksheet to be used prior to the main review and interview stage. It was recognized that self-ratings by subordinates were often conservative. At the meeting with their supervisor it was found that the discussion was very interactive and did not take on any punitive characteristics. Also, by having the individual do his or her own rating, the manager's job was reduced to one of review and comment rather than full-scale creation of the appraisal.

Based on the appraisal ratings, the human resources function coordinates the systematic feedback produced by the "review of the reviewers," providing a summary of a manager's subordinate ratings placed alongside the percentage salary increase granted. The human resources department further adds value by coordinating succession planning, potentials review and training, and development needs analysis using data in the performance management program.

All reviewers and reviewees in the program were surveyed to assess their perception of the program's effectiveness in measuring their contribution to the success of Bonlac. In the first year, nearly 70 percent either strongly or partially agreed that it was effective, with 21 percent undecided. Given the historical level of discontent with performance appraisal systems, this result is quite good. Now, human resources can concentrate on fine-tuning the program.

Internal. The human resources department has developed what it calls a "customerization" process. The purpose is to ensure that all human resources staff identify their clients at the goal

agreement stage of their own performance management programs. Second, human resources management wants to ensure
that these staff members have at least two days per year of offsite
client review feedback sessions. Performance management, motivation, consulting skills, and ways to positively reinforce successes are the agenda for these sessions.

Prior to the two semiannual meetings, Des Tubridy discusses with each client manager what his or her perceptions are
of the various human resources services that were targeted on
that manager's areas of accountability. The results are then fed
back to the appropriate staff person. These data are considered
when determining the performance ratings of the human resources staff.

The customerization program form asks three basic questions and leaves room for open-ended responses. The questions
are as follows:

1. Who are the customers of the human resources department? Name either the departments, sections, or persons
   that are your customers.
2. What do your customers expect from you? List each customer along with the specific expectations that he or she has
   of you.
3. What could the human resources department be doing for
   your customers that it is not doing now? Specify the customers and the services.

It would not cause a problem if the human resources staff
person omitted something on purpose. If he or she did, Des's
informal contact with the key customers later on would uncover
an unexpressed need or expectation.

Once the human resources function has been custom-
erized, the next stage involves the presentation of survey results,
proposed programs, and implementation plans to all management groups throughout the organization. The meetings start at
the top with the executive committee and proceed throughout
all decentralized manufacturing business units. Functional divisions and departments are involved subsequently.

To complete the system, the human resources function has established a set of effectiveness areas, together with measurable criteria. It has also scheduled review periods for the human resources staff. These review periods are linked to the performance management program and drive data analysis and interpretation. In a nutshell, this key step keeps the program from becoming a paper exercise.

To position and market itself, the human resources department distributes a brochure describing its professional services to all clients at these presentations. In 1989, a quarterly newsletter called *HR Feedback* was started. It is issued to clients throughout the company. Its purpose is to inform clients about the various human resources activities and to discuss, anonymously, successful case studies handled by the human resources staff. Des believes that this document provides a valuable channel for raising client awareness of the services provided by the human resources function. This is exactly what I was talking about in the positioning chapter. This is a position message in action.

Through programs such as the ones described here, the human resources staff is adapting its function to the role of profit enhancer. By working and planning in conjunction with senior management, the human resources group will develop the organization's human resources into an effective and competitive edge for Bonlac.

Author's comment: This is an example that is typical of human value management. A major organizational need was identified, and an appropriate system was then designed, implemented, and tested with the customer. It is now maintained as part of the management system of the organization. Success is built like this: one small step at a time. Actions position human resources. Successful business results position human resources as more than an interfering bureaucracy. By piling up a consistent series of successes for the client, the human resources function becomes known as a value-adding partner.

Swiss Bank Corporation
New York
(Prepared by Mike Mitchell and the human resources staff)

When Mike Mitchell joined Swiss Bank (New York) in late 1985 as vice-president of human resources for its U.S. operations, he inherited a rigidly structured staff that functioned as personnel record keepers and rule enforcers. Innovation was not encouraged, and risk taking was generally avoided. Thus, Mike set out to develop a repositioning strategy that he eventually named Operation Phoenix. The goal was to give the human resources function a proactive role in Swiss Bank's overall business strategy.

The Takeoff. Mike found considerable untapped potential in his department. To apply that potential for Swiss Bank, he developed a strategy that would bolster staff self-confidence while simultaneously serving critical bank needs. He realized that change does not take place overnight. Dedication, persistence, and patience would be required. The plan was broken down into manageable steps.

The first step was to gain an understanding of the organization and its competitive marketplace. Human resources needed to know where the bank was going and what market forces might impact its business. This business analysis would then have to be translated into human resources terms.

The next step was to take a critical look at all the department's activities. Meetings were held throughout the bank to answer these questions:

- What is the business of our "customers" (bank personnel)?
- What types of products and services does human resources provide them?
- How does the customer perceive human resources?
- What are the immediate and future needs of the customer?
- Are we meeting them?
- How can human resources realign itself to provide maximum support to the customer's needs?

From the information gathered, a human resources mission statement was developed to guide the repositioning. It set forth these goals:

- Develop and deliver the highest quality human resources products and services that meaningfully support the needs and vitality of our organization and its employees.
- Create a business strategy for our function that challenges the limitations of the human resources practice and provides the potential for us to become a successful business enterprise in our own right.
- Be the best at what we do.

In support of this mission, a plan was developed and presented to senior management. The plan was presented in a way that would allow management to recognize the value of the realignment. The plan was approved with full commitment and support.

Reorganizing. The approved plan was recommunicated to the human resources staff to ensure that they knew what to expect and what would be required of them. It is important to note that not all staff members will make a smooth transition to a new operating style. Thus, lines of communication had to be kept open. Regular meetings were held to discuss progress, relay information, and improve teamwork. Individual accomplishments were shared and achievements celebrated. Fears were acknowledged.

The previously existing five units, which had become quite rigid, were realigned into three focused functions:

Planning is responsible for developing new human resources products and services that directly respond to business issues or opportunities. This group has no day-to-day responsibilities that would get in the way of expedient product development.

Marketing is responsible for delivering day-to-day human resources products and services to customers, ensuring that customer needs are addressed, and responding to business needs of the line units.

Systems and Administration is responsible for day-to-day delivery of traditional human resources products and services (payroll, record keeping, benefits administration).

An awareness of how important it is to maintain communication with one's customers prompted the installation of a cordless hotline. This is staffed from nine to five every workday and longer on special occasions. The number is in every orientation kit and is listed in the Swiss Bank telephone directory. With a cordless phone, it is easy to walk the telephone to someone more familiar with the topic for an immediate answer. For complex inquiries an answer is guaranteed within two business days.

A customer service team was created to handle reception duties and monitor general customer service provided by human resources. Outstanding performance by this team is recognized with special year-end bonuses.

In the early stages of repositioning, there was a need for human resources to have a winner to gain credibility. Two opportunities presented themselves. One was the need for a performance-based compensation strategy; the other was the need for an effective and meaningful performance management and career development system. The answer to both of these needs was the Horizon system.

Horizon is not perceived as a human resources program. Because the line organization was involved in its development, it is seen as a management tool. It has four components:

- Business planning identifies business goals and translates them into human resource needs.
- Performance management helps the employee identify performance goals that directly support the business plan.
- Human resources planning matches employee development plans with the bank's human resource needs: an integrated succession planning, recruiting, and training plan.
- Career planning provides a communication channel for

employees to convey career aspirations and developmental needs to their manager.

Many companies have components such as these. But few have successfully integrated them and connected them to their business plans and strategies.

Mid-Course Adjustments. To keep the program on course and schedule, constant review is necessary. At one point it became apparent that there were some deficiencies in the systems and administration unit. A task force was formed to address the problems. A project plan for short-term improvements was prepared and the necessary corrections made. The goal was zero defects, and that was eventually achieved.

Mike presented management with a long-range operations plan that would solidify the gains made to date. Having shown that the staff was adding value to the bank, he had no problem in obtaining approval and the resources to make it work. This program is a living proof that when you show return on investment, management consistently provides the resources.

Taken as a whole, Mike's initiative yielded a wealth of insights:

1. The model that Mike used created a team that has the flexibility and motivation to handle very large projects in record time.

2. The three primary functions of planning, marketing, and administration must be maintained in a balanced state, they must be integrated, and they must share a common perception of their customer service mission.

3. The use of cross-functional project teams and task forces allows the group to respond to crises, broadens staff skills, and forges vital alliances between the functions.

4. Involving carefully chosen personnel from the company in human resources developments strengthens the link between human resources and the rest of the bank.

5. Repositioning is dynamic and requires ongoing adap-

tation, tremendous effort and commitment, and unwavering, supportive leadership.

Author's comment: There is no question that Mike Mitchell and his team have pulled it off. The repositioning is firmly in place, and now it is a matter of building on it. To me, the most critical aspect of the program was not the conceptualization, although that was excellent, but rather Mike's total commitment to and full support of the idea. I was involved in the early days when it was still a half-formed idea in the minds of some people on his staff. Mike maintained a positive, caring, but firm attitude that was the foundation on which the structure was eventually built. The commitment to helping customers achieve their goals and adding value paid off every time that human resources needed support from the bank.

7

Researching and Developing
Markets for Human Resources

WHAT IS OUR business is not determined by the pro-
ducer, but the customer . . . by the want the customer
satisfies when he buys the product or service.
                                                    Peter Drucker

It is through your marketing plan that you analyze your
marketplace and the customers who make it up. Marketing
plans are prescriptive in that they point out what you can and
must do to successfully service your customers. The purpose of a
marketing plan is to stimulate. It is both the last planning step
and the first action step that you take in designing and delivering your programs, products, and services.

Up to now, your focus has been inward — on your strategy,
your vision, and your position. Now you must turn outward and
focus on the marketplace. The key questions are: How is your
marketplace segmented? Who are your customers? What do they
really need and want? What are their attitudes toward your type
of service?

To market effectively you must learn how your market
works. There are dynamics unique to every market. If you leave
one company and go to another, you have to learn who the
players are, what the accepted style is, whether business is good,
bad, or indifferent, and a multitude of other factors and forces
before you can begin to operate effectively. When you know how
that market works — that is, what affects the buying decisions —
you can connect yourself and your products to the buyers.

Market segmentation is the first strategic action step that
"puts the ball in play." How are you going to win the position you
want to occupy in the mind of your customers?

Research claims that buyers fit into four categories: About

181

2 to 5 percent are eager to be the first to buy a new product. They are the innovators of society. Another 12 to 15 percent, the early adopters, enter the market as soon as the product starts to look promising. The masses, from 60 to 70 percent, buy after a product is established. The last 10 to 15 percent buy only when they have to. If you study your customers, you will soon learn who fits into which category. You will be more successful if you can isolate the leaders who make up the top 15 to 20 percent of your customers and sell to them first. Once they start using and talking about your product, the majority will follow their lead.

Successful marketing develops customers, not just products. In marketing, you are building long-term relationships. If you always approach customers from a "product" standpoint, you will be forced to reestablish your relationship with them every time that you introduce a new product. The product approach does not create loyalty. It makes selling a very time-consuming business, and it gives you the appearance of being self-centered rather than customer focused.

In earlier chapters I talked about the death of the captive market. I mentioned the survey of chief executive officers who said they were telling managers to obtain their support services from the most cost-effective source even if they have to go outside the company. This may not have happened to you, yet. But it is coming in some form, soon.

Administrative functions were originally established because organizations had grown in size and complexity to the point where managers could not supervise large groups of unskilled workers and at the same time take care of all the paper work needed to keep the organization functioning. That situation is now changing. Downsizing, computer communications, and global competition are broadening the span of control and making it imperative for managers to control costs. In my work I constantly come across human resources departments that have been compelled to set up accurate and defensible chargeback systems or adopt a zero-base budgeting process. That being the reality of the human resources marketplace of the 1990s, it makes good sense to begin to look at your market now and develop plans to cope with its demands.

The notion of marketing is frightening to some human resources practitioners and anathema to others. I doubt that many of our colleagues chose the human resources field because they liked selling. Many of us were no doubt surprised to find once we were in human resources that a large portion of our success would be dependent on our ability to persuade, or, in other words, to sell.

Russ Cunningham at Pacific Gas & Electric claims that the ability to sell is one of the two most important facets of human resources operations. Along with professionalism, Russ emphasizes that if you can't sell your products and services within the company, it doesn't matter how technically beautiful they are.

One of the most popular topics I lecture on is "How to Sell Your Products and Services." College human resources administration curricula do not include courses on persuasion or marketing. Yet, these will be two of the most critical skills for human resource managers in the emerging market. You will have to "sell" a lot of new ideas in the next decade, including some that you haven't even heard of today. To sell effectively you have to understand your marketplace. The market is not a monolith. It is composed of many types of people. They share some common needs, but they also have idiosyncratic needs, values, and opinions. If you are not aware of key needs or sources of resistance, it will be very difficult for you and your staff to market your services.

Customer Perceptions

Ries and Trout (1989) have called marketing the battlefield of the mind. In Chapter Six I presented their view that the customer's mind is made up of slots or positions that are filled with perceptions. This thesis implies that you are not dealing with something objective but instead are operating in a subjective arena. Your products and services, which are concrete things or actions, do not exist within the minds of your customers. The really important matter is their perception of you. To obtain the cooperation, support, resources, and respect that you want, you have to confirm or change your customers' perceptions. You are first a marketer and second a human resources specialist.

You do not mold perceptions by trying to brainwash your customers. Nor is it a question of trying to change the environment. Ries and Trout claim that the way to deal with perceptions is by making changes in your organization's operating style or its products and services so that it will be able to serve its customers' needs. To paraphrase them:

> When the boat is leaking, don't waste your time trying to
> drain the lake. Fix the boat.

Rethink the way you approach your customers. Try a style that will help them perceive you as someone who helps THEM achieve THEIR objectives.

Effective marketers don't stop with good plans. They go out and sell them. Miles Flannigan at Bridgestone Australia puts it simply: "Marketing human resources to organizational customers is achieved through effective identification of customer needs and delivery of programs designed to satisfy those specific needs." That's a pretty unequivocal statement.

A human resources friend on Wall Street fills in that basic premise. He says, "Be a salesman. Make calls. Meet your clients on their turf. See what's going on in their marketplace. Tell them which of your products can help them. Describe the features and benefits. Show the prospect how to get and use the product. If you want to build an image of value, nothing beats performance as it relates to customer needs."

To understand the customer's viewpoint, pretend you are a line supervisor with all the pressures that this implies. You have management on your back to get the product out faster while at the same time cutting costs. You have anxious, uncertain employees who don't know if they are going to get caught in the next layoff. You may have a union rep who, for whatever reasons, is posturing and flexing his muscles in your area. On top of all that, a staff person approaches you and says, "I have a piece of work for you to do for me." It could be a new personnel program, a revised purchase order form, or a different accounting procedure. "Please see to it that all employees are informed about this and that the proper forms are filled in and sent to my office by next Monday." How do you feel about the staffer who just laid this extra job on you?

Now try it this way. The same situation, the same pressures, another staff person approaches you and says, "Based on what you told me at our last meeting about what you're trying to get done, I think I can help you. I have a program here that I will help you install. It should make your people feel both more secure and more motivated." Which of the two staff people would you rather deal with?

The ultimate product or service might be the same in both cases. In both, you may have to communicate with the employees and see to it that the forms are promptly completed and returned. The difference is that in the second case the staff person has determined that there is a personnel program that can help you achieve your objectives. When the program is presented in that light, it makes sense for you to cooperate, because it is in your best interests to do so.

Wouldn't you agree that all personnel programs are designed to help the organization achieve its objectives? You don't offer programs, products, and services at random, do you? You don't suggest something simply because you like to do it, do you? Surely you always design, develop, and deliver programs that support the organization's goals. The only thing missing is that human resources often fails to show its customers how its programs service their needs.

What does your customer really want and need? The one thing that the customer does not want is your product or service. What customers want is to have their problems solved, their opportunities realized, and their objectives met. When your products and services clearly do that, your customers will have positive perceptions of you.

William Davidow explains the tricky business of filling customers' needs. He notes, for example, that sometimes even customers don't know what they want or need. He further points out that customer needs do not go away but that the optimal way of satisfying them changes. It is up to the provider, the seller, to keep on top of changing customer needs. Davidow spent the early years of his career in Hewlett-Packard's marketing department before moving to Intel, where he eventually rose to head the sales and marketing function. His thesis is that sellers sometimes lose track of buyers' needs, and he offers examples of what he calls marketing myopia:

"The static and dying industries of America are not the only ones suffering from marketing myopia. Many dynamic high-tech companies are afflicted with the same disease. Most of the mainframe computer companies never successfully made the transition to minicomputers, and most minicomputer companies missed out on PCs. In the semiconductor industry, a rash of new companies popped up to exploit exciting new market niches in semicustom and custom circuits just at the time when everyone thought the semiconductor business was too expensive to enter. Marketing myopia is a dangerous disease. It attacks those who are not constantly searching for better ways to serve their customers' needs. And it is easily contracted in rapidly changing environments" (Davidow, 1986, p.171).

I realize that you are not selling semiconductors or computer hardware, but the point applies to anyone who is selling anything, especially in today's ever changing market. Irv Margol, executive vice-president for management services at Security Pacific National Bank and a twenty-five-year veteran of human resources management, is one of the most insightful men I have ever known. When we were talking recently about marketing human resources services, he reminded me of the classic question: "If you were a line manager responsible for the achievement of certain financial and production goals, would you buy what you are selling?" If the answer is yes, the next question is why? Could you demonstrate that it would add value to your operation to buy what human resources is offering?

Winning by Letting Go

As hard as it may be to change your approach, give up a cherished belief, or abandon a central value, when the environment changes it's time to jettison your old ideas and attitudes.

The way you win is to let go of a method that worked in the old environment and adopt one that will work in the new market. This is hard to do. It is painful to admit that you are wasting your time with an approach that is no longer functional. That's very similar to dealing with a personal tragedy, where individuals go through the stages of denial, anger, and acceptance of the inevitable.

In order to get on with your life you have to accept that circumstances change. Your market has changed. The old, captive market is gone. It died a couple of years ago. You have to adopt new attitudes and practices to deal with the new market environment.

People often start or join a business because they have fallen in love with a product or service. Sometimes the infatuation developed from a hobby. It's great to enjoy a hobby, but it's often suicidal to try to make a living at it. Human resources people get infatuated with their professional tools also. For all our complaining we really love our profession. We do derive a great deal of satisfaction from the good that we do for our organizations and the people who work in them. But sometimes we try to force our products and services onto our customers. For example, I know a manager who is an expert on the Hay compensation system. He has gone from company to company "Haying them." Although the Hay plan is an excellent compensation system, it may not be appropriate for every company at every stage of its life. That is an example of the inside-out approach I referred to in Chapter Five. It mistakenly focuses on products or services, not on the needs of the customer.

Mike Kami (1988) states that the inside-out method is built on "four deadly sins":

1. Complacency. Don't rock the boat. What was good enough in the past will be good enough in the future. Nothing ever really changes. The more things change, the more they stay the same. How many platitudes have you heard that are excuses for not wanting to deal with change?

I once worked for a man who called a staff meeting early one morning and told the assembled (and sleepy) staff, "The number one objective this year is to keep out of trouble." That certainly woke us up. We didn't even know we were in trouble. He wanted to maintain the status quo and instead aroused our anxiety.

2. Blindness. This is the failure to recognize change. Blindness may result from either ignorance of the marketplace or just plain stupidity. The "not-invented-here" syndrome is a classic example. There was a great line in an old Jimmy Stewart movie, *The Flight of the Phoenix*, that expresses this type of blindness very well. In the film, one of the characters said to another, "You act as though stupidity were a virtue." Unwillingness to see condemns us to being hit on the back of the head by high-velocity, low-flying changes.

3. Megalomania. Kami calls this the "I-know-best syndrome." Unwillingness to accept the fact that no one knows best in all circumstances and at all times can lead a manager to try to shove his or her ideas down the throats of gagging customers. The result is predictable.

4. Greed. This is how Kami describes the short-term focus. Everything is sacrificed to current goals. Of all the inside-out sins, human resource managers probably commit this one the least. Most of you have a longer-term outlook than your customers. If anything, you spend too much of your time trying to convince them to adopt a longer-term perspective.

Moving with the Market

In *The Regis Touch*, Silicon Valley's resident marketing guru talks about recent market changes (McKenna, 1986). He argues that in today's world the traditional product-focused marketing program is an anachronism. It does no good to bombard already saturated customers with still more information to convince them that they should buy a product or service. Instead, he suggests three steps. First, understand your market. Accept it for whatever it is. This is the reality that you must deal with. Second, move with your market. Don't try to force it to come to you. The power of the market is always greater than the power of one marketer. Third, form relationships. While information is fleeting, relationships have a permanence that can be very powerful.

In this information-rich world, people might not remember what someone said yesterday, but they do remember what others do. John Nichols at Systematix devotes a lot of time to what he calls "front-end consensus building" before acting. He believes that it pays off to spend time and resources to understand his managers' needs and problems first. Then, when he works with them, they are together able to get it right the first time.

What Could Be. What was is no longer important. The pendulum will never swing back to its previous position. What will be, no one knows. There are too many possibilities to predict the future. The critical issue for any marketer, whether he is selling soap flakes, computers, hamburgers, or personnel programs, is What could be? The marketplace is not nearly as static today as it was in the 1950s and 1960s. It is dynamic, driven by the social, political, economic, and technological forces that I mentioned at the start of this book. Toffler (1970) probably said it as well as anyone when he claimed in *Future Shock* that change happens so quickly and relentlessly these days that what was truth yesterday is fiction today.

Dynamic markets are exciting. They offer endless possibilities because needs shift so rapidly. If you choose to look at today's marketplace as a source of opportunity, you can become very excited over it. This kind of emotion is stimulating. It can fuel your motivation and give you enthusiasm for selling your product and perseverance in the face of rejection. But emotion can also mislead you. If you fall in love with your products, you may fail to see the market. You must approach and study your market objectively and dispassionately in order to truly understand it.

The Market as an Asset. Accountants treat products in inventory as assets. Inventory to me is a liability. When I have software packages on my shelves, I don't look at them as an asset. They are an expense that needs to be turned into revenue.

To me, the market is an asset. In the strictest accounting sense you might not classify your market as an asset because you don't own it. Nevertheless, I consider my markets to be assets because of the opportunity that they represent for me. An asset is something of value and the market certainly represents value to me. This notion may clash with generally accepted accounting principles, but we are not trying to become CPAs. The market-asset image allows me to feel very positive about my market. Your market—the employees and managers of your organization—can be an asset or a liability depending on how you look at it. If you understand it and are well positioned within it, the market clearly has value for you. Without it, you are out of business.

It is through understanding the many facets of your market and working with it in functional, constructive ways that you realize value both for yourself and for your customers. You are both caught in the same market. What benefits your customers benefits you. So let's look at your market segment.

Researching Your Market. A market is not a monolith. It has many segments and niches. The questions for you to answer are: How is your market segmented? Who are the various customers? What needs and expectations do they have that you can fulfill? Which needs are shared and which are unique to each customer?

There are many ways of finding the answers to these questions. You can interview people one at a time. This is one of the best methods because it gives you maximum control of the research. You have the opportunity to ask questions and to watch for nonverbal as well as verbal clues. You can survey whole groups or representative samples. A well-constructed survey can yield a lot of useful data. Just be careful that you don't ask leading questions. Also, don't ask people to respond to questions that they are not qualified to answer. For example, it is usually not effective to give people a list of programs or services and ask them to pick the ones that they want or need. Often they can't really do that because they don't know what each choice implies. Remember, they don't want your products anyway. They want to have their needs satisfied, and sometimes they are simply unable to select the product that will achieve this. A third common method is to use focus groups. These are becoming increasingly popular among researchers, although advertisers have used this method for years. It does have certain drawbacks in that some people may find themselves dominated by other members of the group. They may go along rather than confront more vocal individuals. Later, they became dissatisfied because they didn't get what they wanted. It doesn't matter that it is their own fault. You still have an unhappy customer.

No matter which method or combination of methods you use, the objective is to isolate customers according to their interests, needs, and expectations. A handy way to tabulate the data is to group customers by their needs, either manually or on a computer. Where the need or expectation is unique, that person or group becomes a separate file. Into this file you put information that you gather from various sources about the idiosyncrasies of the individual or the group. Over time you will develop a history of needs and solutions that will give you solid insights into each customer. This is exactly what effective sales-people do. They build customer files. Later, when we talk about how to sell your programs, you will see how critical this information is to making a successful sale.

Grouping Your Customers. Most of your customers can be classi-fied into groups. One of your principal individual customers is the chief executive officer of your organization. Years ago, the chairman of a bank I worked for admonished me because I hadn't served one of his requests promptly. He said in a very nice, fatherly way, "Jac, you really ought to take better care of me. I am, after all, the chairman of the board." Of course, he was absolutely right.

There are other individuals to whom you must pay special attention. These might be department heads, general managers, or certain high-powered professionals. So, this is one market segment: special individuals.

Customer groups can be defined by level — for example, top managers, middle managers, first-level supervisors, and rank-and-file employees. Groups can also be defined by func-tion: the accounting department, manufacturing, research and development, sales, field service, the loan department in a bank, the nurses in a large hospital, or the actuaries in an insurance company. There are external customers such as community groups, regulatory agencies, and even vendors who are trying to sell you a service or consultants who are helping you complete a project. All of them depend on you for something, and they all have something of value to give you in return.

Building Your Marketing Strategy

Once you have assembled sufficient data to develop a marketing strategy, you can start to pull together data from your customer files and prepare a marketing strategy worksheet. The worksheet, be it a piece of paper or a computer file, is an outline of the key market opportunities and obligations that you wish to address. But you might be wondering how the word *obligation* got into a discussion of marketing. In the free market the only obligation you have is to survive. In the marketplace we are talking about, human resources must service certain needs of its customers within the organization. There is no question of ignoring some needs or expectations. The only issue is one of priority or timing.

Exhibit 6 is a sample Customer Analysis Worksheet. On it, you can list all your major customers, their needs and expectations, and the priority you assign to each.

This form is merely a guide. You will probably want more space for each customer or customer group. So, design a form that suits your needs, and then try to analyze all the needs and expectations that your customers have of you. If you are stuck, recall what it is that people in each group come to talk to you about. What interests, needs, and expectations do they mention? You will probably come up with a lot of generalizations—for example, information and communication, pay and benefits, support, advice, training, counseling, recruiting, and so forth. That is fine. In the next step you will convert these general needs into specific marketing strategies. For now, just jot down on the form all the issues that you can think of.

Once your worksheet is filled in, you will have a general picture of your current "market drivers." Market drivers are your

Exhibit 6. Customer Analysis Worksheet.

List all major expectations or needs that each customer has where human resources products and services can be applied.

Customers	*Expectations or Needs*
Chief executive officer	
Top management	
Mid management	
First-line supervision	
All employees	
Departments	
Individuals	
Outsiders	
Others	

key customers and their needs, that is, the opportunities that you can exploit through your products and services. In using the term *exploit* here, I am not suggesting that you try to serve only your own ends. I am thinking instead of the dictionary's primary definition of the term: "to turn to practical account." It is through the timely and effective servicing of these key customer needs that you will both contribute to the organization's goals and find success for yourself.

As you may recall, the chemical industry was being whip-sawed by unstable market forces in the early 1980s. Change was constant. Top management of a British chemical company needed to know what the skill and experience base of its work force looked like before it could make strategic moves. The company's managers did not have a clear picture of their work force. The information technology staff stepped in and ran a study that yielded future staff demand estimates from manage-ment. It matched these estimates against a computerized skill base. These profiles allowed the staff to predict that there would be shortages in certain skill areas. As a result, managers ordered appropriate recruitment, training, or retraining. In this way a high-priority need, in fact a survival imperative, was solved through market- and customer-need analysis.

Your worksheet will yield a list of needs that should be prioritized. Since you can't do everything at once, you have to give some needs precedence over others. This is where your market strategy starts to emerge. You must make decisions about who is going to be served first and with what programs.

Before you start prioritizing, ask yourself this question: What is the need behind the product or service? No one wants a benefit program, per se. They want the value or personal benefit that the program will give them. People don't want wages or salaries. They want the financial security, status, and other bene-fits that their pay represents. When you think about it, isn't a need often shrouded by some traditional request for a program? What happens is that the manager, who is an amateur when it comes to human resources services, senses a problem or oppor-tunity. He or she diagnoses the problem and decides that human resources program X is the solution. But the manager may not in fact select the right program for that problem. Your responsi-bility, as the professional human resources practitioner, is to ask questions until you either confirm or change the diagnosis. You are looking for the illness that the symptom sometimes covers.

You can prioritize within a category. That is, if an indi-vidual or a group has several needs, you can simply compare these needs to one another and decide which are the most important. Or, you can list all the items and then prioritize the total picture. The second method usually works better. The combinations and sequences grow geometrically as the number of needs and expectations grows. The process yields a fairly representative, although static, picture of your market. It is sort of a snapshot in time. However, the market is dynamic. You can't turn it on, work one issue, and turn it back off. While you are attending to one customer, others will be tapping their feet impatiently waiting their turn. You can run yourself ragged trying to respond to all customers every time they ring your bell. Pretty soon you will look like, and be treated like, Pavlov's dog. You stand a much better chance of serving many customers effectively while keeping your stress level under control if you work from a strategy. This prioritizing method will help you continually monitor your situation. Without it you can lose track of which customer should be served next. And if you start to act confused, your customers will sooner or later lose confidence in you and look for other vendors to satisfy their needs.

Market analysis should yield a clear picture of your playing field. When it is conducted in an orderly, unhurried manner, it will disclose what your market looks like, who the drivers are, and what you should do in what order. In other words, this kind of analysis will allow you to approach your market like a professional marketer. You will greatly enhance your chances of effectively serving your customers. You will know what the market looked like when you started out. When new issues surface, you will quickly become aware of them because they will change your overall picture of the market. This will allow you to be more proactive and responsive in serving your customers.

Exhibit 7 gives an example of the Market Opportunity Summary. This form, or a variation of it, can be used to pull together the many items that you identified on your Customer Analysis Worksheet. By now, you have accomplished three basic tasks. You have identified your customers, each of whom represents a market segment or niche. You have brainstormed all the items in their areas that relate to your services, and this has provided you with a description of your market opportunities. Then, you have looked at all the major items and asked yourself what your customers really want or need.

Exhibit 7. Market Opportunity Summary.

List all customers in the left-hand column. With a short sentence, describe their need/your opportunity in the center column. Prioritize the items as high, medium, or low.

Customer	Need/Opportunity	Priority
Chief executive officer		
Top management		
Mid management		
First-line supervision		
All employees		
Departments		
Individuals		
Outsiders		
Others		

You can't get the answers to these questions while sitting in the human resources department talking to your colleagues. John Stapleton of International Minerals and Chemicals tells his people that they have to get out into their organizations and find out why managers are doing what they're doing and asking what they're asking. John describes it as locating the business needs. "This is how you add value," he explains.

I asked Irv Margol (of Security Pacific National Bank) what he tells people who join his human resources staff about preparing themselves to be effective marketers within the bank. His comments carried the same message as John's. "Before you do anything, learn how the function that you're going to service works. Where do they get their customers? What are the customers' needs and demands? You need to talk about their business, not your old employer's world. Bridge the gap between yourself and them by learning their vernacular. Get a copy of the business plan. Learn how they make and spend money. See that staff functions are an expense item. When you feel you are comfortable with all that, then you can talk in a useful manner with your clients. But don't ask them what their problems are. They might be doing great and would resent the question. Instead, talk about what is working for them. Find out how you can institutionalize the good things they are doing. Ask them how come it's working well in one area but not in another. They know. Now, you have a target of opportunity where you can go in and add value to their operation. Finally, involve others. Today's problems are complex. Many minds are better than one, so bring together several types of people so that the solution will be the best possible. Ownership will develop and self-interest will be eliminated."

To return to the Market Opportunity Summary (Exhibit 7), it is time to prioritize. For each customer, you should describe in a short sentence what the opportunity or obligation is. This goes into the center column (Need/Opportunity) of the summary. Finally, in the right-hand column you should indicate the priority of each item. You will then have a comprehensive and specific picture of your market in terms of what to go after first.

This exercise tells you where your opportunities and obligations lie. The next question will be, How capable and prepared are you to handle them? The assessment phase coming up in the next chapter will help answer that.

The Marketing Lesson

Market analysis is critically important in a marketplace that is changing as rapidly as yours probably is. You might think that it doesn't make any sense and is indeed a waste of time to try to research a moving target. On the contrary, it is because the target is so elusive that you must study it.

Only by understanding as much as you can about the basic driving forces of your marketplace can you hope to keep up with it. If you have only a vague idea of what is going on, you will be unable to interpret the changes that occur. You will constantly chase shadows and fads because you have no basis for separating the important from the unimportant. Importance will be a question of who is putting the most pressure on you. Even though you may have a long history with your organization, if you don't stop to analyze how your market is changing, you probably won't be around long enough to explain it to someone else. But if you do pause and think, you will become an indispensable member of the team.

At MCI Communications marketing is the driving force. Bob Levit and his associates run the human resources function with a business and marketing perspective. They see themselves as value-adding contributors in a highly competitive marketplace. They have reinforced that vision to the point that the staff now talks about it as though it were second nature.

The number one strategic issue at MCI is to double its market share in four years. The company believes that it can change the business of telecommunications. Before you write that off as bravado, remember that it was MCI's chairman, W. G. McGowan, who took on AT&T almost singlehandedly in the late 1970s when it was America's biggest monopoly.

I asked Bob and his colleague Mitra Chappell how human resources development fits into that ambitious goal. Their answer was, by providing an environment in which people can think and act independently. They are supporting an individualistic culture of self-initiating risk takers who focus on results and achievement. That is their market—the culture of MCI. Human resources intends to be the champion of that culture, maintaining the heritage while the company continues to grow. All administrative and development programs will try to reinforce that vision. Human resources programs will focus on the specific skills and attitudes that have been identified as

MCI's competitive edge. My sense is that this is an organization that is steadily moving ahead, while some of the other telecommunications companies are still struggling to adopt a competitive culture.

One of the most frequent questions I'm asked is how do you lead a department to change its relationship to its market. The answer is: one step at a time. Successful delivery of one program often opens the door to other opportunities. Time after time I have seen human resources professionals take over departments that for the most part were not respected within their organizations. They built credibility and opened doors by selecting a problem that had a high priority and then fixing it. When they showed that they could fix one problem, people gave them opportunities to fix others. Having demonstrated their competence over time, they were eventually given a place on the management team.

Examples of this are endless. Let me give you just one.

While interviewing for the job of human resources manager in a data services company in the Midwest, the applicant was repeatedly told that the department had developed a reputation for being unable to deliver needed services. The man recognized that credibility was the first order of business. So long as the department was viewed negatively, it would be unable to make any significant contributions.

His first act was to change the name of the department from personnel to human resources. He then made a tour of the company, talking with people at all levels and looking for an important problem that he could undertake to solve. Keep in mind that throughout this research phase he still had to perform the basic administrative obligations of the department. After a while, he isolated a number of issues that most people agreed needed attention. Eventually, he settled on the compensation plan. Although it was more complex than some of the other opportunities, he recognized that everyone is always interested in the question of pay.

Rather than design a new pay plan, the manager designed a new process for compensation. He took a very simple plan and pulled together task forces for the exempt and nonexempt levels. Despite the fact that people didn't yet trust the human resources function, they did want to get their oar in when it came to talking about pay. It was easy to get the people he wanted on the task forces. From there on it was simply a matter of doing his homework thoroughly before each task force meeting. The groups met and hammered out pay policy under his subtle but expert guidance. When the new compensation plan was finally implemented, it was a great success. The manager had won the skeptics over by coming to understand their needs and demonstrating his ability to lead.

At the end of six months he ran a simple attitude survey and found that most people felt the pay policy and pay levels were fair. Naturally, he reported the results to management, along with financial ratios which showed that compensation as a percentage of operating expense was down slightly. In every direction that he looked, he found a satisfied customer.

This positive publicity began to change the image of the department. On the basis of that one successful program, he was able to gain the confidence of both management and employees. He followed it up by proposing a management training program that would help solve some operating problems. Management supported this initiative and gave him the resources to try it. Using a marketing approach, he had made the first critical sale that, in turn, made it possible for him to introduce other programs.

Conclusion

Markets have segments. Your market is no different. There are some needs common to all employees from the chief executive officer down to the newest recruit. For example, everyone needs to be paid, but the structure of the compensation package is vastly different than that of the operatives. Everyone needs information, but different groups need different kinds of information if they are to do their job. Customers have expectations of the human resources function. Some expectations can and should be serviced, while others may appropriately be transferred to other entities.

The best way to serve a customer in an organization is to focus on the effects of your programs, not on the programs themselves. What types of benefits do they produce for different types of customers? Don't ask a person what he or she wants in the way of human resources programs. The most effective way to serve your customers is to ask them what they are trying to achieve. Then you, as the human resources professional, should decide what you have to offer that will help the customers achieve their objectives. Consider what happens when you go to a doctor. He or she does not show you a list of treatments and ask which one you would like. The doctor first diagnoses the problem and then prescribes the remedy that will be most efficacious. You, as a professional, should proceed in the same way. People depend on you to tell them how and where human resources can be effective. I learned that years ago when I went to work for a new company. I asked the chief executive what he wanted from the human resources department. He said, "You tell me. You are supposed to be the expert."

People in marketing and sales always seem very energetic and positive. It isn't just because they are paid better than employees in some other functions, although that doesn't hurt. It is also because they work on the revenue-generating side of the business.

Staff departments spend a lot of their time thinking about how they can keep expenses down. The problem with this is that as they work harder to squeeze another ounce of yield out of their people and equipment, the amount of gain from each unit spent decreases. They quickly reach the point of diminishing returns. Besides, they will never drive the expense level down to zero.

On the other side, marketing people think mostly about how they can sell more. And they can never outsell their market. Their world is, practically speaking, limitless. They can always justify spending resources because they can project a return on the investment. Marketing never has to justify its existence.

The moral of the story is simple: It is a lot more fun to be a value-adding function than to be a cost-cutter. When you focus on customer needs rather than on human resources products, you increase your chances for success, recognition, and having some fun in the process.

> Business makes a grave mistake when it perceives itself as producing products rather than satisfying customer needs.
>
> Theodore Levitt

References

Davidow, W. H. *Marketing High Technology*. New York: Free Press, 1986.

Kami, M. *Trigger Points*. New York: McGraw-Hill, 1988.

McKenna, R. *The Regis Touch*. Reading, Mass.: Addison-Wesley, 1986.

Ries, A., and Trout, J. *Bottom-Up Marketing*. New York: McGraw-Hill, 1989.

Toffler, A. *Future Shock*. New York: Random House, 1970.

Case Studies — Chapter Seven

Baptist Medical Centers
Birmingham, Alabama
(From discussions with Vic Buzachero, vice-president of human
resources)

Marketing is a top priority for the human resources group at the Baptist Medical Centers (BMC) of Birmingham, Alabama, a multiunit diversified health care corporation. The basic strategy employed by the group is to develop its people as a competitive advantage in the health care marketplace and thus to position the organization as the leading regional health care system in the South. This strategy directly links human resources efforts to the organization's mission and vision. It shifts the key human resources executive's emphasis from maintenance of human resources programs to developing the organization's employees.

The direct link to the execution of the organization's vision means that the human resources professionals join with line management in formulating and implementing strategy. All involvement is guided by the dominant orientation of the human resources group to be people centered and market driven. In other words, when working with line management, the human resources group begins with the assumption that people are the most volatile and potentially valuable resource that management has. Therefore, people must be at the center of all planning. Since human resources is market driven, its main customer is the line manager. With people as the product and management as the customer, the agenda for the human resources management team is to recognize people needs through the organizational needs and create goal congruence.

During the next five years, the following will be the key strategic issues facing both the organization and the human resources group:

- Declining market share in terms of patient days, admissions, and revenue

- Declining productivity, defined as the ratio of expenses to adjusted net operating revenue
- Being a technological leader

To meet these needs, the human resources group began by refining the Executive Development Program to have a double focus: to meet individual career aspirations and to meet the organization's strategic needs. The program begins with an extensive value orientation for all executives and moves through specific skill developments as defined through individual and organizational assessments. In addition, extensive computer training and computer-assisted instruction have been introduced in all divisions and at all levels.

To respond to a declining market, BMC has begun to emphasize sales. It first set up a guest relations program and has moved through service management to a focus on basic values. These values include compassionate care, innovation, performance, education, and research. Behaviors to illustrate each value are modeled and institutionalized in all human resources systems at BMC. This approach produced almost immediate results, and the organization began to see a reversal of its declining market share within two years. Additionally, the organization has begun to hire and develop salespeople who build relationships with physicians. This should lead to improvements in patient care and an increasing demand for BMC's services.

To attack the productivity issue, human resources has designed variable compensation programs for all levels of employees. Incentives create focus on key result areas, and innovative compensation programs have increased staffing flexibility and decreased fixed compensation costs.

Finally, development of the human resources staff is viewed as a typical business problem. The BMC human resources group attacks business problems by looking for solutions that generate revenue. The HR Executive Development Conference, designed principally for BMC staff, draws on nationally renowned speakers and is marketed to external non-health care personnel. This not only helps the conference pay for itself or even make a profit but also establishes a network of experts for the BMC group to draw upon as needed. Solutions coming out of the conference include a for-profit temporary employment agency, a travel agency, and a human resources consulting practice and management contracts.

To develop the human resources group to deliver business solutions, human resources executives must perform at levels above technical functionality. Currently, the human resources group's development is focused on the following subjects: (1) financial knowledge, (2) selling skills, (3) negotiation skills, and (4) product knowledge.

Each human resources director participates in the annual planning retreats, and the human resources executives are actively involved in the strategic planning process at the corporate and divisional levels.

Author's comment: BMC found itself on a downward slide. To halt and eventually reverse that trend, it had to take some drastic steps. The center's management decided to launch a strong marketing campaign. The human resources function, under Vic's leadership, did the same. In this case, however, the market was two dimensional. First, there was the standard market of human resources, namely, the organization. Vic then saw a second market outside the company. He found that he could sell his internal training conference to human resources personnel throughout the Southeast. He brought in speakers from outside the area and turned the program into an event.

This is the type of aggressive, creative action that is sometimes required. Twenty years ago when I was at Wells Fargo Bank in San Francisco I suggested that we market the bank's skills and facilities to the outside world. However, at that time, the bank's business was so good that no one wanted to do it. Within a few years, when the cost of the training center became a recognizable burden, the bank did begin to rent space to local schools for night classes. When times change, tactics also have to change.

Dorbyl Limited
Bedfordview, South Africa
(From discussions and material supplied by Edwin Vorster, group
manpower director)

Dorbyl is a diversified heavy manufacturing and engineering company located in Bedfordview, South Africa.* It
manufactures and markets automotive components, mining
equipment, and steel shapes, plate, and sheets and is engaged in
distribution of industrial and agricultural equipment. Dorbyl
employs nearly 24,000 people and is growing at about 20 percent per year with sales greater than two billion rand in 1988
(U.S. $1.00 is equal to 2.60 rand in July 1989).

In 1985, Edwin Vorster moved from Dorbyl's finance department to head the corporate human resources department.
Edwin does not take no for an answer. On the day of my last visit
with him at Dorbyl's headquarters outside of Johannesburg he
needed an overhead projector. After his secretary Paula failed to
find one that was not in use, Edwin took matters into his own
hands. He charged down the corridor from our meeting room
and minutes later returned with a projector which he had
"liberated" from another meeting.

In 1985, Edwin says there were twenty-seven people in the
corporate human resources department performing a personnel administration function. They were providing no leadership
and minimal operating support to line management. There was
little connection between that group of paper pushers and
company operations.

---

* Because of the situation in South Africa, some readers may feel it is
inappropriate to include an example from that country. In the author's
opinion, the business leadership of the Republic of South Africa (RSA) is one
of the most effective tools for reform. To many of South Africa's executives,
affirmative action is more than a concept. It is a competitive strategy. Many of
South Africa's corporations have instituted a variety of programs to help the
native population obtain positions and advance into management. Separate
black/white pay scales have been dissolved in these companies, and "people
of colour" are getting a chance. The author does not claim that there are not
many cases of discrimination in the RSA. However, the author believes that it
is better to support positive efforts than to inhibit them through isolation.

In Edwin's opinion, line management carries the primary responsibility for human resources. He believes that the corporate human resources group should do only those tasks and functions which the line cannot do. Based on my own observations, I would describe the function of the corporate human resources department at Dorbyl as strategic adviser to line management. But the department provides more than advice. It motivates line management to effectively manage the company's human assets. The department clearly serves much more than a processing function. The closest it comes to a processing role is in providing employee benefits by contracting with the insurance carrier to process claims. The payroll function is performed by the accounting department, and all central processing work is farmed out to contractors.

Edwin's view can be summarized as follows: we give advice to line management, but they are accountable to us when it comes to making investment decisions regarding the utilization of people. That position does not imply that Edwin's small group does not work hard to orchestrate the decision making. The corporate human resources staff consists of a half dozen people in the headquarters office who oversee benefits, labor relations, and manpower planning/development. There is another group of eleven people assigned to line divisions where they sit on the division's board of directors and act as advisers to the managing directors and their line executives. Within each of the divisions there is a line personnel staff. These line personnel people are generalists. Edwin advocates hiring specialists as needed for research, development, or consulting. His position is that in-house specialists become co-opted by the system and are not as free to generate the best solution as is an outsider.

Edwin's marketing of his concept was particularly intriguing. When I asked him how he sold it to top management his answer was characteristically direct and to the point. He said, "I told them that this is the best thing we can do for your business." What he proposed to do was reempower line management with the authority and ability to manage their own employees. In many companies corporate HR hoards authority, under the guise of keeping the company out of court. Edwin points out that if line managers can run a multimillion-rand division they can also learn how to manage their human assets. Furthermore, managing people in a country with huge skill shortages and highly sensitive social issues cannot be left to a group of corporate staff specialists who often have little knowledge of division-level operational imperatives and problems.

Corporate philosophy and general policies are supported through a mechanism of high-level committees. The purpose of the committees is to integrate the human issues with the financial and production decisions and to effectively transfer human asset management to the line executives.

There are four major vehicles by which manpower programs and decisions are formulated:

1. The Manpower Committee of the Board is composed of three members of Dorbyl's board of directors and Edwin Vorster. They meet quarterly to determine general directions for manpower management.
2. The Group Executive Directors Meeting is composed of the chief executive officer and chief financial officer of Dorbyl, the three executive directors of Dorbyl's three major lines of business, and Edwin. They meet weekly to review strategic data and issues.
3. The Managing Directors Meeting is composed of the ten line general managers and Edwin. They meet monthly to review and act on operating problems and plans.
4. The Division Manpower Focus Meetings are composed of the chief executive officer, the managing directors and their direct reports, and Edwin. The division management meets annually to present their manpower plan for the year, discuss the status of certain items, and review progress of the preceding year.

The top ten priorities for discussion in the 1988 focus meetings were organization structuring and development, succession planning, manpower sourcing and retention, manpower assessment, manpower utilization, training and development, remuneration management, industrial relations, manpower information systems, and employee benefits.

I had the opportunity to review some of the meeting books prepared by line and executive management for these meetings. A great deal of statistical analysis of employee-related issues was displayed on numerous graphs and tables. For example, absenteeism, overtime costs, staffing ratios, turnover, and manpower needs were integrated with business plans for the next three years. It is clear that over the past five years Edwin has been successful in turning over the management of human assets to the company rather than keeping it as the prerogative of the human resources department.

I have seldom seen elsewhere the total integration of human asset management and business management that Edwin has achieved in Dorbyl. He started marketing this idea at the top of the company with D. B. Mostert, group chief executive of Dorbyl Limited. Having gained Mr. Mostert's approval to test the change, Edwin then convinced two of the business units to try it. When the plan worked and other divisions saw that Mr. Mostert supported it, the rest of the managing directors wanted to become involved. Edwin recruited the best people he could find, whether they were line managers or human resources professionals, and made them the manpower planning directors on the board of each subsidiary company. Now every subsidiary has both a manpower person from the corporate level on its board and a personnel generalist who is the line manpower manager for the subsidiary. Control resides in the hands of the managing director. The corporate manpower person's job is to transform corporate philosophy into management practice. Edwin believes that his concept works because*he was able to sell this critical position to the board of each subsidiary.

The lesson in this case is that it is not difficult to sell even a radical change if you can show that there is a sound business reason for the change. When we try to market our ideas using only altruistic benefits as the selling points it is an uphill battle.

8

Assessing
the Human Resource Capacity
of the Organization

> I WILL STUDY and get ready and perhaps my chance will
> come.
>
> Abraham Lincoln

Will Pape, chief information officer for VeriFone, claims that success in today's marketplace requires people to be trilingual, that is, to have three distinct communicative capabilities. A person must first be technically competent. No matter whether he is a manager or an individual professional contributor, the person must be able to discuss the technology knowingly and carry out the tasks called for in his job description. Second, almost all professional jobs, and certainly all managerial positions, require interaction with other people. These others might be professional peers, subordinates, superiors, or outsiders such as vendors, customers, or community groups. Interpersonal skills are a prerequisite for getting along with others, influencing them, and persuading them to help you achieve your objectives. Finally, people have to be able to speak the language of business, which is numbers. Every kind of work is becoming increasingly complex and less visible as electronic technology takes the place of mechanics and physical labor. To understand what is needed, to plan and describe objectives so that anyone can understand them, to monitor progress and make reasoned, efficient mid-course corrections, and to recognize and evaluate outcomes and impacts, a person must be able to apply basic arithmetical functions and simple statistical analyses and be able to communicate by means of a numerical vocabulary.

210

Functional capacity is determined by the relative power of the positive and negative forces that exist in a given environment. Capability is not an absolute. It is an expression of the relationship of certain personal factors to relevant external factors. An individual's capacity to perform is more than just the sum of his talents, knowledge, and skills. Capability is dependent not only on an individual's competence but also on his objectives and the strength and direction of the strategic forces in his environment. Unlike the creation and communication of a vision, where the principal focus is internal, a capability analysis must also have an external focus. The individual must therefore understand not only himself but also his environment. Indeed, when the issue of capacity assessment is taken beyond the individual to an organizational function, it then becomes clear that the surrounding environment is a major influence on a group's ability to fulfill its potential and attain its goals.

There are two fundamental questions to be answered by a capacity assessment. One is, What are the key capabilities required to meet the function's objectives? The other question is, How will environmental forces support or inhibit the performance of the group? It is difficult to answer the first question without knowing the answer to the second one. Using an extreme example, if all the external forces were positive, the group would not need a great deal of assertiveness and persistence to achieve its goals. So, before thinking about what we can accomplish, we have to look at the organization in which we intend to operate.

Organizational Strategy and HR Capacity Requirements

Sometimes solutions can be found by asking indirect questions. That is, because organizations are systems of interrelated parts, it is possible to look at one area to find clues as to what is needed in another. This is the case with organizational strategy and capacity assessment. You are certainly aware that your company's strategic plan has a bearing on your objectives. These, in turn, point to the resources that you will require. Therefore, by asking some strategic questions, you should get clues as to the work you are going to have to do in support of the strategy. Only then should you ask yourself whether or not you have the human, financial, technological, and organizational resources to do that.

George Odiorne (1984, p. 269) provides a list of questions in his book on the strategic management of human resources that exemplify what I am suggesting:

1. Market Orientation. Are we market centered or technology centered? Do we make things for the sales department to sell, or do we find market opportunities and invent things to fit?

2. Service. How completely do we wish to follow up our product?

3. Top down or bottom up? Do we have the top management (board, etc.) come up with the numbers for sales and growth and work back from the numbers at lower levels? Or do we collect the bottom-up goals and cumulate them to find the corporate goals?

4. Indicators. What is the best indicator (or indicators) of total organization success? Dollar profit? Percent profit? Earnings per share? Return on investment? Return on gross assets? Market share?

5. Pricing. Are we a market skimmer? A price cutter? Are we in price competition or nonprice competition?

6. Ethics. Are we a "straight arrow" company, or do we consider ourselves "rough and tough" in dealing with competitors, suppliers, employers, customers?

7. Systems. Do we rely more on experience and personal know-how of managers or on systems such as computers and analytical models?

8. Incentives. Do we aim at sharing our profits and successes widely with employees, with just a few managers, or not at all?

9. Employee growth. Do we spend resources to grow our own people, or do we let them take care of that themselves and hire others from outside when a new demand for talent crops up?

10. Technology. Are we a basic inventor and exploiter

of our own research, or do we wait for others and assume a second-bite-of-the-apple approach to new technology?

11. Products. Are we a Cadillac, a medium-price, or a low-price product company, or perhaps all of them?

12. Compensation. Where do we wish to stand on employee compensation with respect to the community and competitive firms? Higher, the same, or lower?

13. Community relations. Are we a community leader, a middle-of-the-road citizen, or low profile and silent?

14. Government relations. Do we respond when required, do we permit some affirmative actions toward government, or do we assume positive leadership and work to affect government?

Questions 5 through 10 provide good examples of my point. There are clues in the answers to these questions that tell you what is central to your organization. The answers to those questions are important to human resources because they affect issues such as hiring, paying, employee and labor relations, training, and culture. Let's take them one at a time.

Pricing: This has implications for hiring and paying. A company that is a high-volume, low-price marketer tends to look for different types of skills in its salespeople than does a company that competes on quality rather than price. This is evident if you enter a discount department store right after shopping at Neiman-Marcus.

Ethics: Read the question under this heading very carefully. Doesn't it have numerous implications for employee and labor relations? Are you staffed to handle the ethical implications of your corporation's strategy?

Systems: This is clearly a cultural issue. It refers to your expectations of the human element versus the systems element. An organization that values personal know-how must train and psychologically support its people. By contrast, an organization that runs by the numbers will put its resources into hardware and software. This suggests a different kind of relationship of the company to the individual and of one employee to another. The implications of systems decisions are almost always far-reaching.

Incentives: This is a compensation and benefits issue. How is pay strategically used to stimulate performance?

Employee growth: Hiring, training, and career development are the issues here. Do you have the capacity to satisfy the organization's needs to develop its people? Situation number one above is a case spot on this point.

Technology: Another hiring issue comes up here. Basic applied research companies need different types of people than do second-source and knock-off manufacturers and distributors. This points to secondary questions about pay and training that I am sure have occurred to you already.

It should be obvious to you by now how all these elements are tied together. This further supports the view that human resources needs to be involved in the strategy formulation of your organization. The strategic business plan is your marching order. Once you have become familiar with it, you have to decide if you have the capacity to support it. Even if you cannot influence the strategy, at least you will be prepared to react to it before the organization tries to do something that requires human resources that are not available.

It is imperative in capacity assessment to look ahead. What is past cannot be recovered. The underlying question now is, What are the key organizational capabilities required for success? I'm speaking of the capabilities of both the organization and human resources. The strategy tells you where the organization wants to go. It is the responsibility of management to marshal the resources to get there. It is the job of human resources to guide as well as support the acquisition, maintenance, development, and application of the human assets. This then brings you to the basic question of how the key strategic imperatives of the organization match with the ability of human resources to support them. Now, we are talking about the strengths and limitations of human resources as they relate to the imperatives of the organization and to the external opportunities and threats that may impact the performance of human resources. This is capacity assessment.

Situation Analysis

Capacity assessment starts by acknowledging that you are part of a larger environment. Besides you and your staff, there are other forces in the environment that collectively might be called situational factors. Environmental factors and forces need to be identified, evaluated, and tracked to provide management with a notion of what is possible and what is required. This applies as much to the human resources department as it does to an entire enterprise. If you learn to understand your environmental factors, you may be able to develop a strategy or tactic that will change them in your favor. This means you may be able to proactively shape events in a way that benefits your function and your customers within the organization.

Environmental Scanning. The first of two steps in a situational analysis is the environmental scan. The environment can be divided into four factors and looked at internally and externally. There is the internal environment, which includes factors as they currently exist inside your department, and there are external factors that exist outside your department. The factor categories are the same; only their location is different. The factors are human, financial, technological, and organizational. Exhibit 8 shows a way of arraying them for analysis.

In each of those areas you would look for the factors that affect your ability to perform. Following are some examples of the types of factors that you would place in the various cells on the Internal side:

Human: Staff size, skills, aspirations, values, team spirit, experience, personalities, relationships, turnover rate, morale, motivational levels, and department leadership.

Financial: Size, flexibility, and source of budget; allocations or fees for services; expandability; current allocation among units within human resources; and pay levels.

Technology: Facilities and equipment, level of technology available, product quality, process efficiency, customer service requirements, and the HRIS.

Organizational: Work flow and work load; structure; ad-

Exhibit 8. Environmental Analysis.

List, without evaluating, all the current and foreseeable factors and forces
that should be noted for their possible impact on the strategic operation of
the human resources department. Consider the department as a whole and
its sections as the Internal and the organization as the External.

Internal	*External*
1. Human _____	_____
_____	_____
_____	_____
_____	_____
2. Financial _____	_____
_____	_____
_____	_____
_____	_____
3. Technological _____	_____
_____	_____
_____	_____
_____	_____
4. Organizational _____	_____
_____	_____
_____	_____
_____	_____

---

ministrative, operational, control, and reward systems; culture;
and promotional methods.

In the External column you would look at the same types
of factors, but in terms of the people, finances, technology, and
organizational issues of your customer — the organization — and
its surrounding environment. You could add a third column for
the outside world. But for simplicity of illustration, I have
lumped the two together. Keep in mind that the forms and
illustrations I am presenting are generalizations meant to give
you an idea of a concept or its expression. You have to apply the
knowledge and design forms, procedures, and systems that are
appropriate and useful in your own business.

Some of the factors in the external environment of the
organization and its world are:

Human: Line and staff personnel of the various functional groups; their abilities, experience, potential for growth, values, and relationships; corporate management style; cooperation; and philosophy. In addition, don't forget the relationship that exists between your people and the external employees and management staff.

Financial: Organizational profitability, cash-flow position, order backlogs, balance-sheet ratios, investor and analyst relations, tax situation, and financial leverage.

Technology: Type of business of the organization, quality control, inventory control, facilities and equipment, production capacity.

Organizational: Operating systems and span of control, communications lines and protocols, marketing and distribution systems, MIS, advertising, flexibility, and responsiveness.

You may disagree with my categorizations and that is fine. I don't worry too much about putting everything into the right slot. Just make sure that you have everything of consequence accounted for.

The environment external to the organization should also be considered. As I mentioned above, you can drop it into the External column or list it separately. In volatile times such as these you may want to view the environment outside the organization as a separate issue. In either case, there are at least seven categories of factors and forces that you will want to review.

1. Society: Shifts in customer needs and preferences, along with demographic trends in the population.
2. Government: Legislation and enforcement practices.
3. Economy: Interest rates, exchange rates, cost-of-living trends, national debt, and balance of trade.
4. Competitors: Changes in technology, new competitors, and pricing and product changes.
5. Suppliers: New vendors, changes in supply channels, and costs of materials.
6. Market: Product obsolescence and the opening of new markets.
7. Technology: Changes in production methods, information-

handling methods, and equipment available in the marketplace.

If this process is conducted as a group exercise, you will develop some insights into the views that your staff has of your department and of the organization in which it resides. Quite often their perspective will be different from yours. That is as it should be. They are not standing in the same place as you are. Welcome their different views. They can provide a great learning experience if you remain open to them.

Factor Evaluation. This is the second step in situation analysis. All the factors should be reviewed and assessed from the standpoint of their positive or negative force or power. A factor can fall into one of four categories. If it is internal, it will be either a strength or a limitation. If it is external, it will be either an opportunity or a threat. Of course, any factor has the potential to be either positive or negative. The question is what is the current state of each one. Your objective will be to move as many factors as possible from the negative side to the positive, or at least to neutralize the negative ones. If you can't figure out which side a factor falls on, this may mean that it is not important at the moment.

Definitions of the four evaluations are as follows:

Strength: A capability or resource that a department can apply to achieve its objectives and carry out its plan.

Limitation: A defect, weakness, or fault that could keep the department from meeting its objectives or plan.

Opportunity: Any positive condition, individual, or situation—often a trend, change, or undiscovered need—that supports a demand for a product or service that the human resources department can deliver effectively.

Threat: Any unfavorable condition, individual, or situation that could be a barrier, a problem, or a potential danger to the department's environment or staff.

Exhibit 9 provides a form that can be used to categorize each factor.

One way to assess the leadership of a function is to see if it

Exhibit 9. Factor Evaluation Forms.

Assume a given situation and consider each factor and force listed in the two environments in Exhibit 8. Place each relevant item in one of the four categories below as they relate to the situation you have in mind.

Strength	*Limitation*
_____	_____
_____	_____
_____	_____
_____	_____
_____	_____
_____	_____

Opportunity	*Threat*
_____	_____
_____	_____
_____	_____
_____	_____
_____	_____
_____	_____

is capable of transforming negative factors into positives. If there are skill deficiencies, budget overruns, technology gaps, or organizational blocks, what is the department's leadership doing about it? A large part of managerial and, for that matter, professional competence has to do with problem solving. The winners are those who find a way to turn apparent problems into opportunities, to diffuse threats, and to overcome limitations. The losers are the ones who complain about their lack of support.

How to Solve Capacity Shortfalls

The major complaint that I have heard from close to 15,000 human resources people is "I don't have enough _____!" You fill in the blank: people, money, space, equipment, power, credibility? As I pointed out above, the winners don't complain

much, they just set out to get what they need. The following
examples—one from England, the other from the United
States—show how two different groups, faced with a deficiency,
went after the resources that they needed.

Datastream International. In June 1986, this British information
services company hired its first training professional. At that
time, it had 386 employees. It was a fast-growth, technology-
driven business whose employees required more than the normal amount of training. By January 1989, the number of employees had risen to 620 as a result of growth and acquisition.
Consider Table 7, which was presented by Craig McCoy, senior
training executive, to the human resources manager.

A supporting and amplifying narrative detailed the level
of training provided; for example, 449 events had been presented or coordinated by one person in one year! Clearly, no
attention could be paid to quality. Budget and facilities have
improved, but there is still inadequate staff to optimize the
department's resources.

The narrative concluded by emphasizing the penny-wise,
pound-foolish philosophy of running training programs in this
fashion. A proposal was made to hire a junior trainer. The cost
of a staff trainer would be offset by a reduction in the funds
currently being spent on outside trainer-consultants.

The package was submitted to senior management. Upon
receiving an initial response from management, human resources prepared a follow-up that addressed the managing director's specific questions. It detailed the direct cost savings,
which amount to over £9,600. It also pointed out the lost opportunities and poorer quality that result when it is not possible to
properly prepare and deliver training. Twelve training courses
and their costs were displayed. By this point it had become clear
that it made good business sense to invest in the junior trainer.
There was really no choice for management except to approve
the recommendation, and it did.

VeriFone. A leader in the transaction automation industry, this is
another fast-growing company determined to run "lean and

Table 7. Analysis of Training Requirements.

Indicator/Phenomenon	Market Conditions	Impact
Actual establishment	386 in June 1986 620 in January 1989	Training needs of about 250 extra staff to be met (that is, 60% increase in customer base)
Number of senior posts filled (directors, managers, asst. managers, and equivalent)	50 in June 1986 89 in January 1989	Nearly 40 new managerial posts created, requiring significant management development and training input and support
Age profile	Over 75% of staff aged under 35 32 of 61 managers aged under 35	Predominantly young, inexperienced staff and management requiring significant training
Education profile	Nearly 50% of managers are not university graduates	Several implications: 1. Their powers of analytical reasoning have not been developed through education. 2. Knowledge of field has not been deepened by intensive education. 3. We may have a pool of managers with limited long-term potential and already struggling.
Environmental changes since 1986	Deregulation of stock exchange	Need to provide wider and increasingly sophisicated market with new services
	Black Monday	Increased client problems and difficulty in maintaining growth
	(Corporate parent) impact	1. Need to adopt corporate P&Ps and upgrade some of our lesser systems 2. Need to control costs in line with corporate targets, requiring better resource management
	Takeover	Challenge of managing a new business, adopting our structure, and increasing people 'management skills of our senior management
	Technological/strategic changes; for example, 24-hour-day globalization, new software, competition	Increased need for technical training to cope with new technology and procedures
Overall		Significant increase in the need for all types of training support

mean" as it expands. The business is spread across the United States in a number of relatively small sales and service offices, and it also has several overseas locations. Office services, which include receptionist/clerical/telephones, procurement, facilities management, finance, and human resources, are under the supervision of an office manager. These managers found themselves spending up to 40 percent of their time performing clerical and even janitorial duties as backup to the small administrative staff. They were extremely frustrated and felt undervalued and underappreciated. They had repeatedly complained to management about being overworked and having to spend their time on tasks of little apparent consequence. There was no time to use their experience and skills to carry out the value-adding functions for which they were qualified and supposedly had been hired.

As an example of the negative paybacks from this arrangement, the office managers seldom had time for budget analysis and inventory management. I'm certain the irony is not lost on you. Cost control, a key element in the senior management's "lean and mean" strategy, was impossible under these circumstances. Instead, the office managers were spending their time running copies for line managers, handling the call director at the reception desk, taking out the trash, and coping with other nonmanagerial demands. Although they were proud of the effort they were putting out for the company, they were angry and frustrated at their inability to do the work that they knew needed to be done to cut costs and add value to the company.

While working with them on a performance measurement system, I became acutely aware of their feelings of hopelessness. After a long discussion of the problem and their feelings, I asked them what they were not doing that would add value. That is, if they could get rid of some of the clerical work, what would they do that would help the company achieve its objectives? They quickly went through a list of activities. I asked them what concrete dollar value would accrue from doing these tasks. The following is a sketch of their replies:

- Budget analysis: cost control; projecting overruns so that additional costs can be avoided

- Machine maintenance: establishing and monitoring a schedule of preventative maintenance and thus helping to eliminate costly and untimely breakdowns
- Equipment research: better purchasing decisions yielding better prices and the most appropriate equipment
- Physical inventory: waste management to reduce expense and instill cost consciousness in employees
- Vendor research: choosing the best vendor and thus increasing the chances of good service as well as good prices
- Space planning: better space utilization, improved employee morale, and less need to move people and expand into more square footage
- Fixed assets management: security, safety, control, and forward planning
- Policies and procedures: clarity for supervisors and employees as a way of saving time, reducing confusion, and showing everyone that management is working at equity and simplicity

As a result of this discussion, the office managers realized that they could approach senior management from a business manager standpoint rather than as beggars. This revelation totally changed their outlook. At the time of this writing, they are working with their supervisor, Kay Tokunaga, the director of administration, to prepare a cost-benefit analysis that shows how their function is wasting rather than saving money. Some people would hesitate to present this kind of proposal to management. However, these staff members, who are all women ranging in age from their late twenties to their mid fifties, have enough confidence in their case to submit it to the corporate vice-president for administration. Their proposal will be presented as a return-on-investment analysis meant to demonstrate that current practices run counter to the organization's goal achievement programs. In my view, only the most nearsighted and obstinate of executives would be able to deny the value of their proposal. It will be clearly documented in their proposal that each day that management fails to respond to their needs, the company will be losing money and missing opportunities. I have met their boss, and while he is very cost-conscious, he knows value when he sees it. He will certainly recognize the payback for acting on their proposal.

Qualitative Analysis Techniques

There are a number of useful analytical techniques for making strategic decisions. For example, there are various quantitative methods, and I will address these in greater detail in Chapter Ten. Qualitative methods also play a part in providing fresh insights. Gap analysis is commonly used in strategic planning. It helps the analyst see the difference between what an organization wants to achieve and where the current momentum is likely to take it. Human resources planners frequently apply it in making manpower projections. In this chapter, however, I will focus on life cycle profiling, which can yield valuable insights when applied to current human resources programs.

Every product or service has a life cycle. Knowing where your major products and services are in their cycle is a prerequisite to allocation and optimization of resources. Most managers do a decent enough job of getting a new program off the ground and into the marketplace. But some then make the mistake of forgetting that nothing lasts forever. Compensation and benefit programs must be modified or even replaced as conditions change. Training programs come, and should go, as customer needs change. Recruiting strategies and campaigns shift with the labor market. Employee relations services are instituted and dropped as the employee population ages or governmental regulations change. The alert manager keeps an eye out for change. The life cycle profile should be used every year or so to determine the position of each major program that human resources is running. This is an easy method to implement, and it yields the insights needed to efficiently allocate resources. Managers who use this method often find that they can release resources from one program for utilization in another, thereby avoiding the need to prepare a request for additional staff or equipment.

Life Cycle Method

Most products and services have four stages or phases to their life cycle: the introductory, growth, maturity, and decline phases. Table 8 shows the four phases and the resource commitments that each requires.

This table will make sense if you keep in mind the human resources concept that we have been using. Your department must carry out the same functions as any other business. There is research and development activity even if you don't have a section called that. Many of the initiatives that we discussed in earlier chapters are actually research activities. There is also a finance entity. It is called your budget. From this you draw funds to develop and conduct your programs. There is a marketing activity that is supposed to promote cooperation and participation in your programs. There is a production activity to ensure that prototype services are put into production and delivered to the customers within the organization. And, yes, there is a personnel activity by which people in human resources are assigned responsibilities in one of the above activities. You may think that this is an interesting but impractical model. But I know of several human resources departments that are organized exactly along these lines. The names of the functions even coincide with this concept. You may have noticed if you read the Swiss Bank case study at the end of Chapter Six that Mike Mitchell has organized his group in this way with great success.

Let's look at the model with an eye toward how resources are assigned and withdrawn during each phase of the life cycle. The introductory phase is characterized by a heavy commitment to designing, building, publicizing, launching, and supporting the new program. A relatively large amount of your best resources must be expended to get the program off to a strong start. Experienced staff are assigned to this crucial phase. It wouldn't make sense to put a junior staffer in charge of a major program. The risk would be too high. During the introductory phase the less experienced must follow the lead of the senior staff.

In the growth phase, a flexible attitude is maintained so

Table 8. Phases and Resource Allocations During the Life Cycle.

Function	Introduction	Growth	Maturity	Decline
Personnel	Assign senior staff to the development and initial delivery stages.	Begin to train junior staff to deliver the program.	Phase in junior staff and reassign senior staff to new projects.	Maintain skeleton staff support.
Finance	Allocate funds to cover design, development, and marketing expenses.	Continue support as needed or until program becomes self-sustaining.	Allocate funds to developing custom versions or special features.	Stop spending; liquidate unused resources.
Research and development	Design first version and modify based on test feedback.	Monitor application, research-enhanced versions, and new products.	Design special features and begin to shift resources to develop new products.	Withdraw all resources and support.
Marketing	Begin publicity, develop interest in program, and gain acceptance.	Continue to promote by reporting results with stories of use and success.	Offer customized versions, special features, or discount pricing.	Phase out support and shift to new products and services.
Production	Conduct test version and rework based on revised design.	Continue to deliver standard version with minor changes based on user feedback.	Reduce production costs for standard version; add custom or special features.	Begin to shift resources to build and deliver new programs.

that resources can be directed quickly to serve unforeseeable needs. It is difficult to anticipate what might happen with a new program. So, it is necessary to keep an eye out for unexpected bugs in the system. Also, this may be the time to begin to move the juniors up into positions of more responsibility. The senior staff members are still in charge, but the junior takes a more active and visible role. How fast this occurs is a function of the complexity of the program and the ability of the junior. This is also the time to look at other functions. Their role is probably changing too. As a program grows, it usually gathers support from customers and accordingly requires the expenditure of fewer resources.

When the program reaches maturity, the junior staff members take over and the more experienced people can be reassigned to new duties. Redeployment is the hallmark of this phase. Programs become rather predictable at this stage, and controls can be put in place to reduce operating costs and increase efficiency. I run into people all the time who have been in charge of a program from its inception well into its declining phase. In most cases they should long ago have been reassigned. New projects keep people fresh, young in spirit, and motivated. I know that some employees get into ruts and after a while become too lazy to budge. The point is, don't let them become too comfortable. Sooner rather than later those staffers will become obsolete and have to be moved out or put into a job with no status or significance to ride out the years until retirement.

The declining phase is characterized by gradual withdrawal of all support as demand for the program fades. The program will eventually be closed down, and the only role to be played now is that of a caretaker or maybe an undertaker. Close it up. Turn your attention and resources to something of greater value. There are times, of course, when a program is remodeled, gets a face lift, so to speak, and is then relaunched in a new improved form. In that case, the assignment of resources is dictated by the complexity of the modifications to be made. It is like a new program.

At Seiko Instruments in Japan, Ako Ue is the general manager of the personnel and labor relations department.

When Seiko introduced factory automation, Ako realized that his function had to respond by refocusing its efforts. As a result of the automation project, Seiko was able to produce more with a smaller labor force. Some of personnel's traditional programs were now obsolete. Instead of continuing to train factory workers to run the old system, personnel had to retrain them as electrical technicians or as salespersons. Concurrently, the recruitment function revamped its standard hiring programs and designed a campaign to hire a large number of engineers to staff the new factory.

In another direction, Seiko is on the way to becoming a global company. This will mean a significant increase in overseas operations. But the company is facing a shortage of bilingual managers who can function in a cross-cultural environment. The personnel department is therefore formulating a strategy around this key management issue. A career development program is being designed to ready people for overseas assignment. In this way Ako's staff is showing it has the capacity to serve changing needs quickly.

Restructuring and Resizing Human Resources

In most cases, a capacity assessment will uncover the need for some degree of change. From the middle of the last decade through the end of the 1980s, downsizing and decentralizing have become regular occurrences for human resources departments. Not long ago I encountered a case in which a major U.S. corporation had decided to cut its human resources function. The president asked for a plan to reduce it by 50 percent! It is clear that he wanted to get the attention of that department, and he did. Now, negotiations and plans are under way to make some type of substantive change. What will happen is anyone's guess at this stage. The larger question is, Isn't there a better way to go about structuring human resources than this cyclical buildup and cutback method that we currently use? Peter Drucker once said that judging from the evidence, it was the job of every staff department manager to build the largest staff possible. His facetious comment was based on the reward system in place during the 1960s and 1970s: the larger the staff, the bigger the paycheck.

Stan Davis makes a strong case for a different approach to staff sizing. He calls it the value-added approach: Davis confirms what I told you earlier about the old idea that position power is based on the number of people and the size of the budget managed. I agree with Davis and Drucker that we need reward systems that provide managers with incentives to run the most efficient staffs and budgets possible. Staff reductions and resizings should be based on the objectives that a function is required to achieve. Across-the-board reductions are not necessarily the best path to organizational efficiency. They are just the easiest and most obvious way. As Davis (1987, p. 72) puts it: "Chopping people, without first transforming the method for determining how many were needed to begin with, is a short-term palliative that is bound to produce the same crisis over again in a short time." He goes on to liken this method to a crash diet that achieves a short-term, impermanent loss in weight but does not lay the groundwork for keeping weight off by changing eating habits.

Resizing is probably a better way to go about restructuring a department. According to consultant Anthony Tasca, the difference between resizing and downsizing is that the former is a strategic planning step and the latter is simply a tactical reaction to earlier mistakes. Resizing follows the model that we have been discussing. It first clarifies the organization's vision and position. Then it looks at the market that the organization is trying to serve. It is only after these steps have been taken that the size and composition of the staff come into question. At this point decisions to keep or lay off, retrain or reassign can be made with a purpose and set of goals in mind.

What Lies Ahead?

I estimate that as many as 75 percent of the human resources departments of American companies have gone through significant downsizing exercises between 1984 and 1989. If the life cycle profile of personnel departments hasn't changed, we can expect a buildup again in the early 1990s. I don't think that we will see a return to the large corporate human resources departments of the 1970s for at least ten years. But I suspect that we may see some general restaffing as early as 1991. And if we haven't learned anything, we will see layoffs starting again by 1995. I have watched one human resources department for twenty years. It has gone through four complete cycles of growth and decimation. That includes four vice-presidents of human resources, none of whom survived the cycles.

The only solution that I can imagine for modulating this boom-and-bust cycle is too obvious. Would you accuse me of being simplistic if I suggested that functions should be staffed in direct relationship to their performance imperatives? Some people will say that we have always done this. I have been in business since 1959 and around human resources functions since 1969, and I haven't seen much science used in arriving at staff-loading decisions. Why is it so difficult to build algorithms that link business objectives with staffing levels for human resources departments? I think it can be done. At the very least we should be able to reduce the variance by a factor of 50 percent.

Consider this. The organization decides what its operating objectives will be in the coming year. If it is a manufacturing business, there is an anticipated build plan for each month. Human resources can design a program that will convert that plan into a forecast of the number of employees needed in each job group each month. Furthermore, it can adjust the forecast for changes in production methods or product design or to accommodate the introduction of various forms of technology. Human resources can estimate, based on data in our national data bank and on labor market trend data, how much it will cost to hire and train the people. Human resources can build experience curves into the forecasting model to refine the projections even further. And it can predict how many human resources staff members will be needed to support the business plan.

Take, for example, a manufacturer with a $100 million annual payroll. If we can improve efficiency in hiring and utilization of employees in that company by just 1 percent, we will save the company $1 million in direct costs plus related support costs. That adds more than $1 million to the pretax profit line. It is worth the equivalent of $6 to $7 million in gross sales revenue. My example is for a company with about 4,000 employees. Blow that up to a mid-size organization of, say, 25,000 employees. Do the multiplication and you will see the value of the program.

We can do the same thing for service businesses. Banks, hospitals, and retailers have many part-time employees. My experience in working with many of these businesses is that they may as well use the back of an envelope for their planning. With all the technology at their disposal, why aren't chief executives demanding a more effective human capacity planning model? There are only the faintest signs that scientific methods are being applied to staff loading.

The bottom line for human resources is this: If the customer — the organization — doesn't know from one month to the next what level of service it will need, how can human resources be expected to staff itself efficiently? It is well past time for organizations to utilize computer models and scientific methods to halt the ebb and flow of bodies through organizations. It is not only stupid and inefficient, it is unethical to treat employees and their families like unfeeling objects. Given the pressure for social responsibility, it is only a matter of time before the government will step in with legislation making it virtually impossible to modify a work force. All the signs are clear. Already certain legislation, such as the requirement that long-term advance notice be given before a plant can be closed, is a reality. The history of labor legislation is based on reaction to abusive practices. Management doesn't have much time left to act if it wants to maintain any control over its right to hire and fire.

Conclusion

There are three skills that people need today in positions of responsibility: (1) interpersonal skills to get along with and to persuade others, (2) technical skills to do their job, and (3) quantitative skills to objectively measure their work and communicate their problems and progress.

The capacity to perform is determined by more than individual competence. Everyone works in an environment composed of positive and negative forces. Success requires that a person achieve a positive balance of forces in his or her favor. These forces are found both within the department and outside in the larger organization. A situation analysis can be used to scan the environment to locate the relevant factors, which fall into four categories: human, financial, technological, and organizational. Once the factors have been identified, they can be classified as positive or negative forces. Internally, that is, within the human resources department, a factor can be either a strength or a limitation. Externally, in the organization or the outside world, the items can represent either opportunities or threats. The capacity to perform depends on a person's ability to realign these forces in his or her favor.

The other major form of capacity assessment stems from program life cycle profiling. In this method, each major human resources program is subjected to a life cycle analysis. The programs are spotted along a life cycle. An analysis of resource allocations is then conducted to determine if the department is applying the right amount of each resource to the program, given its position on the cycle wave.

Capacity shortfalls can be remedied. The best way to do this is to build an objective, business-related case that will almost compel management to support your request. In the two examples described in this chapter, staff members built a case for an investment that management would find it difficult to turn down.

An organization's strategy affects capacity requirements. It is obvious that a given strategy implies certain types and levels of performance. Decisions within marketing and sales, production, research and development, customer service, management style, and corporate culture all affect human resources. It is the job of the human resources professional staff and management to look ahead, through the business plan, to the short- and long-term performance implications.

It is my firm belief that we can do a much better job of capacity planning and management if we are willing to discipline ourselves to the task and utilize the technology currently available. With computer models we can forecast the number and types of human assets needed to service a business plan. Furthermore, we can calculate the cost of hiring and training employees. We can factor in losses for turnover and productivity learning curves. As human resources departments are built up and torn down, we can do a better job of resizing them if we take the time to develop a clear picture of what we expect from them. In brief, we can do a much better job of managing the costly human asset and the not-so-costly human resources department if we focus on why the function exists and then apply a little scientific methodology so that we can manage proactively rather than simply react after the fact.

> Do few things, but do them well.
>
> Francis of Asissi

References

Davis, S. M. *Future Perfect*. Reading, Mass.: Addison-Wesley, 1987.

Odiorne, G. S. *Strategic Management of Human Resources: A Portfolio Approach*. San Francisco: Jossey-Bass, 1984.

Case Studies — Chapter Eight

Benj. Franklin Savings & Loan Association
Portland, Oregon
(From material prepared by Carolyn Magura, assistant vice-president and compensation and benefits manager, and the staff in the compensation, benefits, and systems area)

During these frustrating, litigious, complex times, have you and your staff ever:

- Requested and been denied an increase in staff?
- Felt overwhelmed when an employee left because you would inherit the work?
- Been convinced that the work controls you and not you the work?

The following case depicts one human resources department's success in achieving results on each of the above questions — primarily because it implemented a human resource assessment process. The chronology of events leading to success, along with employee reactions and organizational results, is summarized here.

> I remember feeling overwhelmed, overworked, frustrated, unappreciated, with no goals and objectives, and I couldn't see any end to the situation.
> Diane Coon,
> Compensation

Benj. Franklin is a middle-sized savings and loan association (the largest in the Pacific Northwest) with 1,700 employees in six states.

Year One. The need to develop and implement a workload tracking and measurement system came about as we assessed our relationship with management:

- We had a poor reputation because of producing inconsistent and inaccurate data.
- We were perceived as being policemen or bureaucratic roadblocks.
- We were viewed as always being "busy" but not knowing what we were doing.

In our own minds, we were a small staff of dedicated employees, very busy with process and paper work. Some of us were unsure of what we should be doing or if our department was as effective as it could be. Our problem was that we had nothing with which to compare ourselves. We were constantly expected to take on more duties as the company grew with no additional staff (one personal computer for the entire department), and we could see no way to change that trend. So, we decided to design and install a system for tracking and measuring work loads. The key to doing it would be total desire and commitment.

To provide the context for our system, we took the following steps:

1. We developed human resource goals. (Do we want to be the industry's benefits leader, or in the top 75 percent of companies? Do we pay at or above the market rate? Do we want cradle-to-grave benefits? Do we want "equity" or quality?)
2. We developed accurate and comprehensive performance standards and career ladders for ourselves.
3. We began tracking our work in fifteen-minute intervals, by hand, and all products of that work (number of jobs evaluated, employees hired, merit increases processed, and so on). Eventually, we were able to tell not only how much we had done but how long it took on average to complete a transaction. This would give us a target to shoot at for improvement and would help demonstrate the proper staffing level when we went to management for help.

The employees hated tracking the work. The process was perceived as make-work. To quote an employee at the time, "I couldn't see the result of this. What was the purpose? What would it achieve?" There was skepticism that anything would be done with the data. We measured the work anyway.

Year Two. This year we computerized the work-load tracking and measurement system and began to develop flow charts for each process and function. The employees liked the idea of computerizing the measurement system but resisted the flow charts and still didn't like tracking the work.

Year Three. This year we began to benefit from our work:

1. We streamlined the measurement and tracking process to decrease the time involved.
2. We established Year Two as the baseline for quarterly measurement and comparison of activity to measure our efficiency.
3. We established three major maintenance objectives against which we could measure results: cost containment, employee satisfaction, and enhancing systems (curing identified problems).
4. We recognized that the flow-chart process allowed us to fill a vacancy with 50 percent less learning time.
5. We justified and achieved nine promotions among six positions within a three-year period.
6. We justified an increase in the FTE from five to nine.
7. We justified an increase in the number of personal computers from one for all of human resources to four in the compensation/benefits/systems functions.
8. We received approval to effect an integrated HRIS/payroll system.
9. We accomplished outstanding functional results.

In addition, through a program to contain the costs of employee benefits, we decreased corporate benefit spending by approximately $376,000 (1.2 percent of payroll) and saved employees about $496,000 (1.5 percent of payroll). We also converted the defined-contribution retirement plan to a 401(k) plan, thereby increasing employee participation from 70 to 87 percent, and we initiated an employee reimbursement program with a 20 percent initial participation rate versus the usual 12 percent. Finally, when we implemented an employee stock purchase plan, the initial participation rate was again high: 30 percent versus the normal 20 percent.

What's Next? (Year Four). We will use the current statistics as a springboard to move to a proactive consultancy process based on a partnership with management.

Our goals of increasing morale and self-confidence have been met. We are beginning to believe that we have control of our work rather than the other way around. We are confident of being able to achieve our new goals because we already have a track record of success.

Probably the best testimony to the success of our measurement process can be seen in the following quotations from initially reluctant and resisting participants: "The biggest change I see is that now we use a thought process in doing our work rather than doing it out of habit. Because of our measurement system, I *own* my work. I am always thinking of ways I can become more efficient and, now, more effective as a consultant to my customers. I believe that we can succeed because I see how far we have come" (Diane Coon, compensation).

"I still hate to track the work; I always have hated to track the work. The difference is, now I can see where we have come, where we are going, and that I have made a difference. This gives me the motivation to measure" (Anita Humble, systems).

Author's comment: Having seen their reports, I can understand why they have been able to take control of their environment. With the data they have generated they can defend themselves against anyone who would accuse them of inefficiency, they have data to back up requests for more resources, and they can show how they are contributing to organizational goals. Best of all, they know better than anyone else how good they are. They built their system and they are in control.

Televerket
Stockholm, Sweden
*(Prepared from discussions with Olle Alsen, manager of human
resources strategic planning at Televerket, and Donna Hamlin, an
American consultant)*

Televerket is the Swedish telecommunications company.
For many years it was a national monopoly in a socialist state.
The Swedish telecommunications market was protected from
foreign competition. When the Socialist party lost power, however, things began to change. Large, powerful foreign companies began vying for the opportunity to supply equipment in
this market, and Televerket had to face all the changes that occur
when a monopoly gives way to a free market. In the past, as with
all monopolies, Televerket had no incentives to look outside
itself. The company was complacent. In time, Televerket's top
management recognized that its operating managers didn't understand strategic management principles. In order to respond
to the new market threats, the company decided it needed to
learn how to think strategically not only at the top but throughout the company. Human resources was given the responsibility
to set up a program to effect this change.

To their credit, management of the human resources department realized that it did not know very much about strategic
management. In order to carry out their mandate, they felt that
they had to prepare themselves first.

HR's management wanted the department to take an activ-
ist position in the company. Previously, human resources was the
traditional reactive bureaucracy. While that may have been satisfactory in a monopoly, it would not be acceptable in a market-
driven business. There was a clear need for human resources to
become involved at the heart of the major business problem of
the decade at Televerket.

A change of the most fundamental type had been man-
dated by market conditions. And, when a company is forced to
develop a new strategy, human resources must be there to say
what is possible in the areas of human redevelopment and
redeployment. In a socialist state you cannot fire people. That

means you either train them or ignore them. The second choice is not tenable. You also have to attract new people, and recruiting and development strategies need to be designed to accomplish this.

The human resources department engaged an American firm, Hamlin Harkins Ltd., to design training that would help it bridge the gap between a monopolistic environment and the free market. A three-week program was designed as the first step in expanding the capacity of the human resources staff to deal with its mandate. The training included not only classroom work but also a tour of companies in Sweden and the United States. Its objectives were that every participant would

- Have sufficient knowledge of Televerket's market, business, and activities to participate in and contribute to the strategic business plan.
- Have a professional identity as a human resources manager and help employees develop, become competent in the new market, and maintain positive attitudes among all employees.
- Be able to work actively with both tactical and strategic issues.

The curriculum included the following themes and subjects:

- Business planning and human resources planning
- The telecommunications market and Televerket's market position
- Integration of business planning activities and human resources
- Organizational knowledge and professional identity
- Strategic business planning
- Communications
- Human resources in the future
- Internationalization of the telecommunications industry

It was hoped that this experience would help the participants begin to emphasize strategic thinking and positioning.

A new way of managing is now in evidence at Televerket. Competition, marketing, strategy, and similar free market concepts now characterize Televerket's management model. This means that the human resources staff, as well as line personnel, have to catch on to the new model. However, for those who cannot or will not do this there are specialist positions available.

As part of the new style, human resources has established key performance measures that will help the department track its effectiveness. Human resources has always had access to information on costs, salaries, turnover, and training, as well as to lost-time data on accidents and sickness. But this information was never analyzed in a systematic way. That is the purpose of the key performance measures. There are six of them:

1. Personnel head count
2. Ratio of personnel to productive time
3. Short- and long-term sickness periods
4. Mobility: three separation and transfer rates
5. Training days per employee and ratio of training cost and production time
6. Several types of salary figures: distribution of salaries within a given unit and types of work, bonuses, and overtime

This system will be experimented with, refined, and expanded as experience and need dictate. Proof that it is working for human resources and Televerket comes from the top corporate staff officer. He stated that the project had served as a catalyst for the human resources staff and gotten them motivated. Their training program is now being worked into the organization as a whole. Before, managers were scared of the competitive marketplace. Now that human resources has become a bearer of the solution, managers are becoming more confident. With that confidence has come the courage to focus on the external environment. The transformation is nowhere near complete, but there is movement. Televerket is beginning to compete.

Author's comment: It is exceedingly difficult to change a culture, whether it is the culture of a whole company or of one function, such as human resources. In this case human resources was given the mandate to lead a culture change. The department was wise enough to run a capacity assessment on itself before it tried to change the company. If human resources had not internalized the change within itself first, it is unlikely that the department would have known how to carry it through the organization or had the credibility to pull it off.

9

Deciding and Acting on
Key Success Points and Options

SUCCESSFUL INDIVIDUALS HAVE game plans and purposes
that are clearly defined and to which they constantly
refer.

Dennis Waitley

There is a fundamental question, the answer to which is
crucial to the operation of any enterprise. It can be stated very
simply:

What do we have to do to be successful?

Strategic planners spend their time analyzing, extrapolat-
ing, and conjecturing. Managers act. Strategic managers do
both. At issue is the seductive nature of planning. At the onset of
the planning process things tend to go slowly as the team
struggles to get into a rhythm. After a time, team members get
the hang of it, and the process begins to flow. Soon, they are
roaring along laying graph after table into a book that grows
thicker by the day. Group think tends to set in, and penetrating
questions are brushed aside with comments such as, "We discussed that a month ago and settled it then." When this syndrome begins to dominate, plan relevance suffers. Now is the
time to ask the success question.

Underlying the question is the assumption that the answer to this question cannot be found in the company's history. It
implies an attitude that says, "Don't give me all that fancy
analysis. Just answer this." It does not allow for any en-
cumbrances, qualifiers, or disclaimers. It demands the clearest,
most unequivocal, straightforward answer that you can muster.

Actually, it requires about eight answers of that kind—one for each of these eight basic categories:

Marketing of your services   Being innovative
Managing your people   Being productive
Managing your finances   Being ethical
Managing your facilities   Being effective

Key Success Points (KSPs)

KSPs highlight the fields in which an individual must excel in order to be successful in an organization. The basic process is simple to understand. It goes like this:

1. For each of the eight KSPs, talk to a person or persons who could help you answer the question as it relates to the KSP. Make a list of their opinions. When all interviews have been completed, sort the responses into a list of key success points and then evaluate them. You will probably uncover some differences of opinion. That is why you need to talk to several people. Exhibit 10 is a sample of a KSP worksheet that you can use when talking with each of your customers.

2. Compare the KSPs to the objectives and goals coming out of your strategic plan. The idea is to see if they are compatible. Several problems can appear at this point. One is that the answers coming from your respondents may not be compatible with what you were planning to do. Another is that you may not want to follow their suggestions. A third might be that you don't have what you need to meet their expectations. Then what?

Ask yourself why their opinions are different from yours. Do your customers have an outdated view of what you have to offer them? If you are just joining the department, you may find that your predecessors operated in a way that is counter to what you have in mind. This may be why you were hired. Senior management may want a change, but middle management may still have the old model in mind. In this case you need to go back to your customers. Sell them on your approach and how it will help them.

Exhibit 10. KSP Worksheet.

For each KSP list the statements made during the interview.

Marketing our
   services

_____

Managing our
   people

_____

Managing our
   finances

_____

Managing our
   facilities

_____

Being
   innovative

_____

Being
   productive

_____

Being
   ethical

_____

Being
   effective

_____

Q: What do you have to do to be successful—in terms of marketing your services?

A: I need to call on the customers who have the old view of human resources and sell them on the value of my approach and methods.

What happens if the customers buy your approach and

then make demands that you can't fulfill with your current staff? Assuming you want to do what was suggested, you have now come upon questions for some of the eight fields.

Q: What do you have to do to be successful in terms of managing your people (or finances) (or facilities)?

A: I have to make a case for additions to staff (or increases in budget) (or more efficient spaces or better equipment).

Do you see how it works? Once again we discover that organizations are systems of interrelated parts. Problems, deficiencies, and solutions in one place can affect or point to opportunities in another.

3. The third and final step comes when you have all the data in and have reached decisions about what you intend to do with them. This step deals with the setting of objectives and methods for measuring success. Here, we are talking about indexes of performance. The question is, How will you know if the department has been successful on these points? Whenever possible, the answers should be quantifiable. The more specific an answer, the easier it will be to find hard data indexes and the easier it will be to demonstrate that you are being successful. Exhibit 11 is a sample Key Success Objective form.

The Driving Force

It is not always apparent which of the key success points are the most important ones. In the end, of course, each of the eight fields is important, but at any point in time one may be more important than the others. In addition, there are elements in the organization or its marketplace that cause decisions to be made in particular ways. These are called *driving forces*. Tregoe and Zimmerman(1980) define the driving force as "the primary determiner of the scope of future products and markets" (p. 40). Failure to recognize the driving force can lead you to attend to needs of lesser importance. Tregoe and Zimmerman outline eleven areas that can be driving forces: (1) products offered, (2) services offered, (3) market needs, (4) customer needs, (5) technology, (6) production capability, (7) method of sale, (8) method

Exhibit 11. Key Success Objectives.

For each KSP write at least one action objective, following the basic rules of management by objectives. For each objective, show the indicator of performance. The measure should be as specific and quantifiable as possible.

Key Success Point	Action Objective	Performance Measure
Marketing our services		
Managing our people		
Managing our finances		
Managing our facilities		
Being innovative		
Being productive		
Being ethical		
Being effective		

Comments:

of distribution, (9) natural resources, (10) size or growth rate, and (11) financial return or profit.

What is it that is driving your organization today? How can you find out if you don't know? The answer, as always, is to be alert and to listen. People, especially managers, talk about the driving force. If you hear supervisors and managers constantly discussing what is important, it is a good bet that this is the principal driving force of the moment. If you are continuously hearing people talk about expense control, you would win if you bet on number 11, financial return or profit. If you are in a high-tech company, the driving force is probably number 5, technology. In insurance companies it might be products offered, market needs, or even method of sale. Mining and paper companies often are driven by natural resource issues. Knowing the driving force helps you focus on problems or opportunities that will have high impact and thus be key success points.

Banks are driven these days by intense competition and new regulations that often cut profit margins. At the same time, banks have always had volatile labor forces, particularly at the teller level. With that in mind, Pat Brown at First Tennessee Bank developed an in-house temporary teller service. When people applied for teller jobs and were not accepted for one reason or another, even though they were qualified applicants, Pat offered them work through her in-house temporary pool. This kept some of them available for later permanent job offers. It also saved the bank $200,000 in temporary agency fees in 1988. This service has grown to be so responsive and reliable that some branch managers will let a position remain open rather than accept a temporary employee from an agency.

When you step back to analyze what Pat did, you can see that she looked at the primary driving force, cost control, applied her knowledge of the bank's high teller turnover, and selected the key success points of innovation and effectiveness. She then combined the primary driving force with the key success points to come up with the critical action, namely, the establishment of the in-house temporary teller pool.

The Force/Success/Action Matrix

Ask yourself, what is the primary driving force and what is the secondary driving force, if there is one? Tregoe and Zimmerman claim that there is only one primary driving force at a time. I won't disagree except to say that in my twenty-three years of experience as an employee and manager I have found that the difference between the primary driving force and a secondary force is often very small. In addition, in today's marketplace the half-life of a primary force is much shorter than it was in the 1960s and 1970s. Organizations are competitive environments. From time to time marketing wins out over manufacturing or technology development over profits. I believe, in fact, that there is a volatile hierarchy of forces that is subject to change without notice.

After you have identified the force or forces, you should then look at the KSPs. What did your research tell you had to be done to be successful? Find that cell where the force or forces and success points meet (Table 9). Focus on what type of intervention — what critical action — you can apply at that crossroad that will lead to a big payoff for the organization, its employees, and you.

Marketing Services

The KSP that seems most difficult for human resources practitioners to grasp at first is the marketing of services. When I ask them in my seminar to give me examples of marketing, quite often they come up with a program that solves a specific problem. Marketing is not a program. Marketing is a process. I am talking about selling, persuading, influencing, and gaining cooperation.

Batya Rosenfeld from Intel Scientific in Haifa, Israel, knows what I mean. When I asked about KSPs in her situation, one example she came up with was getting buy-in. About a year ago she realized that her salary system needed revision. She wanted to develop a three-part indexing system that would ensure her of optimal competitiveness while at the same time stay in line with Intel's ability to pay. To market this idea she spent a considerable amount of time talking to key management players. Once she felt that she had the backing she needed, she formally proposed the idea and it was approved. She tied her system to local market competition, Intel in the United States, and Intel Scientific's capacity to pay. The system went in without any problems. An attitude survey of employees later showed that they understood and accepted it. Within a year it achieved its monetary goals. But, according to Batya, it all hinged on her getting the support of management before the formal proposal was made.

Bob Coon at Daisy Systems in Silicon Valley uses a marketing technique that he calls "preambling." He can turn a potentially negative situation into a marketing opportunity with this technique. When there is bad news that has to be communicated, Bob starts his conversation by telling the manager that he has some information that the person is not going to want to hear, but that he or she shouldn't worry because Bob has it under control. This puts the person at ease, and Bob can then present the problem to a calm, prepared listener and sell the solution. What might have been an antacid case suddenly becomes simply a problem that Bob is reporting along with the solution. It gives the manager a sense of security knowing that Bob is on the job. A history of this type of behavior has earned him the respect of Daisy's management. Now, when there is controversy in the boardroom about some human resources issue, the chief executive consistently supports Bob's position against any opposition.

Marketing in a different direction helped Bob Albright at the Huntington Bank in Columbus, Ohio, service an important driving force for the bank, namely, financial return. Bob's colleagues are working in several areas that are helping the company reduce costs.

When controlling expenses is the highest priority, training is usually cut, even though this is one of the most short-sighted of management practices. But Huntington Bank is clearly not taking this approach. The bank's marketing strategy is to become a relationship bank. That is, it wants to link an employee to each customer. A number of banks are thumping

Table 9. The Driving Force/Key Success Point/Critical Action Matrix.

KSP Driving Force	Marketing Services	Managing People	Managing Finances	Managing Facilities	Being Innovative	Being Productive	Being Ethical	Being Effective
Products								
Services								
Market								
Customer								
Technology								
Production								

Sales method

Distribution

Natural resources

Size or growth rate

Financial return or profit

that tub right now, but it has a hollow ring. In most cases, all the banks have done is crank up their advertising departments but not changed their bank operations or lending functions or increased their employee training. But Huntington Bank is serious about its program. The training function that Albright leads convinced management that it could play a critical role. Not only did the bank assign an employee to each customer but it works with the training department to train employees specifically for the new job and the new relationship. Employees are taught a bankwide style of customer service. They also learn about the bank's products and competitors' products. Bank officers are supported with videotapes and product profiles that they use at monthly department meetings. This leverages the training staff's time and resources and makes the program a banking office manager's program, not a training department program. As a result of this and other training-driven actions, the bank has received a flood of letters from happy customers, and its highly ambitious financial targets are being hit.

Marketing skills are critically important. Ironically, according to every chief executive with whom I have discussed marketing, human resources practitioners are generally poor salespeople. Perhaps human resource professionals should take courses in persuasion and salesmanship rather than in state-of-the-art human resources technology. If you can't sell your service, it doesn't matter how good it is. When a product sits on your shelf, it is not an asset. It is a sunk cost. You have to get it off the shelf and into the market or you are fundamentally out of business.

Managing Human Resources for Success

Another area where human resources managers seem to have problems is in the management of their function. My experience with most large human resources departments is that they are a system of feudal baronies. Each functional head tends to run his or her little castle either behind some type of organizational "moat" or in open warfare with the barons and baronesses who run the other functions. This is, of course, dysfunctional, but that is not my point. In Chapter Five I talked about the vision that the chief human resources officer needs to communicate. One purpose of the vision is to give the troops a flag around which they can rally. The vision tells them where to focus their attention and what to value as they plan their work.

In the early 1980s the A. T. Kearney Company conducted a series of studies on how corporations that were leaders in productivity were running their companies. The research went into all aspects of each business, including the human resources function. Kearney found that in those companies that it defined as leaders, the profiles of the human resources departments were quite different from the profiles of the same function in other companies studied. The basic difference was that the human resources departments in the leaders played a strategic role in their companies and the others played an administrative role. Two quotations reveal the different position and focus:

> *Leading company HR executive*: "Our efforts are focused on the human resource implications of the corporate strategic plans. We identify opportunities and constraints that might arise from the human resource, and then we remove the obstacles."

> *Nonleading company HR manager*: "We make a continued effort to keep up with the latest developments in the literature with programs such as profit sharing, quality of work life, and participative management."

Doesn't that remind you of the difference between the Value Team and the Expense Team that I described in Chapter Five? The management of these two approaches is diametrically opposed. When you think about the three KSPs of managing your people, finances, and facilities, which approach do you take? Do you make proposals for resource increases based on the need to run programs or for the purpose of directly serving your organization's business goals? The first approach is expense based while the second is based on return on investment. To be successful you need to show your staff the differences between those approaches and imbue them with the value-adding approach.

Periodically, there needs to be some form of review of a human resources department's management practices and operating procedures. The normal response here is to run an audit. Audits have never captured my fancy because they smack of administration. I hope I made it clear long ago that I do not view human resources as an administrative expense center. While it is useful to be assured that all the posters required by law have been put on the walls and the files are accurate and complete, no one will ever promote you for a perfect audit. If they do, you are in deep trouble because they are telling you that they value form over function.

The Gannett Co. uses a "personnel review checklist" for field audits of personnel functions at its various media properties. On the surface it looks quite a bit like a standard audit form. But if you take the time to read some of the 214 items spread over nineteen human resource, safety, security, and facilities functions, you can see that it has the potential to be much more than an audit. I have reproduced a few of the items in the following list so that you can see what I mean:

3. Does the personnel plan fit into the unit's business plan?

24. Do you know what percentage of unit budget is (a) payroll and (b) benefits?

36. Are employees helped to be cost-conscious health care consumers through education?

69. Are efforts made to forecast staffing needs?

112. Are analyses made regarding performance rating trends?

121. Are the results of training assessed?

139. Do employees periodically attend meetings with the unit executive to share information and make suggestions?

151. Does Personnel visit with night-side employees on a regular basis?

210. Does Personnel conduct cost-effectiveness analysis of
a. cost per hire?

b.   benefits as a percent of payroll?
c.   turnover?
d.   cost per trainee?
e.   orientation?
f.   record keeping?
g.   cost per employee?

Gannett obviously pays attention to items beyond neat files and convenient availability of the employee handbook. To be successful managers today, human resources executives need the value-adding orientation that typifies the leading companies in Kearney's study.

Being Innovative, Productive, Ethical, and Effective

The final four KSPs offer the greatest opportunity for human resources staffs both to have some fun and to make a difference. Throughout the book I have offered examples of innovation. One can hardly survive, much less excel, without being innovative these days. Yet, there is a fine line between being innovative and just making changes. I remember talking to a trainer years ago at Wells Fargo Bank where I was working. He was angry because he had been passed over for promotion. When he stopped fuming long enough to ask me if I had any clues as to why he had not been promoted, I made the mistake of telling him the truth. I said, "My friend, you are not seen as a person who keeps up with needed changes in our training curriculum. The banking industry in California is moving into a new era of high competition, and we need to support that with changes in our programs."

He glowered at me and almost shouted, "That's not true. I make changes all the time. Practically every time I run Basic Management Development I add or change a group exercise or some reading material."

That was the end of the conversation. He was not focusing on the evolving needs of his customers. He was buried in his program. Two years later he was let go, and the last I knew of him he was teaching in a community college and "doing a little consulting."

Productivity has become a generic term that covers any type of improvement in an organization, from greater time and motion efficiency to increased organizational effectiveness. I am not interested in getting into a semantic battle, so call it what you will. For me, there isn't much difference between productivity and efficiency. The dictionary I use defines the term *productive* as "producing readily or abundantly." Synonyms are "profitable," "fertile," and "fruitful." The term *efficient* is defined as "competent or adequate in performance or operation." Productivity and efficiency are mathematically calculated the same way, but the concept of productivity is a little more potent. Usage has established the implication than being productive is more than being efficient. The best definition of effectiveness is attributed to Peter Drucker. He allegedly said, "Efficiency is doing things right, and effectiveness is doing the right things."

However you describe productivity, it comes down to improving the input-to-output ratio. I have been preaching since the mid 1970s that it is possible to measure the productivity gains that result from human resources work. In the next chapter you will find many examples of measures of productivity improvement brought about by the human resources function.

Ethics are front-page news these days. Insider trading scandals on Wall Street, government contractor frauds, unfair labor practices, and the responsibility of corporations for the social welfare needs of employees are examples. Being ethical has to do with fairness and equity in our dealings with employees. I congratulate you, my professional colleagues, on your record in this arena. You have done a good job of being the corporate conscience. Sometimes, though, I am taken aback when I read stories about incredibly stupid actions that some companies have taken against their employees.

Recently I read of the settlement of an age discrimination case. Three senior middle managers won a $3.8 million suit against their company. They introduced a tape of a sales meeting in which an executive boasted that because of a change in organization at headquarters, the average age of employees had become a lot younger, and, therefore, they would be ready to spend many hours day and night to help get the job done. As if that weren't enough, the personnel manager testified that he made a list of employees over age fifty-five when he learned that the work force would be reduced. And we wonder why the human resources department is not respected.

Effectiveness can be summed up as a matter of doing those things that support corporate goals. It not only covers a productivity or quality improvement but implies that the change was relevant to the organization's strategy and objectives. The case studies at the end of this chapter provide excellent examples of effectiveness.

Developing Strategic Options

There are always many ways to solve a problem or take advantage of an opportunity. When we are faced with a choice it is usually not simply a matter of saying yes or no. The world is not a binary environment. It is a continuum. Eastern philosophies long ago refuted the on-off, black-white notions of early Western logicians. We are beginning to accept the androgynous nature of human beings. We need to remember that whenever we are faced with apparent black-white choices in other subjects. There are many shades of gray available to us.

There are at least ten options that can be considered for any situation. Each employs a unique form, offers certain advantages and disadvantages, and has a different probability of being successful. They are the form of critical action that in your opinion will be most effective. Options should be examined as early as will be useful in the planning stage as well as at any point during the action stage of a situation. The point to keep in mind is that there is always a solution to a problem.

The following list gives ten options and briefly describes each of them:

0. Status quo. Continue current operations and activities. Do not respond to or change anything.
1. Concentration. Direct your effort toward improving your

basic product/service line. Focus more on your current problems and opportunities.

2. Horizontal integration. Gain control of your market by bringing inside a human resource process that is currently being conducted by someone else.

3. Vertical integration. Become more self-sufficient with part of an HR process. Bring inside some part of the design, development, delivery, or evaluation of the process that has been contracted outside.

4. Diversification. Expand into functions other than human resources if it is in the best interests of the organization.

5. Joint venture. Combine resources with other units for the purpose of expanding capability, sharing costs, or spreading risks.

6. Retrenchment. Reduce the level of service or shift some resources from one activity to another to improve performance or solve a problem.

7. Divestiture. Transfer a responsibility to another department that can handle it so that you can focus your attention on more important issues.

8. Liquidation. Stop offering a product or service and reallocate resources to servicing other objectives.

9. Innovation. Do something new. Add a new program or revise a current product or service to meet a changing need.

You have probably used most of these options at some point in your career. Let me give you some examples of the creative ways in which our colleagues have applied the strategic option concept.

Status Quo. Some HR practitioners think that whenever someone rings their bell, they are obliged to salivate. They're not. There are times when the best thing to do is to do nothing. Haven't you had the experience of someone's telling you about a situation in your company and suggesting that you get involved? Rather than grabbing your sword and charging into the fray, you took a look at what was happening and decided that, if left alone, the problem would work itself out. Many personnel problems work themselves out without your help. If you let it lie, it might die of its own irrelevance.

Concentration. Alex d'Arbeloff, cofounder of Teradyne, Inc., advised, "Concentrate your resources to win." Mark Twain wasn't as elegant but his advice is just as clear: "Put all your eggs in one basket and— WATCH THAT BASKET!"

Years ago I read a story about two men having lunch at a Wall Street restaurant. One diner noticed that practically everyone who came into the restaurant went over to the table of a certain man and talked to him for a moment. The observer asked his companion the name of the man who was attracting so much attention. The reply was, "That is Mr. X. He knows more about municipal bonds than anyone else in the world."

There is great power in concentration. I have seen consultants fail when they billed themselves as generalists. I have seen managers fail when they tried to take on too much. I have seen professionals fail when they got into areas where their knowledge was limited. Knowing when to stick to your knitting is a valuable piece of wisdom. You don't have to solve all the problems in your organization. Do what you do well and refer the other issues to someone who is prepared to handle them.

Simplification is a form of concentration. When Jay King joined Central Community Hospitals in Fresno, California, he found a compensation system with 193 job ranges for an organization of about 4,000 employees. He reduced these ranges to 35 through retitling them and grouping them into job families. The outcome was a system that was more efficient to administer, easier to explain, and simpler for employees to understand. The results were fewer complaints to handle and more satisfied employees.

Horizontal Integration. There are times when a human resources function is farmed out to someone else in the company or when someone else decides that he or she can do it better and stops using your department. If you believe that you should be responsible for the function because you are better able to carry it out, build a case to get it back. Many years ago I joined a company as the personnel director and found that the hiring of professionals and managers was being handled directly by line managers. For the most part they were using search firms, even for lower-level positions that were not difficult to fill. I decided to make a case to get that function back in personnel where I thought it belonged.

Rather than go directly to the line managers, I went to the accounting department first. I told them that I knew that they often received invoices related to these hires and that they didn't know who had authorized them or if the amounts were correct. I offered them a deal. If they would give me all the invoices that seemed to contain hiring-related expenses, I would find out to whom they belonged and obtain signatures and an account number on the invoices. In this way, accounting could stop wasting time playing private eye and spend its time carrying out its own responsibilities. Accounting thought that was a fine idea.

Now that I had the data coming to me, I could go to the line managers and explain to them how I could do the job faster and more cheaply and still give them well-qualified candidates. I assured them that while they would still have control over the hiring decision, my people would handle the search process, thereby saving them the trouble of reviewing resumes. We would also be able to save them money because we knew how to handle the employment agencies. The line managers also agreed to this arrangement because, like the accountants, they could then spend their time practicing their profession instead of mine. Of course, not every manager went with me the first time that I approached him or her. But the word soon got around, and within six months I had integrated the process with the rest of human resources.

Vertical Integration. This option deals with part of a process. Instead of using a consultant to design and conduct a training program, you might have the specialist design it and then run it yourself. This tactic is probably familiar to you. As times and conditions change, you contract part of a job out to someone and later bring it back in when you have the personnel necessary to handle it or you want to save money. Programming, writing employment advertisements, survey interviews, and a dozen other tasks can be integrated or dispersed as conditions dictate. The most common example is hiring a full-time permanent staffer and terminating a contract for outside services. We saw an example of that in the Datastream case in Chapter Eight.

Diversification. When Jim Lynch was human resources manager at the semiconductor division at GenRad, Inc., he got into diversification out of necessity. It started when the facilities manager left and Jim was asked to take on that job, in addition to the human resources function. It was supposed to be a temporary assignment, but he did such a good job that he was given other service departments. At one time or another, Jim managed MIS, telecommunications, and facilities in addition to human resources.

However, once he had a function running well, Jim would bring in a new manager and give the department to another group to supervise. He developed a reputation as a turnaround specialist and a solid businessman. Whenever he wanted something for personnel, he was certain to get it, because of the respect he had gained during his diversification tours.

Joint Venture. At a southern manufacturer of sheet rock and related building products, the driving force is the sales staff. A highly competitive, cyclical, and low-margin market demands well-trained salespeople and sales managers. To gain a competitive advantage the sales management development and corporate management development departments are jointly developing a sales and sales management success profiling system. They believe that there are three advantages to the company in this system. First of all, it will help the sales managers do a better job of selecting and hiring sales staff. This will lead to an increase in the average gross sales per person. Second, by having more competent sales personnel, the company can cut turnover. Third, the system will help the company identify the best potential sales managers from among its sales force. This is a high-cost investment for the company right now, and many training managers would hesitate to bring up a proposal so costly and seemingly so risky. But the concept has been accepted and is now awaiting funding. The key to making the sale was that the two departments joined forces to deal with a driving force in an innovative way.

Retrenchment. One of the most difficult things for any staff manager to do in the old days was to cut back on a service. Recall Peter Drucker's statement that every staff manager wanted to build a large staff because that was the basis for his or her pay and position. Today, when the move is definitely toward cost-effective management, many organizations are looking for ways to measure performance. Building a large budget and staff will simply not be rewarded. So what should you do?

I suggest you audit your list of activities and conduct some research into the value-adding nature of each of them. In the early chapters I spoke of value management as waste management. I can't tell you how many times I have confronted managers with the idea of retrenchment only to be told that they could not cut back on anything. Yet, shortly afterward they were replaced by new managers who went through the product/service list with a broadsword, hacking programs left and right. Even when they didn't do a very good job at it, top management applauded their efforts. And remember, when we reduce activity in one area, we can always reassign the resources to something more productive.

Divestiture. This is the second reductive option. There are undoubtedly some responsibilities that you wish you didn't have. Be honest. Isn't there a function that you wish you could get rid of? Then, do it.

Take management of the cafeteria as a good example of a no-win job. There are two reasons for you to get it off your job description. One is that there are people in the organization who would probably like to run the cafeteria or supervise an outside vendor's managing of it. They would probably do a good job of it, too. The second reason for considering divestiture is that it is not a key value-adding function. Moreover, "cafeteria manager" is not on the career ladder of corporate officers. How many of your company's vice-presidents ever ran the cafeteria? Turn your attention to the jobs where you can make a real difference, not just reduce heartburn.

Liquidation. This is the final leg on the reduction stool. You know that products or services often outlive their usefulness. The stories are too numerous to be worth mentioning. The point is that it is all right to reallocate your resources to something more important. One of the reasons why human resource managers are constantly crying about lack of resources is that they are pack rats. Once they acquire a responsibility and start to produce something, they don't want to let it go.

I met a new-breed human resources manager recently who joined an organization and the first thing he did was make every section manager justify every product or service in terms of the value it was adding to the company. You can imagine the panic. After he revived the managers, he worked through the process with them and found that they were doing many things that they didn't need to do. After they had reconstructed their responsibility list and found themselves with excess resources, he didn't take them away. Instead he led them in an investigation of the value-adding jobs that they always said they wanted to do but didn't have the time for.

If you decide to liquidate, be ready with a new and more valuable product or service. Then, not only will you not have to worry about losing staff but you will be congratulated for being a cost-effective manager who isn't afraid to take some risks and make the tough decisions.

Innovation. I don't need to say much here. You are already being innovative or you wouldn't be reading this book. Instead, you would be working on your resume because innovation is a survival tactic today. Just be sure that when you offer a new service it is not one that Rose Patten at Manufacturers Life Insurance describes as "having a life of its own." If you can't find a direct link between your service and the organization's business imperative, don't offer it. However, when there is such a link, you will have no problem in showing the impact of your work on the organization's objectives.

Conclusion

The basic question for any person who is trying to be successful in any endeavor is, What do we want to accomplish? I have taken you through a variety of concepts and exercises designed to show you how that question can be answered most effectively. My premise has been that you always follow a process, conscious or otherwise, in trying to increase your chances of being successful. In my opinion, it is better to be aware of the process and use it deliberately rather than leave things to chance.

In this chapter I suggested that you concentrate on three activities:

1. Poll key people in the organization who can respond to the question of what you have to do to be successful in the organization in terms of the KSPs.
2. Compare the responses to the eight KSPs with your strategic plans and, if necessary, make adjustments to keep them parallel.
3. Decide on and execute the critical actions that will take you where you want to go.

There are usually one or two driving forces around which all decisions are made. They may be related to products, markets, technology, resources, or growth or financial objectives. To learn which are the driving forces, pay attention to who wins the arguments at the top of the organization and what their selling points are.

By matrixing driving forces and key success points, you should be able to more easily choose the critical action that will work in your organization. For example, to be successful in a company that is technology driven, your marketing style will have to be tailored to engineers. In a service-driven business such as a bank or insurance company, your marketing style would change and the driving force would also be different. Success requires flexibility.

The fundamental success criterion in any situation is the amount of value that is added. Your actions must produce human, financial, or production value. The following chapter will complete the human value management model by showing you how to locate value, do something to increase it, and demonstrate what and how much value you have contributed.

> Whatever you can do, or think you can do, begin it. For boldness has power and magic and genius in it.
> Goethe

References

ASPA Resource, 1989, *8* (3), 12.

Misa, K. F., and Stein, T. "Strategic HRM and the Bottom Line." *Personnel Administrator*, Oct. 1983, pp. 27–30.

Tregoe, B. B., and Zimmerman, J. W. *Top Management Strategy*. New York: Simon & Schuster, 1980.

Case Studies — Chapter Nine

Boy Scouts of America
National Headquarters
Dallas, Texas
(Developed from materials and conversations with Larry Burk,
compensation manager)

Change is the central fact of life these days, even in a not-for-profit agency such as the Boy Scouts. Over 100 years old, built on so-called middle-class values of courtesy, cleanliness, kindness, friendliness, bravery, reverence, and cheerfulness, it hardly seems a likely candidate for proactive change. Nevertheless, its human resources staff at national headquarters in Dallas, Texas, thinks otherwise. Larry Burk has a vision of human resources as the driving creative force in an organization. He says, "We must want the responsibility for making things work in our companies and want it passionately." Larry adds, "We can't expect it simply to be handed to us on a silver platter because we're wonderful people."

Larry and his associate Richard Christian recognize that of all the key success points the first one that they have to address is the marketing of their services. Not everyone has the same vision of change within the Boy Scouts as these two. They point out that, traditionally, human resources people have not seen themselves as marketers. This misperception, they say, must change. Every opportunity must be taken to market the expertise of human resources. This means being effective communicators, which is more than just a matter of gathering information. It is extremely discouraging and counterproductive for the human resources function to know that a new program will address a problem effectively and then not be able to sell it.

Another key success point — and one that is linked to marketing — is management of the human resources staff. This means that the staff must be trained to take advantage of market opportunities. Burk believes that if we are to create a future for human resources, we will have to undergo a painful redefinition of our character and purpose. In order to sell the value-adding image of human resources, we first have to view ourselves in a new way. This becomes the jumping-off point for aggressively marketing our products and services.

We must prepare ourselves by building skills in areas beyond personnel specialties. Larry states that if he were teaching a class in survival skills to a group of human resources generalists, he would emphasize three skills:

1. Creative problem solving to service customers and build relationships
2. Marketing ideas and programs to sell what you have to offer
3. Quantitative measurement to prove that you are adding value

We must become, if we are not already, the experts at optimizing human potential. Human resources must develop answers to the organization's basic question, How can we best utilize our people to continue to achieve our goals and objectives? Human resources professionals must stay current with what is and isn't working so that when management comes with a problem, we can give them a number of potential solutions. This means that we have to do our homework and maintain our skills in human development and organizational effectiveness. Of course, some people think that these points apply only to the training department. That is not true. All human resources professionals and staff have to take a holistic view. No system, process, or program works in isolation. Each contact with a customer affects the larger system. It is somewhat like trying to heat only part of a room. If there is a central heating system, when you turn up the heat it will soon permeate all parts of the room. Changing a program or solving a problem in one area often affects an adjacent or related issue.

The third key success point that Burk and his associates are focusing on is innovation. Some of what they are doing may not seem innovative to you. The point is they are making the changes and introducing innovative ideas to their market as part of their effort to optimize the effectiveness of the Boy

Scouts. The results are traceable to other key success points, such as productivity and effectiveness.

For example, human resources has introduced a report that tracks the history of each job requisition. This, along with ongoing measurement of the time needed to fill positions, helps the recruiters learn what can and should be done to improve the hiring process.

Major changes in the benefits area include cost containment programs, expanded use of health maintenance organizations, and introduction of dental, wellness, and EAP programs. The latter two programs are being tracked in terms of program utilization and relationship to cost factors such as sickness and accident rates. This is a key point. It is not enough to put a program in place and then let it run. The issue of cost effectiveness and return on investment cannot be shrouded in the social welfare aspect of the program. Management has a right to expect financial as well as human value results from an investment.

Training is also a major thrust in the organization's human potential movement. Management classes have increased by 67 percent and the number of participants by 79 percent in the past two years. Pretesting and posttesting are routinely used to measure learning changes in most courses. Written action plans based on the training with follow-up ensure that courses are building competence and producing positive changes within the organization.

The effects of these and other innovations, improvements, and initiatives can be seen in organizational indexes such as turnover of professional staff. The professional group turnover rate has dropped from over 20 percent in the late 1970s to 13.8 percent in 1988. This macro index demonstrates that there is value in human resources work. Skeptics would say that other factors may have caused the change and that human resources therefore cannot take credit for it. Compare that to fund-raising efforts at the Boy Scouts. If the development department takes in 20 percent more dollars in one year than in the previous year, doesn't it get credit for that? One could say that people were just feeling more generous or that business was better and so companies could increase their corporate support, and on and on.

All of that might be true, but the development people will still be congratulated for a job well done. The same principle should apply to human resources.

In 1988, the human resources department at Boy Scouts of America introduced a performance measurement system to track its own effectiveness. Exhibit 12 shows a portion of the report. It displays six macro measures (without data), along with annotations that explain the indexes and note other organizational studies that are under way.

Larry concluded our last conversation by emphasizing his position. The image that the human resources staff should create is one of single-minded dedication to customer service, whether that customer is the chief executive or the newest employee.

Author's comment: Venerable institutions such as the Boy Scouts are often more innovative than the general public suspects. I spent four years of my early career working for the United Way. I have never seen an organization that was more in tune with the changing demographics of society. We can learn a lot if we keep our eyes and minds open and are willing to accept ideas from all sources. I've learned from working with Larry and Richard. I expect to learn more from them in the future. I like to work with people who say and mean things such as this: "Creating and aggressively marketing initiatives that add value involves risk, and it takes time and energy. But it makes our jobs a lot more fun, and the paybacks in terms of recognition for the work we do and the internal satisfaction make the extra effort more than worthwhile." Thanks, Larry.

J. I. Case do Brasil
Sorocaba São Paulo, Brazil
(From materials and discussions with Raul da Costa Navarro,
formerly industrial relations manager at Case do Brasil's
Sorocaba plant, now with Kibon in São Paulo)

The J. I. Case Company, a division of Tenneco, began manufacturing tractors in Brazil in the early 1970s. At last

Exhibit 12. Personnel Measurement Standards Program.

	Definition	Impact	(A)		(B)	
			Total Survey	BSA Data	BSA Sept. 1987	BSA Sept. 1988
Personnel expense	Personnel expense as a factor of total organizational expense	Reflects small % of revenues expended on personnel programs and services	0.0%	0.0%	0.0%	0.0%
Expense factor	Total organizational expense divided by total number of regular employees	One indicator of employee productivity (low $ equal high productivity)	$000	$000	$000	$000
Total absence rate	Total for exempt/nonexempt employees	Productivity loss as a result of absenteeism	0.0%	0.0%	0.0%	0.0%
Total termination rate	Total for exempt/nonexempt employees	Productivity loss plus high cost of replacing employees	0.0%	0.0%	0.0%	0.0%
Cost/hire	Average cost per hire of each new employee	Managing this number downward saves operating costs for BSA	$000	$000	$000	$000
Time to fill	Total time from receipt of job requisition to candidate acceptance	Managing this number downward increases productivity for BSA	0 days	0 days	0 days	0 days

(A) Compares survey data from 1987 ASPA/Saratoga Institute Human Resources Management Standards Survey of 205 companies nationwide, and BSA data from all national locations July–December 1987.

(B) Compares one month's data – September 1988 – to our base month of September 1987 so that effectiveness standards can be established, meaningful trends identified, and concerns successfully addressed.

check, it employed over 1,100 people and its annual sales were around $70 million. In 1976, the company decided to move its operations from São Bernardo do Campo in the state of São Paulo to Sorocaba, also in São Paulo State, in order to find a space that offered better expansion possibilities along with more favorable labor costs and relationships.

The success of the move would depend on the ability of the company to find, attract, train, and acculturate people to work in what was for most of them a foreign environment, namely, a sophisticated manufacturing system. Sorocaba's industrial base had previously been in the textile industry. The area was essentially rural with a history of low labor costs. However, the school system was not prepared to turn out graduates with manual skills required in heavy manufacturing. In addition, there was a shortage of experienced supervisory and managerial personnel, as well as a dearth of technical knowledge and skills.

The major objective of the project team headed by Raul da Costa Navarro was to ensure a supply of competent people for the plant's operation. People not only had to be trained, but they had to be prepared for the work environment and to accept Case as "the place to work." The company began assembling a human resources team in March of 1976. In August, an office was rented in downtown Sorocaba. A target was set for opening the plant in sixteen months; that is, in December of the following year.

The human resources group developed a strategic plan with the following objectives:

1. Attract and prepare a sufficient number of trained personnel to begin operations at the plant on the target date.
2. Create a positive image of Case in the minds of local government representatives, the press, educators, and the citizenry at large.
3. Establish personnel policies to deal with the conditions at this location. Make adjustments for the differences between the communities of São Bernardo do Campo and Sorocaba.

4. Develop growth productivity indexes and employee cost projections for the project.
5. Develop good communications practices from the beginning with a sensitivity to employee needs so that there would be no situations for a union organizer to exploit.

The human resources staff launched a strong campaign on several fronts simultaneously. One of the first programs targeted people who might want to work for Case. A recruitment, selection, and indoctrination program was designed and implemented. Coincident with that was a program to build a relationship with local schools. Case employees made speeches at schools and presentations at academic events. Likewise, on the broader scale they went about creating a positive company image in the community. Personnel contacts were made with local government heads and agency staffs. This later made it possible to minimize red tape when approvals were needed. Articles were placed in local newspapers, and press releases were made from time to time. Finally, a list of qualified suppliers of needed services was developed. This included canteen service, temporary personnel agencies, medical services, and so on. The human resources staff even went so far as to lead in the building of a local professional human resources association. The aim was to create similar scenarios among local industries so that they would all support better education and training, help create a positive atmosphere for industry, and, in general, make the area a good place for investment.

On the internal side, the team had to prepare facilities and information for Case personnel who were considering transferring from São Bernardo do Campo. A referral service that provided information on hotels, restaurants, transportation, social clubs, real estate agencies, and local facilities was developed. A relocation policy was created. Employees and their families were given information about living standards and housing conditions in Sorocaba. Human resources also helped the spouses of employees find work in Sorocaba and provided information on schools. Finally, when it came time to move, the human resources staff handled that process, too.

At the time, the move was the most significant investment decision that the J. I. Case Company had made outside the United States. It turned out to be a highly successful decision. The plant was inaugurated on December 8, 1977. It exceeded its production targets within the first year by about 10 percent, without any labor strife or government intervention.

Author's comment: This case shows that when competent human resources professionals are put on a project and given the resources to carry it out, they can make a tremendous difference in the level of business success. Consider another scenario. Assume for the moment that an insensitive project manager had been assigned to carry out this move. Without an appreciation for the labor, government, and community forces, the project could have turned into a disaster. It takes so little to turn one upset bureaucrat or job applicant into a wall of defiance. The difference can be literally millions of dollars in lost investment. Human resources people need to point out the value that they are adding to business decisions. You cannot expect that someone will recognize your brilliance if, through a misguided sense of modesty, you do not total up a few figures and present them occasionally to management.

10

Evaluating
the Value-Added Effects
of Human Resources

MORE PEOPLE WILL understand what you are talking
about if you tell it to them in their own language.
Alan C. Elliott

Contrary to the biblical admonition, every manager must
serve two masters. One is internal to the department or function
that he or she manages. The other is the external market that the
function services. The chief executive officer looks after the
operating efficiency of the company while simultaneously being
concerned with the growth in sales and profits that comes from
putting quality products on the market at competitive prices.
The manufacturing manager is charged with building a quality
product at the lowest unit cost possible while concurrently
ensuring that shipments to customers are on schedule. Research
and development directors must guide their scientists and technicians in finding innovative designs that will meet new needs in
the marketplace. Sales managers monitor the cost of sales while
simultaneously keeping an eye on customer satisfaction and
demands for product improvements. It doesn't matter whether
we are talking about product or service businesses; everyone has
to operate internally as efficiently as possible while at the same
time performing as effectively as possible in the marketplace.
This applies to administrators in a hospital, loan and operations officers in a bank, actuaries in an insurance company,
transmission line managers in a utility, mine supervisors, airline
operations officers, and human resources directors.

In the human resources department we try to be efficient
and productive while designing and delivering quality products

274

and services. This is our internal focus. Externally, we look to the needs of our customers—the employees and managers of the organization—to analyze what we can do for them that will help them achieve their goals. It is not uncommon for staff departments in particular to become so deeply involved in services that they forget to stay abreast of the changing needs of their customers. I often hear human resources staff members say that they are customer focused. However, when I ask them to give me examples of their customers' operating objectives, they can't do it. Simply responding to the yanking of one's chain is not being customer oriented. Reactive management is nothing more than a survival mechanism. The strategic human value manager looks for specific customer objectives and tries to respond in the most innovative, timely, and cost-effective manner. That's what this book has been about: how to go from vision to critical action. The octagon in Figure 8 provides a simplified, graphic example of this imperative.

The human resources octagon shows the many service functions that reside within a standard human resources department. Those functions exist for only one reason: to contribute to customer goals, examples of which are listed in the center rectangle. The dark arrows indicate that the primary focus is on the customer. The light arrows indicate that the secondary focus is on the efficiency, productivity, and quality of the operation of the human resources department. This is the dual focus of human resources strategic management. Value measurement describes the qualitative and quantitative worth of products and services provided by the human resources department in terms of what they contributed to the customer's goals.

Effects of Human Resources

In Chapter Five I showed you a model of one way to look at the job of human resources. Table 10 is a copy of what you saw there. But now look at the model from the standpoint of the types of value-adding effects that can be measured. These are the outcomes and impacts that human resources can show as a result of its work within the organization.

Figure 8. Human Resources Octagon.

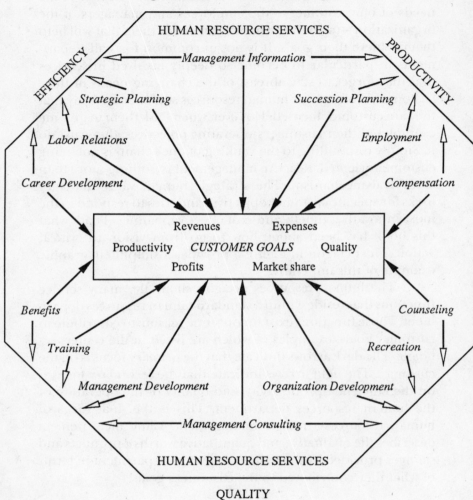

Whether or not anyone is aware of it, your programs, products, and services do affect the various operating functions of your organization. For decades, line managers have claimed that staff departments are little more than necessary evils. In specific cases, it might appear that way. But if managers were to take the time to look at the effects that the personnel depart-

Table 10. Human Resources Effects Matrix.

Objective:	Help Managers Improve Their			
Functions	Productivity	Quality	Effectiveness	QWL*
Operations				
Producing	Units built	Scrap rate	Ship on time	Safety Stress
Designing	New products	Redraws	Acceptance	Morale
Maintaining	Repairs	Breakdowns	Accidents	Absence
Purchasing	POs filled	Errors	Delivery on time	Turnover Complaints Grievances
Marketing				Employee cooperation
Selling	Units sold	Margins	Repeat sales	Legal actions
Servicing	Calls handled	No recalls	Problem solved	Suggestion program use
Market research	Responsiveness	Good data	Customer saved	EAP use
Advertising and PR	Ads designed	Errors	Responses	Career development Benefits use
Administration				
Info systems	Job cost	Reruns	Faster operations	
HR	CPH	New hires	Company met schedule	
Finance	Invoices processed	Errors	Cash flow up	
Planning	Plan on time	On spec	Predictive	

* QWL issues occur in all departments.

ment has on their units, they would find evidence of those effects everywhere. That evidence might be a mixture of good and bad news, but the point is that any staff function affects the line and other staff departments that it serves—or does not serve. Every minute that a manager or an employee puts in at work is either enhanced or hindered by the actions, or inaction, of staff departments. Staff functions build and maintain administrative systems that create a large part of the work environment. They cannot help but affect the organization. The only question left is how can human resources affect it as positively as possible? For that, we need both a strategy and management processes.

Table 10 displays just a few of the kinds of effects that you as a human resources practitioner have on the outputs and working environment of the rest of your organization. As you follow a line across a function, you will find examples of productivity, quality, or effectiveness improvements for that function. In the right-hand column are a number of environmental factors that human resources affects. They are not function specific; hence they can be found in any of the departments in the left-hand column. I have illustrated this by placing them in a column that runs down the length of all functions.

Many human resources practitioners have a problem seeing the connections between their work and the operation of their companies. The impact of support programs such as benefits seems to be especially invisible. The way to find a connection is to ask what the purpose of a benefit program is. For example, why do companies have an employer-supported health insurance plan? One of the reasons is to be competitive. Today it is difficult for large companies to hire people if they don't offer health insurance. So, one effect of having a health plan is that it becomes easier to hire better-quality employees. Since high performers usually have choices about where they will work, an employer with a good health plan has a competitive advantage in hiring over one who doesn't.

Another reason for having a high-quality health insurance plan is to help employees be more productive. If you have comprehensive protection, your employee will not have to worry about paying a crushing medical bill. In today's market most plans cap the employee's annual out-of-pocket cost at several thousand dollars. The purpose of a health plan is to provide both peace of mind and financial security. Given that, instead of wasting time worrying on the job, employees will focus on doing their work. That may be a cold economic way of looking at it, but it is nevertheless true.

Consider the effects of more obvious human resources services. Clearly, the recruiting function has a very strong impact on the cost, time, quantity, and quality of hiring. At

Memorial Sloan-Kettering Cancer Center in New York City, Ed Kleinert faces a tremendous supply-demand imbalance for nursing and other professional positions. One innovative critical action that he took was to set up an 800 number that allows applicants to call in and work through a list of jobs using their phone keys. Job seekers can find the job information that they need before sending in a resume or talking to a recruiter. In another program, Ed has computerized data from advertising responses. He knows the response rate, quality, and quantity of applicants and hires from several different sources. Compare this approach to the story I told you in an earlier chapter about the recruiting manager who simply broadcast her requisitions to all sources and prayed for a hit.

Melva Diamante, who works with Ed, has been running a performance measuring system for about four years. In the beginning she didn't like the assignment because of the extra work it represented. But once she started to use the data for analysis and reporting, she found a change of attitude in management. Managers came to see her and the department in a new light. As a result, her operating budget has more than doubled, and she has been able to consistently show a return on investment with the extra resources.

The effects matrix suggests that when the human resources staff goes to work with someone in the organization it can often find data that show the impact that its programs are having on the productivity, quality, effectiveness, or working environment of that part of the organization. Don't hiring, training, paying, counseling, and negotiating efforts pay off in higher productivity, improved quality, and increased unit effectiveness and quality of work life? If they don't, why in the world would anyone hire you to do them? There is no question that they do, the only issue being how much. That is what the models and examples in this chapter will help you demonstrate.

Measuring Human Assets

The traditional model for organizing a human resources department is based on functional responsibilities: employment or staffing, compensation, benefits, employee relations, labor relations, and training or development. This has led many human resources people to develop an activity fixation. I would like to propose a purpose focus. If you accept that employees are assets of the organization in the sense that they have the potential to add value to it, then you might be able to accept the notion of managing them as though they were assets. Human asset management is organized around five purposes. Management must first acquire an asset. Second, it must maintain it. Third, in the case of the human asset, there is value in developing its potential. Fourth, the asset must be applied or put to work. Finally, it must be managed. These five purposes can be set beside the traditional personnel/human resources labels as follows:

Traditional	*Asset Management*
Employment EEO	Acquisition
Compensation Benefits Employee relations Labor relations EAP, and so on	Maintenance
Training Career development	Development
Organizational development Productivity and quality	Application
Supervision	Management

It could be argued that this is just a semantic issue. That is partly true. Semantics is the science of word meaning and as such it is important. People give meaning to words and act in accordance with that imputed meaning. I believe that there are important implications behind the words *acquisition*, *maintenance*, *development*, and *application* that can yield a fresh, more effective view of our work. For example, viewing compensation, benefits, and employee and labor relations functions as collec-tively focused on maintaining the human asset places those functions in a broader perspective. It shows the purpose behind administering benefits, counseling, and negotiating. When you know why you're doing something you usually do it better. This leads to decisions that spring from your vision of the purpose of human resources and the organization's philosophy of human relations. And it is a language that management can relate to. It affects and is affected by corporate culture. The job becomes much more than a daily activity for which there is never enough time, seldom enough recognition, and always plenty of aggrava-tion. In the end, it sets up a more useful, more relevant method for measuring the effectiveness of your work. This yields a higher level of job satisfaction.

Practically all management gurus over the decades have noted that measurement is a fundamental requirement of busi-ness management. Experts such as Tom Peters, Bob Waterman, Phil Crosby, W. E. Deming, and Peter Drucker all insist on it. It is a truism that:

You can't manage what you don't measure.

I would like to follow that with Cramer's Rule:

Anything you measure improves.

Quinn Cramer of Hewlett-Packard may not be as famous as some of the experts mentioned above, but she has more hands-on managerial experience than most of them. The way Quinn explains it is that when you tell your people what is going to be measured and how it can be accomplished, you find that the process or the output invariably improves. This is because most people are competent and can do a better job if they know precisely what is expected of them.

As an illustration of the importance of measurement, and of the ability to speak the language of business, imagine a scene in which the chief executive officer calls in the chief financial officer and asks for a report on last month's revenues. The financial officer says, "Chief, you're going to love it. We made a lot of money last month. Sales were up and expenses were down." The chief executive leans back and smiles. "So tell me," he says, "how much did we make?" The financial officer, beaming broadly, says, "A whole bunch!" The other laughs and says, "Great, could you be a little more specific?" The financial officer replies, "Oh, don't worry, it was a lot." The chief executive leans forward and asks with a note of impatience, "Okay, enough is enough, just how much did we do?" The other officer squirms a bit and says, "Well, I don't know for sure, but it looks like we did a lot better than last month."

How long would the boss put up with these ridiculous responses before he threw the financial officer out? Probably not very long.

However, I have talked with many executives who have had similar conversations with human resources managers. They ask specific questions and get nonspecific answers. I don't know why they even put up with that. What I do know is that line management is becoming increasingly less patient with vague answers when it comes to human resources results. Table 11 is a reproduction of a prop that I use to show the absurdity of the "whole bunch" grammar. I've shown it at least 150 times at seminars and during speeches over the past six years, and it never fails to get a laugh and make the point. Why do human resources people believe it is all right for them to talk in subjective terms about business operations? Don't they see that this is the central cause of their image problem? If they don't speak the language of business, how can they possibly ever earn a spot on the Value Team?

Aversion to Measurement

I have been preaching the gospel of measurement since the late 1970s. I have heard every excuse you can imagine for not implementing measurement systems. I listed them in my first book (Fitz-enz, 1984) and I haven't heard any new ones in the past five years. What I have come to understand is the thinking behind these excuses. The four blocks to measurement are:

Table 11. Just How Many Is a "Whole Bunch"?

Common Phrase	Absolute Value(s)	Common Phrase	Absolute Value(s)
One	1	About a dozen	9 to 15
A couple	2 to 4	A bunch	8 to 15
A few	3 to 5	A whole bunch	9 to 19
Quite a few	3 to 6	Two dozen	22 to 26
Several	3 to 9	About two dozen	21 to 27
Many	3 to 8	A few hundred	75 to 125
Most	4 to 6	A couple hundred	99 to 139
Half a dozen	5 to 7	Two or three hundred	140 to 175
About half a dozen	4 to 8	Half a million	90,000 to 125,000
A lot	6 to 10	A majority	50% + 1
Quite a lot	7 to 11	A clear majority	51%
A whole lot	8 to 17	An overwhelming majority	61% to 70%
Ten	9 to 11	Almost all/everyone	71% to 75%
Around ten	7 to 13	Practically all/everyone	76% to 80%
A dozen	11 to 13	Absolutely all/everyone	86% to 90%

Source: Wiesenberg, 1982.

habit, fear, disagreement, and ignorance. If you decide to put a measurement system in place in your unit, you may run into one or more of these obstacles. Let me describe them and give you some ideas about how to deal with them.

Habit. People get into habits that they don't like to break. They have found a way to operate that works for them and causes them the least amount of effort and grief. Many people feel overworked. Most learn to cope with their work loads and to shift priorities to find time to do the things that are truly important. Others settle into fixed routines and try to avoid climbing out of their ruts. Recently, I was talking with a management group at an insurance company. One of the men in the small group sat through my hour-long presentation in total passivity. Not a word or gesture. At one point I felt like slapping him to see if he was still alive. After the meeting I asked one of the others how it went. She said it achieved its purpose except for Mr. X. Then she said, "But that's just him. He has a full plate and he isn't interested in anything." People like Mr. X won't change their ways unless compelled to by their boss. They are simply marking time until retirement. You will never convince them that measurement has value because "value" is not part of their lexicon.

Fear. Many people fear measurement. Either they have heard of bad experiences or they have themselves been hurt by a measurement system that was used punitively rather than positively. But they can be converted. They can be shown how a measurement program will help them and their people. If you take the time to work on their fears, they will come around.

Last week I started a measurement program with a training manager. He was not particularly happy with the idea, but his boss made it a no-vote situation. We had a preliminary meeting to get better acquainted and to discuss his problems and opportunities. He told me, "If you bring me anything that is going to take much time, I'm not going to be very happy with it." He then went on to tell me how hard he was working, which I didn't doubt, and how frustrated he was with the company for not recognizing the value of his function. At our second meeting we made out a list of six training programs that we might measure and started to analyze them. We began at 10 A.M. By noon we had finished three program designs, and he suggested that we have a working lunch since I had to see another client that afternoon. By two o'clock we had completed the fifth program and decided to stop there. As we relaxed, he stopped talking for a minute and looked thoughtfully at the papers in front of him and the diagrams that we had drawn on the flip charts. I then heard him say to himself, "I'm going to submit this project to the company's Improvement Award Program!" What a change in four hours.

The reason he came so far in such a short time was that his fears had been allayed and he could now see the value of a measurement program. Lethargy is difficult to deal with. But legitimate fears can always be removed if you proceed from a positive, value-adding frame of mind.

Disagreement. This objection is based on the belief that human resources work somehow exists on a higher level than any other endeavor. It is a quasi-religious attitude that is dying out, but is still an issue for some. Ten years ago many human resources people thought that their work really had little to do with helping the organization that employed them. They saw their role as that of corporate conscience. These people were probably better suited for a religious or social welfare vocation.

Even now, however, there are still some people in business who really believe that business is a less than honorable career. Those whose value systems are dominated by concerns for the inherent goodness of people often see organizations as evil places. This attitude allows them to place themselves above the banalities of business and to argue for the "goodness" of people. Of late they have been largely silenced by the pressures to meet organizational objectives. But I still run into them in the middle of strategy and measurement sessions. Often during a break or at a dinner function they will amble up to me and say something like, "Don't you think that this measurement business can go too far?" What they are afraid or too polite to say is, "I don't like the idea of submitting the people side of the business to objective measurement." I always respond to their question by agreeing that anything can go too far. I then quickly point out that they no doubt have the knowledge and experience to know how far this method can go in helping people achieve their operating objectives and advance their careers.

Objections based on value systems are the most difficult to unearth and handle. Watch for the oblique question. Focus your response on the premise that an objective description of "good" work is a more powerful argument than is bleeding heart, subjective terminology. Top executives value people, but they must meet objective business goals or they won't be around to be nice to people. Someone might think that, if the organization is allowed to flounder, current management will be replaced by a more humane group. If so, they have never been part of a turnaround effort. That is one time when humanitarian values are definitely set aside.

Ignorance. This barrier is really the source of all the others. Ignorance comes in two forms. One is misperception. Measurement has a bad reputation in some circles. Ignorant or insecure managers have used measurement as a form of punishment. The stories about measurement projects in staff functions are somewhat similar to the stories the evening news broadcast. Most of the news focuses on apocalyptic subjects: famine, flood, sickness, and war. Sometimes there is a thirty-second human interest story at the end of the broadcast that is designed to show us there is hope, albeit very little. Because there is so much more bad than good news circulating about measurement, many people have a misperception of the process.

The other form of ignorance is simply lack of information. Many of our colleagues are so buried in their work that they just don't know what is going on beyond the edges of their desk. For whatever reason, they focus entirely on the technical aspects of their job and never look at related managerial or organizational issues. These people need to be brought into the light and shown that spending a little time collecting data will help them do their job even better.

The key to dissolving the four barriers to measurement is information. Examples of simple measurement techniques, along with the retelling of success stories, can do more to encourage people to adopt a measurement system than can any type of threat or incentive. In support of that claim, let me take the mystery out of performance measurement by reducing it to its fundamentals.

Building Blocks of Measurement

I have been working on the measurement of staff functions for nearly twenty years since I first discovered the menial position that some of the staff departments occupied within their organizations. I have talked with thousands of people about this subject, and over the years I have looked for ways to reduce what seemed to be a complex subject to the simplest model possible. Figure 9 shows the basic elements of performance measurement and the indexes that are available to describe changes in performance.

Every organization from the smallest to the largest con-

Figure 9. Building Blocks of Measurement.

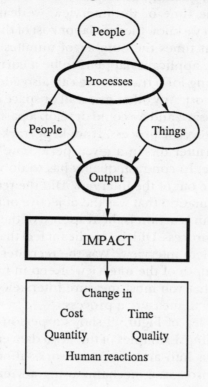

sists of just two production elements: people and things. Everything is either animate or inanimate, alive or not alive.

Process. Processes start and performance springs from the actions of a person. People work either with other people or with things such as equipment, material, or forms. On the left side of Figure 9 you see a person engaged in a process with another person. You can call it an action or a behavior if you like. I use the business term: *process.* An example would be a recruiter using a communicative process with an applicant. To identify this specific communicative process, we give it a categorical name: *interview.* This is the first point of measurement. If necessary, we can measure this process in any of the five ways shown in the figure: cost, time, quantity, quality, and human reactions. If we keep track of the time of the interview, we learn how many minutes it took. If we know the unit labor cost of the recruiter, we can multiply that times the number of minutes the interview consumed. If the applicant happens to be a current employee who is interviewing for a transfer, we can also add in the applicant's unit labor cost. Any other material or space costs could be obtained if necessary, and we could develop a partial or full cost for the entire interview process. If we kept track of how many interviews a recruiter did in a given period, we would have a quantity measure. In contrast, quality has to do with the information that came out of the interview. Did the recruiter obtain the type of information that was the objective of the interview? Finally, the human reaction is the response of the recruiter and applicant to the process. Did the applicant feel that he or she got a fair and complete interview? Was the recruiter satisfied with the scope and depth of the interview? Keep in mind that I am not suggesting that you must measure interviews. I am simply showing you how to measure a process.

The right leg of Figure 9 shows a person involved in a process with a thing. Examples of this are a data entry process: a clerk typing data into an electronic workstation; a repair or manufacturing process: a mechanic using a wrench to tighten or loosen a nut; a balancing process: a bank teller counting money; an examination process: a nurse reading a thermometer or blood pressure gauge. All organizational performance starts at this simple one-on-one level.

Of course, there are also more complex processes. Management is an exercise that is made up of many small processes. I view management more as a concept than as a process. I think of processes as something I can see. I can't see management. But I can see managers going through a number of processes; when these are combined, they add up to management. Managerial performance can be measured as a function of four processes and outcomes. I'll show you how to do that later in this chapter.

In summary, you can see that processes can be measured along the five indexes of cost, time, quantity, quality, and human reactions. The last is any physical, emotional, or psychological response to the process. It includes matters such as supervisory attitudes, employee morale, or customer satisfaction.

Outcomes. The same method applies to measuring outcomes. People engage other people or things in processes for the purpose of achieving some objective. I call this objective an outcome. Using the examples above, we can say that the purpose of an interview is to develop information that will lead to a selection decision. The outcome might be a referral to a hiring supervisor, rejection of the applicant, or a decision to make an offer on the spot. For the person in data entry, the outcome might be a completed document or record. In the case of the mechanic, the outcome could be a machine that serves its function or a subassembly that is attached to a larger system. For the teller, the result might be a cash drawer that balances at the end of the day. For the nurse, an outcome might be an entry on a patient's record or information transmitted orally to the examining physician.

Each of those outcomes can be described in terms of the five indexes. How long did it take to achieve the outcome and how much did it cost? How much was done? What was the error or scrap rate? How satisfied are the affected parties?

One of the major problems that staff departments have always had results from their focus on the activity rather than on the result. When it is a question of hiring, staff members talk endlessly about how many people they interviewed but not about how they might have improved the process or the outcomes. At the process level (Figure 9), the point should be that the efficiency or productivity or quality of the interview process has improved. This is useful information for the staffing manager. At the output level, the outcomes should be considered. Is the cost of hiring employees being held in check in a difficult market? Is the time needed to fill jobs increasing or decreasing? Is the quality of the hires getting better or worse? What is the ratio of requisitions open to those filled? How satisfied are the hiring managers with the service they are receiving? This is the type of information that can be communicated to your top management. Executives don't want to spend time reading about how hard you have worked. But they might be interested in whether or not your results are improving.

Impact. This third and final performance point tries to show what value was obtained from the outcome, and it is here that staff departments often fall down. On the one hand, they have made great contributions to the goals of their organizations. On the other hand, they have failed to demonstrate their achievements, with the result that they have been relegated to the necessary evil category.

What difference did the outcome make on the organization's bottom line or to a customer's objectives? If your customer is paying for your service and you consistently deliver high-quality service on a timely basis and at a reduced cost, you are probably helping the customer in several very direct ways. But you may also be contributing to his or her success in some indirect ways. If you fill an open position quickly, you may enable the customer to meet a schedule or maintain a high level of service. If you successfully counsel a troubled supervisor or employee, you may thereby help the person perform at a higher level of productivity or at a lower accident rate. These outcomes add up to improved unit performance.

Most people accept these kinds of logical, causal demonstrations. But they often fail to see how they can demonstrate the positive contributions of their work. Not long ago I was talking with a new client who was hoping to get started on a measurement system for all administrative functions. He was stuck with his apparent inability of reconciling the presence of intervening factors. His question, which I have heard more times than I can count, was this: "How can I show that the program had the effect I claim it did when there are so many other things going on that could have caused the effect?" Although it is an honest question I still get cross with it because I have answered it several thousand times.

If you think for a moment, however, the answer to his question becomes apparent. You must first gather some data about the situation before you perform a given service. After an appropriate period following implementation of the service, you should gather data on the same situational variables. Throughout the intervening time you must stay close to the customer and watch for causal events. I don't mean that you have to visit the client every day. But what you do need to do is talk with the customer and find out if any fundamentals have changed. Has anything happened to material, prices, facilities, competitors, or other causal forces that may have produced a change in the situation? This is a simple experiment. We are looking for major intervening variables. You might be surprised to find that in most cases nothing very significant has happened. It is true that many small events have an impact every day. But they tend to cancel each other out. Even if a big event comes along, it may or may not have any impact. In either event, it is visible and you can evaluate its effect.

I am not suggesting here that you must be able to prove at the .05 level of statistical significance that you caused a given effect. All you have to do to be seen as an effective member of the Value Team is to demonstrate that you had something to do with the positive change that took place after your intervention. Throughout this book our colleagues have described many examples, large and small, of how they had a favorable effect on their organization's goals. You can do it too if you just try.

Creating Value

Value is a subjective term. What is valuable to me may not be valuable to you. This has long been the problem with human resources. While some practitioners have emphasized the well-being of employees, others have stressed profits. At times these two values seem to be mutually exclusive. One might argue that taking good care of employees always pays off financially in the long run. But it might be difficult to prove that in the short term. So, if we are going to talk about value we need to define it and try to determine what kinds of values there are.

I mentioned in Chapter Three that there are three categories of value: human, production, and financial.

Human values are factors such as security, safety, career growth, morale, cooperation, and job satisfaction. These are the areas that the human resources function has prized as its primary focus for decades. They are basic requirements for happy, effective employees.

Production values cover efficiency, productivity, and quality factors. For years, some human resources professionals have argued that happy employees are productive employees, and there is much evidence to support this point of view.

Financial values deal with money. Gross and net profit margins, cost avoidance, and expense reductions are prime examples of the bottom-line financial measures that drive businesses. Human resources managers are much more aware these days of how they can and must stay focused on financial factors.

So often when I talk to groups or work with clients, I have to assure them that I look for all three types of value. I acknowledge that at times these values can come in conflict with each other. But that does not mean that we can't deal in all three. When you talk with management, you can describe all three types of value to be gained. Although top management may focus on achieving production and financial goals, it also appreciates human values. But if your work hasn't resulted in any financial benefits for your company, it will be nearly impossible to get management to hold still for human interest stories. If you first show examples of the financial impact of your work, management will then be more than happy to discuss human values with you.

Types of Data

Traditionally, business people talk about two types of data: hard and soft. Hard data deal with objective, quantifiable factors. Soft data deal with subjective, qualitative factors. Businesses tend to value hard data because they are less equivocal. In contrast, soft data can mean about what anyone wants them to mean. What Humpty Dumpty scornfully told Alice about words also applies to soft data: "When I use a word it means just what I choose it to mean—neither more nor less."

Table 12 provides a list of hard and soft data terms. If you look closely, you can see the basic difference between them.

Whereas the so-called hard terms are very specific, the soft terms are more general. Businesses run on specific information. The Internal Revenue Service demands it. Banks require it. The Securities and Exchange Commission takes the same view, and so does the management of your company. It seems to me with the rest of the company operating on this level, that human resources has no choice but to also emphasize hard data. We have to shift our vocabulary from the soft side to the hard side where our listeners are.

Hardly a week goes by that I don't hear about another case in which a chief financial officer asked the human resources director for quantitative information. Recently I attended a meeting at the American Electronics Association (AEA) with Jim Norton, who directs the association's northern California region. He told me a typical story of a human resources director, who had called him in a state of mild panic. She had been asked by her chief financial officer for some numbers, and she didn't know how to respond, much less how to develop the data. Jim invited her to his office and showed her numbers from our Human Resources Effectiveness Report as well as numbers that AEA had developed. After being shown the tables and graphs, she looked at him and asked, "What does it mean?" Unless she learns the language of business, she will never go any higher than she is today.

Four Ways to Use Data

Sometimes after I take people through a demonstration of the diagram in Figure 9, they ask me how to use hard data. There are four common uses for hard data:

1. Monitoring current activities and results
2. Identifying and solving problems
3. Forecasting trends
4. Projecting future benefits and values

Monitoring. Most professional business people set quantifiable objectives. They track their operations and watch for deviations

Table 12. Types of Data.

Hard Data		Soft Data	
Output	*Time*	*Work Habits*	*New Skills*
Units Produced	Equipment	Absenteeism	Decisions Made
Tons Manufactured	Downtime	Tardiness	Problems Solved
Items Assembled	Overtime	Visits to the	Conflicts Avoided
Money Collected	On Time	Dispensary	Grievances
Items Sold	Shipments	First Aid	Resolved
Forms Processed	Time to Project	Treatments	Counseling
Loans Approved	Completion	Violations of Safety	Problems Solved
Inventory Turnover	Processing Time	Rules	Listening Skills
Patients Visited	Supervisory Time	Number of	Reading Speed
Applications	Break-in Time for	Communication	Discrimination
Processed	New Employees	Breakdowns	Charges Resolved
Students	Training Time	Excessive Breaks	Intention to Use
Graduated	Meeting Schedules		New Skills
Tasks Completed	Repair Time	*Work Climate*	Frequency of Use of
Output per Man	Efficiency	Number of	New Skills
Hour	Work Stoppages	Grievances	
Productivity	Order Response	Number of	*Development/*
Work Backlog	Late Reporting	Discrimination	*Advancement*
Incentive Bonus	Lost Time Days	Charges	Number of
Shipments		Employee	Promotions
	Quality	Complaints	Number of Pay
Costs	Scrap	Job Satisfaction	Increases
Budget Variances	Waste	Unionization	Number of
Unit Costs	Rejects	Avoidance	Training
Cost by Account	Error Rates	Employee Turnover	Programs
Variable Costs	Rework		Attended
Fixed Costs	Shortages	*Feelings/Attitudes*	Requests for
Overhead Cost	Product Defects	Favorable Reactions	Transfer
Operating Costs	Deviation from	Attitude Changes	Performance
Number of Cost	Standard	Perceptions of Job	Appraisal
Reductions	Product Failures	Responsibilities	Ratings
Project Cost	Inventory	Perceived Changes	Increases in Job
Savings	Adjustments	in Performance	Effectiveness
Accident Costs	Time Card	Employee Loyalty	
Program Costs	Corrections		*Initiative*
Sales Expense	Percentage of Tasks		Implementation of
	Completed		New Ideas
	Properly		Successful
	Number of		Completion of
	Accidents		Projects
			Number of
			Suggestions
			Submitted
			Number of
			Suggestions
			Implemented

Source: Adapted from Phillips, 1983.

from the desired path. With quantitative data you can set goals and objectives for your unit and track your progress. If you set a band of tolerance on either side of the desired track, you can take action quickly when the results aren't meeting your expectations. You can also use these data for periodic reports to management. The question of what to monitor is answered by your objectives. You track only what is important to achieving those objectives.

Identifying. Even if you are a seasoned manager, you will still need data to help solve problems. Experience and intuition are critical to identifying and solving problems, but without data you are just guessing. When you mix data with experience, you gain insights that are just not possible to achieve otherwise. For a smart manager, data and experience work with each other either by validating each other or, if they conflict, by raising a flag of caution. There are many problem-solving techniques for you to apply. Pick one that suits the problem and use hard data.

Forecasting. Management needs to know what to expect. It is very difficult to plan a business expansion without knowledge of the availability and cost of various material and assets. This includes the human asset. By monitoring past trends and introducing current data, you can alert management to shifts, such as impending skills shortages or anticipated increases in hiring costs. Surveys, commissioned research, the trade press, and even newspapers provide data that you can use to predict significant changes.

Projecting. Everyone would like to be able to foretell the future. In business, if you could know what was going to happen as a result of alternative actions, you could have a consistent edge over your competition. A technique you can use for predicting the benefits and values of proposed actions is to work with a customer to project the probable monetary and nonmonetary benefits to be obtained from a future action, such as a training program. This method contrasts with the practice of using an after-the-fact questioning technique to help people locate and value the outcome of some event. I will take you through a sample problem with each technique later in this chapter.

Connecting Human Resources Programs to Outcomes

The question of how to connect your work to some benefit experienced by your customer arises frequently. In the next section I will show you two techniques for solving that problem. Here, I want to describe the underlying principles.

Exhibit 13 is an example of a specific organizational strategy that was translated into a business plan with productivity and quality objectives. Based on those business goals, a grand strategy was set and programmatic objectives were laid out. The programs were delivered and measurements were taken. The results could be traced back to the productivity and quality objectives, and it could be determined if the programs had an effect. It really doesn't matter what percentage of the productivity achievement was a function of the intervention by the human resources department. It is enough for everyone to see and agree that its programs were a big help.

The tried-and-true traditional method of cost-benefit analysis is very straightforward. If you want to show how you are affecting profitability through either expense reduction or revenue increase, the process goes like this:

Problem: Hiring costs for certain skilled trades are too high and are increasing steadily. In addition, the quality of people hired through traditional sources—advertising and employment agencies—is less than you would like.

Reason: There is a general shortage of trained personnel in those trades. This is causing longer, more expensive searches and producing less than satisfactory hires.

Solution: Find a more cost-effective source.

Process: Analyze past hiring records to find where the high-quality and low-cost hires came from.

Answer: Employee referrals constitute the lowest average cost per hire, and they also produce the highest-quality people as measured by performance and tenure. Note: The differential

Exhibit 13. Connecting Human Resources to Unit Business Plan Goals.

*** Organization's Strategy ***

BECOME THE TOP PRODUCTIVITY AND QUALITY COMPANY
IN THIS INDUSTRY WITHIN FIVE YEARS.

*** Unit Business Plans ***

Increase productivity 12%   Improve quality to .01% rejects
Respond to all service calls within 45 minutes

*** HR Grand Strategy ***

1. Design productivity training program for supervisors.
2. Develop quality circles program.
3. Institute incentive plan for customer service reps.

*** HR Business Plan ***

Objectives:

1. Conduct productivity skills I starting July 1.
2. Kick-off quality is no. 1 project starting June 1.
3. Install new performance pay plan for CSRs on January 1.

Action:

Do it!

Measures:

Gather before-and-after data on effects of the program. Prepare report and
deliver it, showing relationship of the HR-led program to unit goals.

---

value of high versus low performance and turnover costs can
also be calculated.

The difference between new method and old method
costs can be worked out as follows:

New Method Costs:

1.	Analysis cost: Staff time	$ 600
2.	Employee Referral (ER) promotion costs	1,500
3.	HR Hires (175@$200)	35,000
	Total	$37,100

Old Method Costs:

Ads and agency hires (175@$605) $105,875

Direct Value Added: $105,875 − $37,100 = $68,775

Indirect Value Added: Increased employee morale as a result of recognition and payments. Better-quality employees; easier to supervise, fewer conflicts, and so on.

Don't make the problem harder to solve than it really is. Look for the easiest, most commonsense solution. That is usually the best one. Even the vaguest of problems will yield to this proven method. Just remember, whatever you can describe in visible terms you can measure at some objective level. Some consultants like to sell you old methods decked out in fancy new labels. Don't be fooled. Just ask yourself these questions:

- What is the problem?
- What is the reason for the problem?
- Why is it a problem: cost, time, quality?
- What would be a workable solution?

Do it! Calculate and compare the old with the new. You probably solved the problem and are able to prove the value added.

Finding Value

I said before that there are two places to find value. One is before the fact. This is called projecting. The other is after the fact. I call that locating.

Projecting. Figure 10 provides an example of a form that you can use for projecting value. The process depends for its success on specificity in all statements. The people working the process must be familiar with the environment in which the hoped-for effects will occur. In the example given in the figure, the trainer works with the client manager who is sending people to the program. Only that manager knows what goes on in his or her environment, and he or she is the person who can best put a value on the outcomes.

1. Outcomes. State specifically, in visible terms, what the trainee will be able to do as a result of the training. It must be a visible action—for example, an improvement in a skill.
2. Beneficiaries. List the people who will benefit from the newly acquired skills. Since many people may benefit, confine the list to the key beneficiaries who will account for most of the effect.
3. Benefits. List the benefits that each beneficiary will receive. For the reason previously stated, you can see why it is necessary for the client manager to work on this.
4. Describe in nonmonetary terms the values of the benefit. For example, reduced stress or increased job satisfaction might produce lower rates of turnover or absenteeism. The client can estimate how much.
5. Put a monetary value on the nonmonetary value of the benefit. I find that line managers have no problem estimating a range of value once you reach this stage. They have done the work throughout this process and it is now easy to project what the change will be worth.

The last step is to make a list of the nonmonetary values and to total the dollar values. Probabilities or percentages of value can be introduced since it is unlikely that total value will be achieved. This result can be compared to the cost of the program and a decision to proceed or not to proceed can be made.

Critics will claim that value projection results in nothing more than an estimate. That is true. Any time that you look into the future you are talking about estimates. No matter how much past data you have for a given operation, there is no guarantee that the future will be a mirror of the past. This applies to sales, costs, production, quality, satisfaction, or any other business indicator. The difference between the value projection technique and a seat-of-the-pants guess is that the former links specific, visible actions throughout the process.

Locating. If you want to find value for an event that has already taken place, there is a questioning technique that is very helpful.

Figure 10. Value Projection Format.

PROGRAM OBJECTIVE (statement of general improvement objective; what training is aimed at fixing)

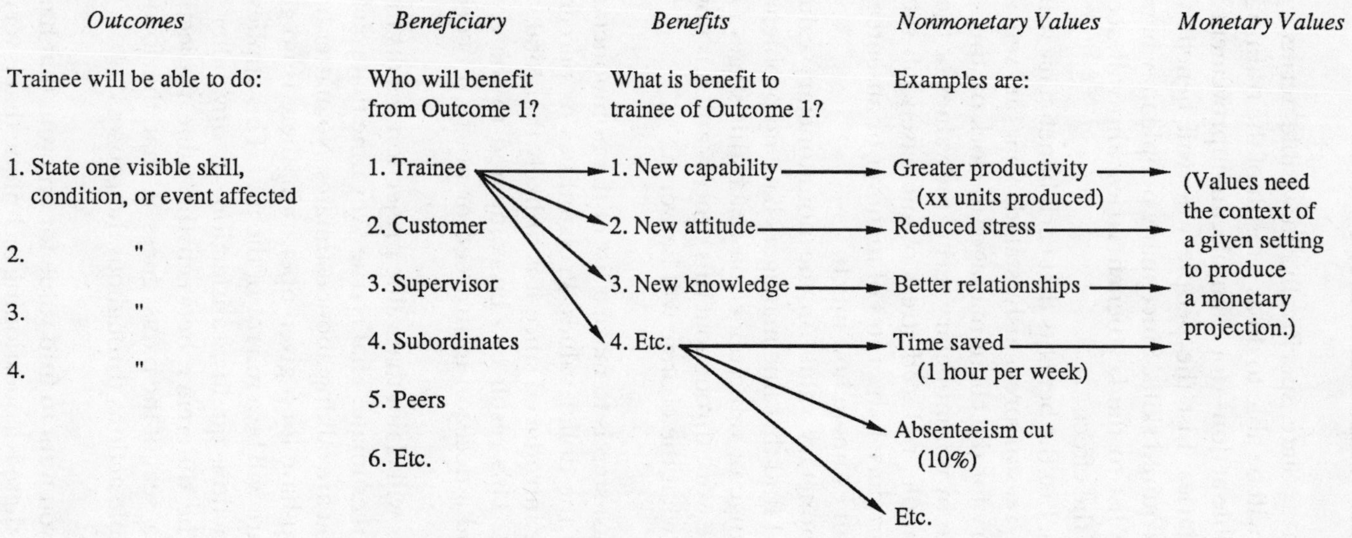

Outcomes	Beneficiary	Benefits	Nonmonetary Values	Monetary Values
Trainee will be able to do:	Who will benefit from Outcome 1?	What is benefit to trainee of Outcome 1?	Examples are:	(Values need the context of a given setting to produce a monetary projection.)
1. State one visible skill, condition, or event affected	1. Trainee	1. New capability	Greater productivity (xx units produced)	
2. "	2. Customer	2. New attitude	Reduced stress	
3. "	3. Supervisor	3. New knowledge	Better relationships	
4. "	4. Subordinates	4. Etc.	Time saved (1 hour per week)	
	5. Peers		Absenteeism cut (10%)	
	6. Etc.		Etc.	

I call it the quantifying interview. This can also be used to estimate the future value of something.

In the following example of a quantifying interview, Tom Trainer (T) talks with Mary Manager (M) about the quantifiable dollar value of a recent training program on managing customer service that Mary attended.

T: Hi, Mary, I hear that last month's customer service training program went well. Several people have told me they are already applying it. We are wondering what value you think it had.

M: I thought it was very practical. I feel much more confident that I can handle special customer problems or requests. I know I am doing a better job of coaching my people on problem calls, but I don't know how you can put a value on that.

T: I'm glad it's making you more confident. But tell me, what do you mean when you say "confident"?

M: Well, first of all, I listen better. I really hear what the customers are saying because I'm more comfortable with my ability to handle their problems. I only get involved when one of my people can't handle the situation. And that's not happening as often now. Sometimes the customer is really upset.

T: I can imagine what it's like. I've had problems with vendors that don't get solved, and after a while I get upset, too. How else does it help?

M: We get to what's bothering customers faster because I let them vent their frustration and then ask a question that takes us right to the root of their problem.

T: Can you always solve their problems?

M: Not always. But I am doing a better job.

T: Can you be more specific?

M: I've had to handle at least three problem calls a day. So far, I haven't lost a customer, and I've probably solved 90 percent of their problems.

T: That's great. How often did you lose one in the past?

M: Well, you don't always know, but I think I lost one or two a month for sure. Usually they had service or capability problems. If we can't help them, I know some leave us for one of our competitors. Several times since the training I've been able to increase the number of services they sign up for by suggesting additional features.

T: No kidding? We ought to put you in sales. How often does this happen?

M: I guess about once a week, at least.

T: That's pretty good. What would you say is the average amount of the dollar value of the new billing?

M: I never thought about it.

T: Would you say it was $5,000 a year?

M: Oh no. Well, once in a while I get one that would probably amount to $5,000 or more. But, usually it's less than that.

T: How often is once in a while? Once a week?

M: Come to think of it, probably at least that. I would say one and a half to two times a week.

T: Okay, how about the other cases? The times when you get a smaller add-on order. How often does that happen, and what do you think is the average amount?

M: Well, I've really been turning them lately. I probably get something more out of a fourth of the calls. Each one might amount to $200 more on a monthly billing.

T: So, not only are you saving a customer a month; in many cases you are turning a problem into an order. That's super.

The key to finding value is to make the invisible visible. In the interview, try to find a description of one or more activities that are subject to visual verification AND that collectively describe the values obtained.

1. Where are the quantifiable benefits? Look for comments about efficiency, productivity, quality, and customer satisfaction.
2. Where do measures of cost, time, quantity, quality, and customer satisfaction or employee morale apply? Which can be converted to dollars?
3. Add up the dollar value of the training for Mary, as you see it.
4. Are there other tracks that could be investigated that might yield additional dollar payoffs?

Measuring Asset Management

Measurement of individual processes and outcomes was the subject of my first book. For those readers who want lists of formulas to choose from, I refer you to that work (Fitz-enz, 1984). There are about fifty formulas and many sample charts and graphs to stimulate your imagination. In this section I am going to give you some examples of the measurement systems that people have built for each of the asset management categories.

Acquisition. In an earlier chapter I mentioned the human re-sources group in a major company that used to collect and report a voluminous amount of activity statistics on its person-nel function. As their industry began to change radically, the company's managers faced the necessity of operating on smaller margins and fixed budgets. The human resources manager decided it was time to revamp the system. He wanted to try an approach that would be more appropriate and useful in the new environment.

In late 1987 I began working with a team of the company's regional human resources managers to put together a set of formulas that would do the job. You should know that the company had experienced a series of layoffs and reorganiza-tions over the past six years. Changing a measurement system is a cultural as well as an operational task. By definition, what gets measured is what is valued. The people had to have faith that by

Table 13. Acquisition Measures at One Company.

Measure	Sort	Levels
Cost per placement	P	E & N
Cost per hire	H	E & N
Process cost	P & H	N
Initial response time	P & H	E
Time to fill	P & H	E
Time to start	P & H	E
No. of jobs received	P & H	E & N
No. of jobs filled	P & H	E & N
No. of open jobs	P & H	E & N
No. tested	P & H	N
No. qualified	P & H	N
Ratios of offers to acceptances	H	E

Note: P = internal placement
H = external hire
E = exempt (nonmanagerial positions)
N = nonexempt positions

abandoning the old system and taking a chance with the new one, they would not be jeopardizing their careers.

A series of meetings and training sessions resulted in the selection and design of a measurement system for the employment function. This system was put in place in mid 1988. The measures chosen are listed in Table 13.

Unfortunately, there is a sad end to this story. In this case, the old culture simply overwhelmed the new system. Benign neglect set in for a time when the new system's champion became distracted by other duties. A year later the system was still struggling to take hold. The moral of the story is: If you want to make big changes you have to make big efforts.

Maintenance. Transamerica Occidental Life Insurance Co. has gone through a series of unsettling changes. The divestiture of a line of business, the downsizing of the remaining functions, and a strong emphasis on operational profitability all hit the employees and managers in 1987 and 1988. In an effort to respond to demands for greater efficiency and effectiveness, Lisa Moriyama led her staff of employee relations professionals in the reorganization of their department and the development of an employee relations tracking system. While this project was being worked out, there were a number of other major re-organizing activities taking place (such as corporate downsizing and the selling of one business line).

The system yields a report for each employee relations consultant—a report that includes the following items:

- Total cases
- Contact type: phone or personal meeting
- Initiated by: manager, employee, employee relations
- Issue type: employee or manager
- Issue category: EEO, general, policy (broken down further)
- Status
- Time spent
- Total cost
- Cost per case
- Cost per issue

This information allows both Lisa Moriyama and her consultants to know what is going on at all times. They know where their resources are being spent and the outcomes of their programs. In short, they have the employee relations functions under control, and they can keep line managers aware of the top human resources issues. In this way, employee relations and management can plan appropriate interventions to prevent or reduce serious problems. If certain people are having chronic problems with human resources issues, the employee relations group can provide specific development activities for them.

Development. Tracking the cost of training is a simple matter. A system can be set up to route all bills over a training manager's desk, where they are coded and given a line item number. The original is sent to accounts payable for processing, and a data entry operator enters the figures in the appropriate cell in the cost-analysis system shown in Table 14. This format can be put on a computerized spreadsheet program that will handle the summing of costs by type and phase.

The other part of development management is the value-adding activities side. One of the most comprehensive approaches that I have seen in a training and development function is in place at Huntington National Bank in Columbus, Ohio. The human resources division is managed with this objective: "Operate Human Resources on a 'return on investment' approach which is in keeping with the company's corporate strategic objectives."

The strategy of the Huntington Institute of Banking (HIB) is equally explicit: "The HIB will offer specific training programs designed to enhance the technical competence of Huntington employees, improve their delivery of services, and provide additional educational opportunities for them to further their careers. Each employee will be versed in the culture, history, traditions, basic beliefs, and values of the Huntington."

Bob Albright is a well-known development professional who has served on the professional staff of the American Bankers Association. With the support of senior line officers and help from his associate Mary Held, Bob has led the development function in carrying out a number of very successful programs, the most visible of which was the creation of the Huntington Institute of Banking.

A system of learning paths that are specific to positions in retail and commercial lending was set up. These paths lead to specialist certificates in customer service, leadership, and lending. After completing courses in basic banking and customer/product skills, employees can study for diplomas in relationship banking at the fundamental and mastery levels. Eventually people will be required to earn certificates and diplomas to qualify for these positions because the courses in the HIB are designed by line specialists.

Application. Many of the success stories I have shared throughout this book focused on improving the efficiency of the human resources operation. When we talk about applications, however, we are moving outside of human resources to look for the impact on the customers' goals. In brief, what can human resources do to help solve operational problems?

The Jack Eckerd Corporation is composed of the Eckerd Drug Company, which is headquartered in Clearwater, Florida, and operates 1,600 drugstores in fourteen Sunbelt states, a pharmacy operation that serves institutional care facilities such as nursing homes, and a chain of vision-care superstores. It has a total of 30,000 employees.

About two years ago, the company became concerned that the pharmacies were not as profitable as they should have been. There was a request for more staff, which is the standard solution to poor performance. Bill Silberman and Wayne Saunders got involved and came to the conclusion that the problem would not be solved by throwing bodies at it. Instead, they worked with the management of pharmacy services and developed a new position called the pharmacy development specialist. The idea was that this specialist would "coach" the pharmacists and help them run their departments as businesses. The responsibilities of the specialist included recruitment of new pharmacists, initial training of them, and support to help them manage inventories and maximize the profitability of the pharmacies. The early feedback from this program has been very positive. This is an example of how human resources departments can help solve a business problem by recommending an innovative solution based on a company's human assets.

Management. According to the principles of value measurement, managers should be measured primarily in terms of the output of their units. However, since managers play pivotal roles in organizations, their full value cannot be measured by one yardstick. Their performance should be viewed from the more complex standpoint of effectiveness. To evaluate the effectiveness of managers, we have to expand the scope of measurement. There are four focal points:

1. Output of the units that he or she manages
2. The manager's personal work on projects
3. The manager's interpersonal skills and relationships
4. Relationship of the unit's output and the two personal factors to the organization's objectives

Table 14. Training Cost Analysis Program.

Phase	Cost					
	A. People	B. Material	C. Equipment	D. Facilities	E. Miscellaneous	X. Total
1. Diagnosis	01 Sal and ben—HR 02 Sal and ben—others 04 Meals and travel—HR 05 Meals and travel—others	07 Office supplies 08 Program materials (diagnostic) 09 Printing	11 Equipment expense allocation 12 Equipment rental 13 Equipment maintenance	15 Facility expense allocation 16 Facility rental	10 Outside services 17. General overhead 18 Other miscellaneous expenses	
	1.1 Subtotal	1.2 Subtotal	1.3 Subtotal	1.4 Subtotal	1.5 Subtotal	1X Total
2. Design and development	01 Sal and ben—HR 02 Sal and ben—others 04 Meals and travel—HR 05 Meals and travel—others	07 Office supplies 08 Program materials (learning) 09 Printing	11 Equipment expense allocation 12 Equipment rental 13 Equipment maintenance	15 Facility expense allocation 16 Facility rental	10 Outside services 17. General overhead 18 Other miscellaneous expenses	
	2.1 Subtotal	2.2 Subtotal	2.3 Subtotal	2.4 Subtotal	2.5 Subtotal	2X Total
3. Delivery	01 Sal and ben—HR 02 Sal and ben—others	07 Office supplies 08 Program materials (learning) 09 Printing	11 Equipment expense allocation 12 Equipment	15 Facility expense allocation 16 Facility rental	10 Outside services 14 Registration fees	

03 Sal and ben—participants 04 Meals and travel—HR 05 Meals and travel—others 06 Meals and travel—participants	07 Office supplies 08 Program materials (evaluation) 09 Printing	rental 13 Equipment maintenance	15 Facility expense allocation 16 Facility rental	17 General overhead 18 Other miscellaneous expenses	
3.1 Subtotal	3.2 Subtotal	3.3 Subtotal	3.4 Subtotal	3.5 Subtotal	3X Total
4. Evaluation 01 Sal and ben—HR 02 Sal and ben—others 03 Sal and ben—participants 04 Meals and travel—HR 05 Meals and travel—others 06 Meals and travel—participants	07 Office supplies 08 Program materials (evaluation) 09 Printing	11 Equipment expense allocation 12 Equipment rental 13 Equipment maintenance	15 Facility expense allocation 16 Facility rental	10 Outside services 17 General overhead 18 Other miscellaneous expenses	
4.1 Subtotal	4.2 Subtotal	4.3 Subtotal	4.4 Subtotal	4.5 Subtotal	4X Total
5AX Total	5BX Total	5CX Total	5DX Total	5EX Total	5XX Total
5X. Total					5XX Total

Table 15. Managerial Effectiveness Matrix.

Factor / Measure	People	Things	Processes	Outputs
Cost				
Time				
Quantity				
Quality				
Human Reactions				

Table 15 is a matrix that reduces the complex nature of managerial work to discrete, measurable outcomes. We already know that organizational measurement can be analyzed in terms of how people interact with things or other people for the purpose of achieving outcomes. We also know that the effects of those activities and events can be measured by looking at costs, time, quantity, quality, and human reactions. If you put all these items in a matrix such as the one found in Table 15, you can make a number of tactical and strategic assessments.

First look down the People column. Ask what the manager has done in regard to managing people from a cost, time, quantity, quality, and human standpoint. Ask the same question as you go down each of the other three columns. When you have answers for all twenty cells, ask what impact these results have had on the organization's business goals. The approach outlined here may sound simplistic, but it covers the essence of the manager's responsibilities. The nine items are the criteria by which you evaluate the contribution of a manager to the organization. There are no other categories. All you have to do is look at the imperatives that a manager was given and analyze them within this matrix to evaluate how effective he or she was.

Conclusion

Value is culturally defined and subjectively expressed. In organizations, value is most often expressed in financial terms. The human resources function, however, defines value in both human and financial terms. It cares about people *and* profitability, and it talks about human, production, and financial values in two ways: quantitatively and qualitatively.

To be effective, the human resources function must connect itself with its customers. It does this by focusing on the customers' goals and providing products and services that support those goals. Human resources professionals are gradually giving up vague, subjective terms for the more specific, objective language of numbers.

But there is still some resistance to measurement—a resistance that is rooted in four factors: habit, fear, disagreement, and ignorance. The solution to enlisting people in measurement systems is to overcome resistance by reducing ignorance through education. They need to be shown that measurement does not take as much time as they think and that it is not a negative, punitive process. Through education they can be brought to see that there is a place for quantitative as well as qualitative language in the human resources profession.

The mechanics of measurement are relatively simple. There are basically three issues to measure: the processes of people working with people or with things, the outcomes that result from these processes, and the impact or difference that the outcome causes. The amount of change in the process, outcome, and impact can be described in terms of one or more of the following: cost, time, quantity, quality, and human reactions.

Value can be found before and after events if you keep one principle in mind: Describe whatever is happening, has happened, or will happen in visible terms. The truism of measurement is:

If you can see it, you can measure it.

Practically speaking, just about everything in organizational life can be broken down and described as a visible act or

condition. With some probing you will usually be able to find a
visible factor that can be quantitatively evaluated. By using the
technique of deductive questioning, you will make the connection between the action and the effects that it produced. By
connecting human resources work with value-adding organizational effects, you will elevate yourself and your function to a
prominent position on the Value Team.

> The things we choose to measure and the way that we
> measure them tell us lots about what we value and how
> we see the world.
>
> Stanley Davis

References

Fitz-enz, J. *How to Measure Human Resources Management*. New
York: McGraw-Hill, 1984.

Phillips, J. J. *Handbook of Training and Evaluation Methods*.
Houston: Gulf Publishing, 1983.

Wiesenberg, M. "Just How Many Is 'a Whole Bunch'?" *InfoWorld*.
Menlo Park, Calif.: InfoWorld Publishing Corp., copyright
1982 by InfoWorld Publishing Corp., a subsidiary of IDG
Communications, Inc., 1060 Marsh Road, Menlo Park, CA
94025.

Case Studies — Chapter Ten

West Coast Utility Company (WCUC)
(Drawn from examples provided by the vice-president of human resources and the staff)

WCUC is one of the largest public utilities in the United States. In the years following World War II, the company doubled in size every ten years. As it grew, however, it also developed a highly centralized, very directive, top-down, semimilitaristic management style. Sensing important changes in the company's marketplace, the chairman ordered a review of the organization and the direction in which it was going. The company was eventually restructured in such a way that its thirteen divisions were reduced to five business units.

In support of the changes, the human resources function involved itself in a number of value-adding activities:

High-performance teams were created, and unions were asked to support changes in the way WCUC operates so that it can become more competitive.

Several cost-containment benefits programs were introduced, including a flexible benefit system that allocates dollars to employees that they can then apply to a wide range of benefit options.

Health awareness programs were introduced as a way to test medical and educational intervention techniques and thus determine the return to employees and the company of various programs and costs. Four pilot programs will evaluate the impact of the company's efforts on medical plan costs, employee utilization, and other indexes.

New approaches were made to collective bargaining. It is hoped that these will educate the union leadership and gain its support for changes in work rules and job definitions. This will eliminate the need for more downsizing and thus protect current jobs.

Testing new employees has become more difficult because of the need to validate each test used in the selection

procedure. So, human resources organized a program to sign
up other electric utilities to support development of indus-
trywide validated tests. In one project the validation study
showed that the difference between an outstanding senior power
plant control operator and one with subpar skills could make a
difference of $500,000 a year in operating efficiency.

College recruiting was assigned to the operating departments. This eliminated seven corporate recruiting positions.
The results are that line departments take a much more active
interest in recruiting, are more responsive to requests for training and public relations visits to campuses, and are claiming
ownership of the new hires once they arrive. College recruitment is now a management program.

The list of cost-avoidance and value-adding projects is
lengthy. In an effort to learn how cost effective these programs
actually are, the corporate human resources group developed a
performance measurement system. This system measures volume and efficiency of services and also provides a sense of
control over program and service costs. It shows the human
resources staff how well they are doing in relation to both
internal goals and external demands. Performance goals are set,
and detailed measures are taken of both productivity and customer satisfaction.

The following are examples of some of the more interesting methods of measuring services and programs at WCUC.

> *Affirmative Action/EEO.* Several charts developed by human
> resources show trends in minority and female repre-
> sentation throughout the company by salary and posi-
> tion level.
> *Benefits.* A matrix of goals showing the key activities of
> plan delivery, adaptation, costs, and communication
> are matched to their cost, quality, time, and employee
> reactions. This unique approach keeps the benefits
> staff focused on the effects of their work.
> *Career management.* Human resources tracks the utilization
> of the job posting system and prepares reports for the
> company as a whole and for each division. Results can

also be sorted as needed according to a variety of demographic variables. Cost advantages and value-adding measures can be computed.

Compensation. Actual versus target costs are computed by the business unit. Management incentive expenditures versus corporate return on equity (ROE) can be compared. Compensation as a percentage of revenue and expense can be tracked and reported to senior management for a division or the entire company.

Computer systems development (CSD). Levels of customer satisfaction are obtained and reported by means of bar charts, both companywide and for each project. CSD is responsible for maintaining the HRIS network. Percentage of computer "up time" or availability is shown on a trend line graph. Any special value-adding data can be shown on a chart or described in a narrative when it occurs.

Employee assistance program. Measurement of case type and volume is maintained according to region, business unit, and the entire company. The number of new cases, continuing cases, and cases closed and the current case load are tracked. Consultation, project, training, and vendor contact data are captured for analysis. Finally, client satisfaction and objective results are reported. All this is maintained with the proper levels of confidentiality.

Employment services. Cost per hire, placement ratios, quality levels of new hires and temporary personnel, and client satisfaction are tracked.

Industrial relations. Grievance settlements, bargaining, and consultation results are reported. Results of negotiations of basic labor contracts are summarized and reported when they occur.

Learning center. Utilization rates, program cost measures, participant evaluations and instructor comments on the training center's management, and budget versus actual cost figures are tracked.

Organization planning and development (OP&D). Value-

added outcomes of OP&D interventions and client satisfaction levels are the basic measures. Quantitative
and qualitative results of survey-guided development
projects and high-performance employee involvement
program results are reported.

Research, development, and analysis. Project completion
data, turnaround times, imputed value, avoided cost,
and client satisfaction with outputs are charted and
reported through narratives.

Suggestion award program. Ratio of savings to costs, savings
per employee and business unit, and received versus
adopted suggestion rates are shown on three charts
which give management a quick but complete view of
the major issues.

Author's comment: The measurement system at WCUC covers nearly 100 activity and result indicators spread across thirteen functional areas in human resources. This sounds like an
enormous load, but when it is spread across those sections and
subsections, most staff have only a few measures to monitor.
Some items are tracked solely for the use of the section manager.
Others are published for use by the vice-president of human
resources or for distribution to other senior managers. The
system was put in place in early 1989.

Designing a system with a group this large—and one that
had been so highly bureaucratic for decades—was not easy.
There was the usual amount of fear and reluctance. But eventually most human resources staff members joined in when they
realized that the information would help them understand what
they had accomplished as well as improve their communications
with people outside of the department. With the gentle but
steady support of the vice-president and his assistant, the program got off the ground in the spring of 1989. One of the
greatest values was the hardest to put a number on. While
working in one section, a supervisor was heard to exclaim, "I
finally see all that the department and myself are doing and it
makes me feel good."

*Government of Western Australia, Department of Computing and
Information Technology (DOCIT)*
Perth
*(From materials and discussions with Jessie Woodyatt, manager of
the human resources branch of DOCIT)*

In 1987–1988, the human resources investment represented 26 percent of the total information technology (IT) budget for the Western Australia public sector. As in many other
regions, there is growing concern in Western Australia about the
cost of government. Although information technology shows
great promise in helping stem the rising cost of government
through improved productivity, in Western Australia there is a
shortage of skilled information science personnel. On top of
that there is a lack of executive awareness and understanding of
how to plan and manage IT to most effectively meet organizational goals.

DOCIT is charged with achieving productivity gains and
better services to the community through improved planning
and management of information technology in the Western
Australia public sector. DOCIT requires agencies to prepare
strategic IT plans that are integrated with their corporate plans
and include human resource implications. Agencies must submit annual budget bids so that five-year forecasts of expenditures can be made to the treasury and the cabinet. DOCIT
makes a report to the government's Computing Budget Committee to provide advice to the government on IT management.
This includes identification of dollar benefits from IT
expenditures.

As the human resources manager for DOCIT, Jessie believes that she has a mandate to guide the agency and the state
government in applying the human side of IT to solve expense
management problems. The approach of the Human Resources
Branch to the human side of IT management has been to encourage agencies to look at human resources activities as an
investment rather than as a cost. At the top, human resources
targets chief executive officers and executive-level managers for

a variety of educational programs to increase their knowledge and understanding of information resource management and its human implications.

Human resources at DOCIT does not duplicate programs or services available on the outside. Instead, it provides policies, guidelines, work aids, and programs that help agencies better manage their IT employees. The human resources staff tackles the areas where agencies are having the most difficulties. They help managers determine the scope of problems, identify solutions, implement strategies, and evaluate solutions. Jessie says her objective is to always add value. The following are some examples of how her staff does just that.

To build awareness among managers of the value added by her approach, she encourages agencies to identify human resources benefits achieved as a result of implementing technology. In 1987–1988 the agencies ranked human resources benefits ahead of nearly all others, including financial and legal benefits. Examples were staff reductions, improved deployment, and productivity gains.

Another example of value-adding work occurred as a consequence of the collection, analysis, and publishing of IT–human resources data. This provided an indication to government decision makers of trends and problem areas and led them to focus their attention and "repair" activity on the areas of greatest need. For example, the statistics showed that over a two-year period of acute staff shortages, only 1.5 percent of the IT investment dollar was spent on training. In addition, a survey showed high turnover and vacancy rates in the applications development group. These types of data are used to lobby the Public Service Commission and agency executives to adopt innovative retention strategies such as special training. When organizations finally increased their training expenditures, they not only upgraded staff skills but could take on new trainees and pay for off-the-job courses. All this contributed to reducing the governmentwide shortage in IT skills and thus increased the ability of agencies to effectively use IT to attain their goals.

Always on the leading edge, Jessie is now guiding the development of competency profiles for IT jobs. That in itself is not extraordinary, but it becomes so when paired with the HR planning manual that her group developed. The HRP manual is a staffing projection tool. With it, even a person who has no experience in human resources planning can anticipate the number of staff and kinds of skills that will be required to meet the demand generated by the installation of IT. The manual includes a step-by-step example that shows the planner a wide range of options when deciding how to meet a skill demand. It goes beyond supply-and-demand issues for IT staff. Another output is the skill demands for organizational users of information technology.

With skill shortages being as severe as they are, the HR Branch tracks separations in great detail. The objective is to prevent turnover or, to put it another way, to retain existing staff. Following are five charts that represent part of the data maintained (Figures 11–15). If you had this information on your company, you would know at least the following:

1. Number of proposed positions by function: Projected growth of each function. If positions are approved, you can begin to build a proactive recruitment program.
2. Resignations by function: Who is quitting? Take steps to find out why. Perhaps of equal importance, why are people staying? Are their reasons for staying positive ones?￢
3. Vacancies by function: Where are the holes? Work is not getting done. Or if it is getting done, it must be at the cost of overtime and employee stress. If this situation continues for a protracted period, it will probably generate a high degree of errors as well as precipitate additional turnover.
4. Vacancies by classification: Who is leaving? Are you losing junior or senior people? What does that imply for succession plans?
5. Average time vacant: How long is it taking to fill jobs? Is it taking more or less time than it used to? Is that a reflection of changes in the market or of something inside the organization?

Figure 11. Number of Proposed Positions by Function.

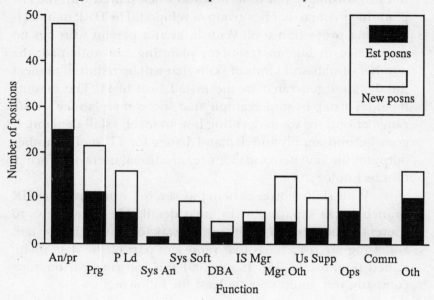

**Figure 12. Resignations by Function
(Given in Percentages).**

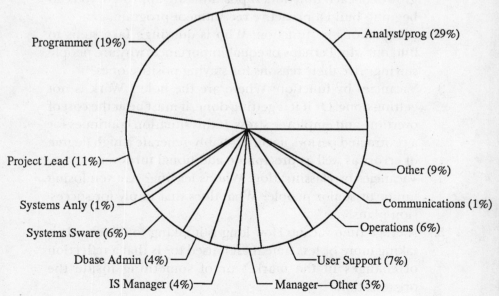

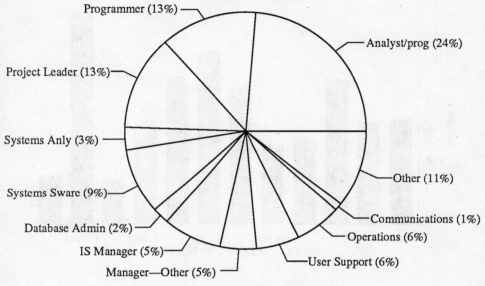

Figure 13. Vacancies by Function (Given in Percentages).

Programmer (13%)
Analyst/prog (24%)
Project Leader (13%)
Systems Anly (3%)
Other (11%)
Systems Sware (9%)
Communications (1%)
Database Admin (2%)
Operations (6%)
IS Manager (5%)
User Support (6%)
Manager—Other (5%)

Figure 14. Vacancies by Classification (Given in Percentages).

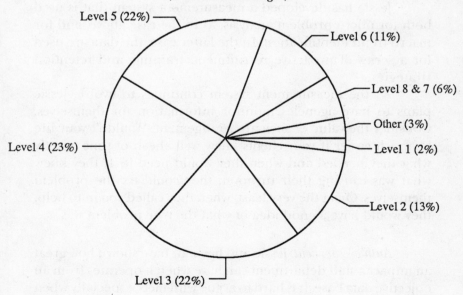

Level 5 (22%)
Level 6 (11%)
Level 8 & 7 (6%)
Other (3%)
Level 4 (23%)
Level 1 (2%)
Level 2 (13%)
Level 3 (22%)

Figure 15. Average Time Vacant (Months).

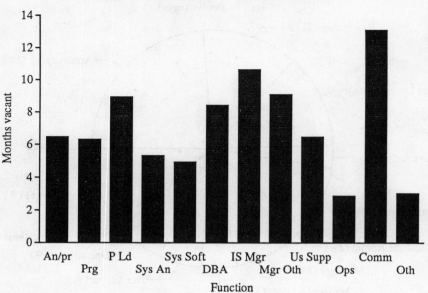

Jessie has developed a measurement system that is used both for micro problem analysis, as in the case above, and for macro trend identification. In the latter case, the data are used for a series of proactive recruitment, training, and retention strategies.

As the measurement system continues to evolve, Jessie plans to have agencies monitor information for themselves. Consider the value of such an arrangement. Wouldn't your life be much easier if your clients knew well ahead of time exactly what they needed and when they would need it? If they knew what was causing their turnover, they could fix the problem themselves. Or, at the very least, when they called you in to help, they would have a good idea of what the true problem was.

Author's comment: Jessie and her staff have shown how great an impact a staff department can have when it operates from an objective data base. It is hard to argue with facts, especially when you have them and your adversary doesn't. In the course of consulting with human resources managers on five continents over a dozen years, I have seen countless examples in which the human resources manager carried the day in the face of traditionally more powerful people just because he or she had harnessed the power of objective data.

11

Conclusion: The Present
and Future States
of Human Value Management

It is very encouraging to work with the forward-looking people in our profession. They are using their imagination, intuition, technical and interpersonal skills, and knowledge of business operations to make truly marvelous contributions to the well-being and profitability of their organizations. There are so many noteworthy, value-adding projects under way that I cannot begin to cover even a small percentage of them. Therefore, I have decided to conclude this chapter, and the book, by mentioning a few examples of the seminal work that is being done in our field. This work focuses on a theme that is central to the growth and development of the human resources profession.

Correlations to the Bottom Line

Human resources professionals have long dreamed of finding a formula that could be applied to organizations to prove that enlightened treatment of employees leads to profits. Two studies were conducted between 1985 and 1988 that looked for evidence in that direction. The first was reported by Dennis Kravetz (1988).

Kravetz looked for correlations between financial results and what he called *human resources progressiveness*. He defined progressiveness as "operating in concert with the current and future workplace, rather than experimenting with radical programs or spending exorbitant amounts of money on human resources programs. A company high in human resources progressiveness understands the critical importance of people to the bottom line and operates with this in mind" (p. 36).

He hypothesized that companies high in human resources progressiveness have enjoyed higher rates of growth in sales and profitability than those that are less progressive. The degree of a company's progressiveness was measured through a questionnaire and interviews. The questionnaire contained fifty-one questions pertaining to human resources progressiveness in the following areas:

- Communications progressiveness
- Degree of emphasis on people in the company culture
- Degree to which management is participative
- Emphasis on creativity and excellence in the workplace
- Extensiveness of career development and training
- Effectiveness in maximizing employee job satisfaction
- Degree of recognition and reward for good performance
- Use of flextime, work at home, and part-time employment
- Degree of decentralization and flattened management hierarchy

The financial success of the companies was tracked over a five-year period ending in 1984. Five hundred companies, most of which were in the *Forbes* 500 list of America's largest companies, were asked to participate. Questionnaires were sent to the chief human resources officer of each company. Some follow-up interviews were conducted to validate the information and obtain additional details on company practices. A total of 150 companies were retained for the final study.

The most progressive companies were found in computers, scientific equipment, and service businesses. The least progressive by Kravetz's criteria were in textiles, metal manufacturing, and machinery. Lest we applaud or condemn whole industries, however, Kravetz noted that individual company characteristics appeared to account more for progressiveness than did type of industry.

His principal conclusion was that highly progressive companies did enjoy significantly better financial results than did the less progressive companies. The key results were as follows:

1. High progressives had 64 percent greater sales growth each year than the less progressive.
2. High progressives were increasing profits each year more than four times as fast as the less progressive.
3. High progressives had profit margins 61 percent greater than the less progressive.
4. High progressives averaged 16.7 percent annual growth in equity compared to 9.3 percent for the less progressive.
5. High progressives showed an average annual increase of 6.2 percent in earnings per share versus an average annual loss of 3.9 percent for the less progressive.
6. Although high progressives had better price-earnings ratios, the difference was not statistically significant at the .05 level.

While it might be argued that progressive human resources practices do not guarantee better financial results, the data seem to prove that the two go hand in hand (see Table 16).

HR Performance and Organizational Effectiveness. In a second study on the same subject, Jack Phillips (1988) examined the relationship between human resources department performance as measured by certain human resource indicators and organizational effectiveness. His hypothesis was similar to Kravetz's in that he looked for relationships between certain human resources issues and organizational performance. But his study differed from Kravetz's in that he took data on both human resources and organizational finances from the ASPA/Saratoga Institute 1986 Human Resources Effectiveness Report. His principal assumptions were as follows:

1. Each human resources program is undertaken either to meet an external requirement or to improve the performance or efficiency of the organization.
2. Since an organization's performance is the sum of the per-

Table 16. Human Resources Progressiveness and Financial Results.

	Highly Progressive Companies	Less Progressive Companies
Average human resources progressiveness score	178.9	127.8
Annualized sales growth, five-year trend	17.5%	10.7%
Annualized profit growth, five-year trend	10.8%	2.6%
Latest annual profit margin	5.3%	3.3%
Percentage of companies having loss in last year	0%	18.0%
Annualized equity growth, five-year trend	16.7%	9.3%
Annualized growth in earnings per share, five-year trend	6.2%	−3.9%
Latest price-earnings ratio	15.1	13.8
Annualized dividend growth, five-year trend	13.4%	9.2%

formance of individuals within the organization, efforts to improve the performance of individuals should improve organizational performance.

3. Most human resources programs designed to improve performance do so, although it is difficult to measure the improvement.

4. Organizational performance is a function of several important variables, with human resources performance being one of them.

5. From one organization to another, there are inconsistencies in the way that human resources performance is measured and evaluated.

6. Most organizations do not pursue a comprehensive approach to the measurement and evaluation of the human resources function.

7. There is no one best formula or measure of human resources performance as it relates to organizational performance.

8. The human resources department will focus more of its

attention on those activities associated with evaluation criteria than those not being measured.

Phillips's intent was to lay the foundation for the development of a human resources effectiveness index. He solicited seventy-six organizations for their reactions to his proposed index. A total of thirty-nine indicated a high degree of interest in such an index and agreed to participate. Potential uses for the index were identified as follows:

- Compare present with past human resources performance within an organization.
- Compare human resources performance in an organization with industry norms.
- Compare human resources performance in an organization with that of other organizations.
- Establish goals and objectives for the human resources function.

The study formulated six measures of human resources performance and four measures of organizational effectiveness. They are shown below.

HR Performance	*Organizational Effectiveness*
$\dfrac{\text{HR Expenses}}{\text{Total Operating Expenses}}$	$\dfrac{\text{Revenue}}{\text{Employees}}$
$\dfrac{\text{Total Compensation Expenses}}{\text{Total Operating Expenses}}$	$\dfrac{\text{Assets}}{\text{Employee Costs}}$
$\dfrac{\text{Total Benefits Expenses}}{\text{Total Operating Expenses}}$	$\dfrac{\text{Operating Income}}{\text{Employee Costs}}$
$\dfrac{\text{Training and Development Expenses}}{\text{Total Employees}}$	$\dfrac{\text{Operating Income}}{\text{Stockholders' Equity}}$
$\dfrac{\text{Employee Days Absence}}{\text{Employees} \times \text{Workdays}}$	

Total Employees Separated

Total Employees

Phillips found that there were significant correlations between independent variables (HR performance) and dependent variables (organizational effectiveness). The strongest relationships were found to exist between organizational effectiveness, on the one hand, and human resources management expenses, compensation expenses, and benefit expenses, on the other. The weakest relationships were between organization effectiveness and training and development expenses, absence rate, and turnover rate. One of the more interesting findings was the inverse link between spending on compensation and benefits and increases in organizational effectiveness.

This study was hampered by a lack of data in some areas. Nevertheless, it is a bold step in the direction of connecting human resources performance to organizational effects.

HR Performance, Employee Attitudes, and Customer Satisfaction. John McLaughlin and George Maurer at Cedars-Sinai Hospital in Los Angeles are working on the formulation of an information system that will pull together data from employee attitude surveys, patient satisfaction reports, and human resources variables. Their objective is to look for correlational or causal effects. The work is just under way, and no results are yet available.

Key Performance Indicators. In Australia, David Proud of Puntimai Associates (according to Proud, a *puntimai* played the role of consultant among the Australian aborigines) is working on a software package that will be the platform for a system of key performance indicators (KPIs) linking human and organizational dependent variables.

In Proud's system, which is being used on an experimental basis at one of Australia's largest banks, the criteria for selecting KPIs are based on a data study of the most recent twenty-four months of operation. Hypothesized KPIs are tested against the actual data. The critical KPIs are then chosen and tested with at least three work groups of 250 employees or more. The operations of the experimental groups would be tracked by means of an action research model for signs of effects in either direction. Over time the system would be monitored and modified as conditions warrant. This study was initiated in early 1989.

Human Asset Management Index. The Saratoga Institute has been working on an indexing system that it believes could provide the foundation for a long-term indicator of organizational effects and change. We have explored various formulations with human resources professionals over the past three years. Their penetrating and insightful commentaries have helped us refine the formulas. At this point we are working with ten formulas that we believe represent a comprehensive but manageable set. Each has been chosen on the basis of its assumed relationship to one of five aspects of organizational health and effectiveness. The formulas currently being studied are shown in Table 17.

In summary, I have tried to show a small sample of the advanced work being done in our field, but there is need to do much more. We are particularly weak in sophisticated forecasting of human resource trends. There is also a need for systems that directly link business plans and human resource plans. Too many resources are being allocated to improving administrative systems and too few are being directed at business problems and opportunities. We have reached the point of diminishing returns on personnel administration. We need to take some risks and begin to utilize the scientific and technical knowledge that we already have. Breakthroughs in human resources management will not result from better record keeping. We have ridden the motivational research and models of the 1960s long enough. Now there is a need for new organizational models and management theories to help us through the turbulence of the 1990s.

Conclusion

I set out to achieve two objectives in this book. First, I wanted to describe for you the new wave of human resources

Table 17. Human Asset Management Index.

Human Operating Expense

$$\frac{\text{Compensation} + \text{Benefits} + \text{HR department expense}}{\text{Organization operating expense}}$$

Example: $\dfrac{\text{Compensation} = \$10M + \text{Benefits} = \$3.5M + \text{HRM} = \$0.5M}{\text{Operating expense} = \$45M}$

Cost to Supervise

$$\frac{\text{Management compensation}}{\text{Total compensation}}$$

Example: $\dfrac{\text{Management compensation} = \$4.5M}{\text{Total compensation} = \$10M}$

Stability Factor

Turnover percent + Nonexempt absence percent

Example: Turnover = 12% + Nonexempt absence = 2.4%

Development Factor

$$\frac{\text{Training expense}}{\text{Operating expense}}$$

Example: $\dfrac{\text{Training expense} = \$1.2M}{\text{Operating expense} = \$45M}$

Productivity Factor

$$\frac{\text{Revenue per employee}}{\text{Compensation/Revenue}}$$

Example: $\dfrac{\text{Revenue per employee} = \$150,000}{\text{Compensation} \div \text{Revenue} = 25\%}$

management that I have observed and, I hope, have contributed to over the past several years. It is clear to me that a change is sweeping the profession. The more effective human resources people have shifted their focus from human resources programs and activities as such to business needs and impacts. They are playing a central role in the management of their enterprises. I have tried to show through examples that this is not an isolated phenomenon. It is a global shift. Just as line managers are searching for new ways to be effective in the new marketplace of the 1990s, human resources professionals are developing new approaches to helping those managers achieve their goals.

The model that they are using starts with a clear vision of human resources as a value-adding function. This self-concept is transmitted through words and actions into a position message that convinces line personnel that human resources is a reservoir of practical, financially aware skills. These human resources managers research their markets and assess their internal capacity to perform in that marketplace. They ask themselves the ultimate pragmatic question: What do I have to do to be successful? Finally, using data from that research and analysis, they set objectives and build measurement systems to help them manage and communicate. I labeled this process human value management for good reason: it is driven by a concern for adding value to the enterprise through the appropriate investment of the human asset. Therein lies the key change. Human resources is learning that its job is not to run programs but to add value through people.

My second objective was to stimulate those human resources people who are looking for a better way. I wanted to share the excitement of the new wave. For those who wonder if their work life can be made more rewarding I hoped to show that it can. For those who doubt that change is possible I hoped to remove that doubt. The underlying question is, If others can do it, why not you? None of the successful people discussed here asked permission to act. Either they sold their ideas or they just charged ahead and carried the day through a display of positive results. They didn't look for excuses to hide behind. They found ways to get what they wanted, never mind the odds. I will feel that the time it took to research and write this book was worth it if you act on what you have read.

I will close by asking you to do one other thing. Many people are contributing to the development of human resources. Everyone who claims to be a professional has a responsibility to make a contribution to his or her profession. This is not satisfied by an annual dues check. It is necessary that each of us go beyond the daily grind of work to think, discuss, and perhaps even write or speak out on issues and methods that will make it easier for our successors to continue a tradition of service to our organizations and to our communities.

Some people tell me they don't really want to work that hard. They want time to enjoy life, to be with their families, or to spend more time on their hobbies. I simply mean to suggest that we should think, learn, analyze, and communicate our insights. This is a reasonable request unless your goal is to die well rested.

References

Kravetz, D. J. *The Human Resources Revolution: Implementing Progressive Management Practices for Bottom-Line Success*. San Francisco: Jossey-Bass, 1988.

Phillips, J. "The Development of a Human Resources Effectiveness Index." Unpublished Ph.D. dissertation, College of Commerce and Business Administration, University of Alabama, Apr. 1988.

Index

ISBN 1-55542-228-4

90000

9 781555 422288